COMPASS POINTS

BOOKS BY EDWARD HOAGLAND

MEMOIR
Compass Points

ESSAY COLLECTIONS
The Courage of Turtles
Walking the Dead Diamond River
Red Wolves and Black Bears
The Edward Hoagland Reader
(edited by Geoffrey Wolff)
The Tugman's Passage
Heart's Desire
Balancing Acts
Tigers & Ice

TRAVEL BOOKS
Notes from the Century Before:
A Journal from British Columbia
African Calliope: A Journey to the Sudan

FICTION
Cat Man
The Circle Home
The Peacock's Tail
Seven Rivers West
The Final Fate of the Alligators

COMPASS POINTS

HOW I LIVED

Edward Hoagland

Pantheon Books

New York

All rights reserved under International and Pan-American Copyright
Conventions. Published in the United States by Pantheon Books, a division
of Random House, Inc., New York, and simultaneously in Canada
by Random House of Canada Limited, Toronto.

Pantheon Books and colophon are registered trademarks of Random House, Inc.

Portions of this book have appeared in *Harper's, Granta, The New Yorker,
Civilization, The American Scholar,* and *Esquire* magazines.
Appreciative acknowledgment is given.

Library of Congress Cataloging-in-Publication Data

Hoagland, Edward.
Compass points : how I lived / Edward Hoagland.
p.   cm.
ISBN 0-375-40246-2
1. Hoagland, Edward.   2. Authors, American—20th century—Biography.
3. Visually handicapped—United States—Biography.   I. Title.
PS3558.O334 Z47 2001   818'.5409—dc21   [B]   00-056512

Random House Web Address: www.randomhouse.com

Book design by Cassandra Pappas

Printed in the United States of America
First Edition
2   4   6   8   9   7   5   3   1

The author wishes to thank Lauren Seidman,
who typed the manuscript with peerless attention.

For Marion Magid, and Steele Commager,
and Ross Wetzsteon, and Joe Flaherty,
and other friends who didn't live long enough
to write their own memoirs.
And to Trudy with love and gratitude.

Contents

COMPASS POINTS

In the Country of the Blind

"*T*he blind eat many a fly," says a fifteenth-century proverb—familiar as recently as sixty years ago, when I was small and blind people were still all over, tap-tapping with their white canes and saddled with dark glasses. The cane, if waved peremptorily, with any luck brought traffic to a halt, and its rhythmic tapping could part a stream of pedestrians and function for the blind person like a kind of radar besides. Power and pathos: because dark glasses were not then an emblem of celebrity or of a fashionable alienation, but of the saddest, sharpest handicap. Ostensibly making it harder to see, they signified instead that the person couldn't see and probably had a face so wooden or profoundly wounded by loneliness that he or she preferred to go incognito. Common problems such as cataracts or glaucoma were not often reversible, whereas today you need to fly to Third World outposts to encounter blindness on such a scale.

This phenomenon of adults who were helpless and pitiable, though in the prime of life, became one of the first moral puzzles children recognized. Old age they knew; jailbirds they knew about; real freaks—like the "waterhead" whom I once visited, painfully imprisoned in an easy chair in a dark cottage, his head bloated to double size—they might also have some vague acquaintance with. But the blind were ordinary folk, innocent of any crime or grotesquerie, of no specific age, who lived in crabby or long-suffering perpetual night. A mean individual I knew used to snicker when he told me how he had snuck into a blind man's house when he was a boy (having watched him leave for his weekly tap-tap trip to the grocery store), and shat into the sink where all his dishes were. And I could hear the desolate groan the blind man must have uttered, coming home, smelling the evidence of what had been done to him and searching for where it was, while he fathomed his impossible position from now on, living alone, as the story spread among the children of the neighborhood.

In the 1950s, however, when I reached my twenties, certain types of people began to adopt dark glasses to convey a different message and as a form of chic. Jazz musicians, for example, could dramatize the underground, persecuted, jokey character of their existence and telegraph the idea that even at night they already knew too much about what was going on to want to see much more. Better for the spirit to be self-absorbed, ironically bemused, optionally blind—a "spade" so savvy that he wore shades. Yet highway troopers, too, wore smoked glasses to mask their emotions and thus look formidably impassive as they delivered news as highly charged as jazz. And many of the newsworthy intellectuals of the era, café-based Existentialists on both sides of the Atlantic, likewise affected sunglasses as a means of demonstrating that a great deal of the passing parade was better left unseen. Impelled by the atrocities of two vast wars, and signature books like *Nausea* and *The Stranger,* they seemed to advocate disguising your identity to forestall repercussions and limit what you let yourself take in of a corrupt, demoralizing world in which the night was better than the day because of what it screened.

I didn't agree with this, and didn't wear dark glasses. Believing in nature and an overshadowing beneficence even in its offshoot, human nature, I wanted to gorge on every waking sight. I loved the city like the country—the hydrants that fountained during the summer like a splashing brook—and wanted therefore to absorb the cruel along with the good. I knew that Americans had responded to the bloody ruination of the Civil War not in a fashion corresponding to Sartre or the theater of the absurd, but by turning west once again to seek the balm of the wild. And if in doing so they had gradually spoiled it, that eventuality was more through overpopulation than by greed or any other classic wickedness. I saw this because my own solution to a sad spell was also to head outdoors and climb a spruce, find a pond, or hitchhike west, where I achieved an acquaintance with the frontiers that were left. In the city, it was to seek the most crowded places, Coney Island, Union Square, the Lower East Side, Times Square, on the same instinctive principle that life in bulk is good. Embracing the fizz and seethe of a metropolis was safer then, as was hitchhiking, but my tropism to crowds has never changed. Rubbing shoulders with thousands of people, my spirits surge in the same way that I grin at seeing a one-year-old, or will approach someone elderly, optimistic at the prospect of talking with him. A basic faith kicks in. It's automatic, not ideological, though I believe life has meaning. I find diversity a comfort in the wilds and in the city—that there are more species than mine, more personalities than me—and believe in God as embodied in the earth and in metropolises. I believe that life is good.

So, night or day, in Alaska or Africa, Bombay, Rome, Istanbul, New York, I never wore dark glasses. I can remember dazzling long wonderful days out in a boat in alligator refuges in Georgia—bird sanctuaries in Texas or Louisiana—scouting with wildlife experts who had some protection for their eyes. But I wanted to see everything just as it really was, in the full spectrum of colors, as a bird or reptile would. In the desert looking for a mountain lion I was the same, and in Greenwich Village, at Andy Warhol parties, I'd no more shade my eyes from the blitz of strobe lights than put in earplugs. I wrote for the purpose of being read in fifty years, and how could you describe a world whose colors you hadn't honestly seen?

But nature played a trick on me. Sunlight kindles cataracts (which I didn't know), and in my fifties I got them bad, compounded by bad retinas. At about the same juncture a bunch of my writer friends died before their time of lung cancer, emphysema, throat ailments, and the like—Edward Abbey, Donald Barthelme, Raymond Carver, Frederick Exley, Richard Yates, and several lesser-known good souls—at least partly because they had ascribed to the equally romantic notion that writers ought to smoke, drink, fuck, carouse, get pie-eyed (whereas I only thought they should fuck). Not all of this chemical imbibery stemmed from the Gallic-Kafka-Beckett idea that life was shitty, which had been in vogue. Nor was it simply macho, though the Hemingway-Mailer axis of behavior was as influential as the Europeans' despair. The hard-living ethos had its best argument in the idea that the mind, like a pinball machine, may need a bit of slamming to light up. Smoking like a chimney, drinking like a fish, or using pot or stronger dope might rev the mind, dramatize the vertiginous character of life, and wipe out humdrum thoughts for a while.

I didn't disagree with the proposition of slamming one's sensibility around. That's why I sometimes walked across the Brooklyn Bridge at dawn, and had driven or hitchhiked across the country eight times. Strangers and the play of expressions across their faces, by the thousand in a single day, were what the city boiled down to for me—Hausa, Chinese, Irish, Navajo, Polish, Puerto Rican—just as it's the scores of species in the woods that make the country as rich as it is: Blackburnian warblers and moccasin flowers, oyster mushrooms and oak worm moths, bigtooth aspen, squirrel corn, and hophornbeam. The city had its music and movies, at the Five Spot and the Thalia, and the emotions of a jam-packed tempo so much faster. Though the city hasn't worn quite as well for me in fifty years of loving it (I love it more at a distance now), from my twenties to mid-thirties I chose to spend the height of the spring and summer in the midst of New York as often as out in the country. Human nature, if cosmopolitan enough, with bodegas and storefront churches, and kielbasa eateries and elderly people sitting in folding chairs on the sidewalk, and numerous infants, was nature to me. I walked by the Hudson River almost daily, when the past night's paroxysm of violence or vomit had abated and the commerce of the day lent the city its terrific thrum: not just the million people, but the million trucks. I had a Bella motor scooter that I'd ride the length and breadth of Manhattan on; or I'd go to a Yankee game and walk all the way home from the Bronx to the East Village, one hundred eighty blocks, as the daylight darkened. Or nose along the classic portal side streets—Elizabeth and Forsyth and Mott and Eldridge and Orchard—off Canal and Delancey, where people were still beginning new American lives. Or amble under the financial towers at Nassau, Whitehall, Pine, and Wall Streets, with that wonderful lift that the beige and creamy and graystone downtown and midtown buildings can give you at midday, when they're so full of sunlight and strivers that optimism is lent to anybody striding through. High buildings: high hopes. Their enhancing identity was catching.

Mute because of a bad stutter, I'd wandered Boston's night neighborhoods with hungry yearning throughout my college years, supposing that just to stare at a single mysterious light in a lonely house with enough longing might cause the woman inside, whoever she was, to sense my presence and slip to the front door and summon me in. In a sensible world, a just and passionate world, it shouldn't be necessary to be able to talk to find a lover. After all, bad guys tend to be the best talkers of all. But I wasn't bold, I was shy, and such adventures didn't happen to me. I was a walker, a witness, but didn't close. For example, I remember a waitress in a café near the old North Station, where the trains from Maine arrived, who left me an extra dessert one time, but I couldn't bring myself to use this as an entree to better things. I'd just walk for five, six, or a dozen miles, feasting my eyes on the lights of the oil refinery in Everett and the half-darkened State Street mini-skyscrapers and the harbor from Commercial Street, where the glistening water, like all ocean water, seethed. Boston's sourball sweetness, with its softer darkness, orangey streetlights, miniature but meta-ethnic neighborhoods—Italians back-to-back with Irish, blacks with Portuguese and Chinese, North End, South End, West End, the weekend street markets at Faneuil Hall, yet Skid Row nearby, Charlestown, East Boston, Roxbury, Somerville, Cambridge, Back Bay—five years of walking in Boston helped prepare me to reassume my native New Yorker status after my teenage years in suburban Connecticut. Then during my two years in the draftee army, mostly stationed as a lab technician at a hospital in Pennsylvania, I had hiked roundabout Philadelphia. After being discharged in 1957, I lived in and explored the hills of San Francisco, the prettiest of local cities. And after marrying, for two and a half years in the early 1960s I'd walked extensively in Paris, London, and Rome, plus wilder environs in Sicily and Spain, with my first wife, Amy. As a writer too, I was visual. My first novel had been set in a circus; the second was about the cruel, graceful art of boxing.

But then, as a family man, I began to forsake the city for wilderness areas during the next quarter-century, in pursuit of ideas for books that excited me. I continued to live in New York, as Audubon, Frederic Remington, Albert Bierstadt, and so many other artists who have made wild places their subject matter have done. (You generally accomplish more in the city because of that inexorable thrum.) It was where my wife's career and lovely daughter's school were. But I did spend three or four months a year drinking from a spring, bathing in a pond, heating with wood, lighting with kerosene, in northern Vermont, and this kept me reasonably honest when I went foraging for stories—my husky in the car—to the Far West and Deep South. When we stopped for gas the dog would jump out the side window to pee and jump right back in.

"Better than havin' a pistol," one hillsman said, when we were halfway through Tennessee. "A pistol can snap, but a dog like that'll go right attum."

When an old-timer who lived by a lake would tell me he moved his difficult bowels every morning by wading hip deep, I knew what he meant. If he loved the frogs' songs as much as the birds', "Same here," I could say. They were, what, three hundred million years old? I had learned to shoot in the army, so I was up to the tin-can contests we sometimes had; or scrambling up a mountainside to an old mine hole. I knew dogs, and therefore wolves; goats, and therefore deer; parrots, and therefore ravens and crows; big exotic wildlife, and therefore little homebody wildlife as well. I knew what I wanted—pristine lore—and that is half the battle.

In 1968, on the untrammeled Omineca River in north-central British Columbia, for example, I met up with a paradigmatic first white family who had settled at the head of a gold rush trail near the last Sekani Indian family to leave this traditional homeland of theirs for a reservation to the south. The Sekanis weren't able to understand why the Canadian homesteaders were taking exclusive possession of the river bench that for generations had been their own special home. But it was an unequal dispute because the Indians had become squatters from the law's standpoint, living on moldy rice and not much else, and able to hold on at all only by doing the washing, shoveling, nail-pounding, road-clearing, firewood-hauling, and garden-digging for the whites. Yet the white family—hard-drivers, intolerant, with the berserk but self-thwarting energy of people who had failed elsewhere and fetched up here—still wanted them out. Whether it was in order to salve their consciences by forgetting that the Sekani tribe had ever existed or because they didn't like dark-skinned folk, they kept up a constant sneering refrain about "dirty, filthy, smelly" Indians in the windowless log hovel down on the gravel-bar beach. They'd built their house a hundred feet higher and a hundred yards back, with the result that the three white kids snuck out at all hours, concealed themselves on top of the embankment, and threw stones down on the Indians' roof, or at their children if they were playing in the dooryard. The savagery of the prank lay of course in the fact that the Sekanis must only grin and bear it. They could neither complain nor retaliate. To throw stones back or even go and protest to the parents would hasten their eviction from what was now a piece of "private property." They were the "niggers of the North," their presence a constant temptation and amusement to the under-entertained white children, and an irritant to the gunsmith/marksman father who wanted to be master of all he surveyed, not to mention his hard-pressed spouse, who hardly needed to imagine spurious dangers—there were enough real ones, like grizzlies—but did so anyway, and who wanted some neighbors, but not these neighbors, "hanging from the trees." The pressure was such the Sekanis were succumbing. That's how the West was won.

The nearest store, ten miles away, was a log cabin with staples like rice, beans, sugar, flour, salt, and tea that a lone placer miner panning for gold in a mountain creek and living off the land as much as he could, would need. I stayed upstairs for a night or two here and wandered the footpaths to visit several of these mild guys, bachelors who'd been living around for at least a decade and had no need of visitors, but were not rude to me. When they went out for a long walk, the old hope of blundering upon a strike would well up again inside them, but otherwise it was like wage labor. So many hours with a shovel and a pan meant so many grains of gold. Each piece of the creek could be counted on for a certain payback. Then I returned to Manson Creek and Fort Saint James and Vanderhoof and Prince George, and home again. It was my third trip to northern British Columbia, in pursuit of my first nonfiction book, *Notes from the Century Before.*

In the guise of a wildlife man, a hook-and-bullet writer for *Sports Illustrated,* I went south also, to Baton Rouge and beyond. People there might tell me how they had "treed a coon" and not mean a raccoon. A plain old hook-and-bullet writer must most likely be a good ole boy, too, so I was privy to the sort of blathering that ostensibly political journalists seldom hear. I went, for instance, to Leander Perez's moored houseboat, south of Venice in one of the hidden tall-marsh-grass "passes" in Plaquemines Parish, at the mouth of the Mississippi River, in 1973. Leander Perez was a fearsome figure, an actual plantation boss and dictator of his county-sized fiefdom south of New Orleans during the 1950s and 1960s, a throwback terrorizer of the local blacks—who set up a kind of mosquito-plagued, barbed-wire "concentration camp" in an old Civil War fort on the river, where he planned to throw "outside agitators," instead of in the county jail. This houseboat was for duck hunting, deal making, whisky drinking, move plotting, card playing, however, and though Perez wasn't there at the time—just his Colombian houseboy—I did get to see the inside anyway because I was traveling with a game warden and a duck biologist, to look at snow geese, garfish, muskrats: things like that. And the decor of the place revolved around the famous trio of little monkeys with their paws fixed to cover either their eyes, mouths, or ears. *See no evil, speak no evil, hear no evil.* Every flat surface had a set of these, carved like chessmen from jade or some variety of malleable wood or semiprecious material to represent the conspiracy of silence that had made his reign possible. The blacks one talked to on the road walked and spoke with an engrained flinch, their faces roasted in a crucible.

In my anti-modernist ebullience I was not, I think, a Pollyanna. I saw the South with a Yankee's acidulous eye and the North with Thoreauvian impatience. (In my teens I'd been more drawn to the Tolstoyan mode, but couldn't sustain such exalted idealism or the literary aspirations to go with it.) Yet acidulousness is not Absurdism. Sunshine and drifting water under a shifting mosaic of leaves, with alligators in the bayou and otters in a creek—I mean, what more do you need to believe? In my travels I was seeing so many alligators and otters (once an alligator eating an otter), and waterfowl in flocks of thousands, whales, seals, walruses, moose, elk, caribou, then African lions and elephants, warthogs, horned toads, striped skunks, black and green porcupines, painted turtles, white-tailed deer, ruby-throated hummingbirds, black-throated cliff swallows, blue warblers, red newts, golden eagles, water buffaloes, desert dromedaries, and little swerving brown bats, how could I not believe? So many creatures in a matrix of ethology that when I was out-of-doors there was never a day I doubted life's divinity. In the city, I went to and loved Beckett's *Krapp's Last Tape, Waiting for Godot,* and Pinter's, Ionesco's, Genet's, and others' brilliant plays—but didn't actually accept the premises of Absurdism. To a naturalist, Absurdism is ultimately absurd. It's a subway/sidewalk/basement philosophy, a starless-moonless-cloudless-night philosophy. But there are few cloudless, starless, moonless nights, and people living in basements and subways for more than a few years have constructed an uncommon life for themselves. Absurdism was like a stopped clock, but time doesn't stop.

MY SENSE of divinity was visual, so I'd never bothered to learn many of the birdcalls in my neck of the woods, and knew my friends by their faces, not the barometer of the voice. I played great music drawn from several centuries all day long, but didn't think of it as a radiant expression of humanity's unique genius—not as great as the visual drama of the clouds and sun, the Hudson or another river rushing by, the pointing firs, fuzzy tamaracks, sheeny willows, generous sweet-sapped maples, or a hawk in a basswood tree.

By 1988 I lived in the country year-round, and as my sight dimmed, I found driving becoming difficult, and began placing sets of binoculars next to the windows I looked out of, or wore them around my neck, using them dozens of times a day. I focused, too, on bookish pursuits, as if my time were short, but postponed thinking about what was wrong with me because I'd always lived for the sake of my work and as if I might die before it was finished anyway. Even in my twenties, I'd made sure each night that the day's accretion was legible enough for somebody else to decipher if I kicked off. I've always anticipated a "disaster" (faith in nature implies that you accept death as natural, often proper), and have always had weak eyes. Nature did not expect us to live to be eighty-four, or even sixty-four. Nature did not expect us to see so much, either—the daily TV catalogue of scandals and catastrophes, far-flung tearjerkers and utter outrages that you'd think some year would end. You'd think that when the massacres of ethnic cleansing are broadcast everywhere, or simpler, accidental tragedies like school buses hit at railroad crossings, they simply would never happen again. People would see the horror on the screen worldwide, and *never do it again.* Not slaughter thousands of people because of their tribe, nor stop a school bus on the railroad tracks.

The doctors I went to for my blindness weren't sure what was really wrong because the underlying culprit, beneath the cataracts, was that my retinas were in terrible shape—"pitted and bulging like a bald tire about to burst," as one surgeon put it. He didn't want to operate; the ordinary cataract procedure would be more dangerous because of the pressure that it would engender on the back of the eye. Indeed, the first three doctors I consulted declined. And they mistook the primary problem I was having with my vision. They thought it must be the retinas, not my clouded lenses, because they could see through my lenses to the back of my eyes so much more clearly than I could see out.

Meanwhile, as my sight dimmed, I began swallowing flies that might be swimming in my juice or soup, and other foreign matter, and voluntarily quit driving and gave my car away because bicyclists now looked like mailboxes posted beside the road, dogs like cardboard boxes, and pedestrians like poplar trees. I was afraid I wouldn't be able to see a child playing there at all. Living in Vermont, I perforce became a long-distance bus rider, and the local line, called Bonanza, was my carrier when I went to Manhattan or Boston. By great good luck, Bonanza happened to have been founded some forty years before by one of my ex-schoolmates, and he still headed the company and was esteemed as a good boss. It was my luck because I'm a shy person and in my previous spates of riding buses for long distances, during my roving youth, I'd never been able to summon the courage to sit up front, surmount my stutter, and strike up a comfortable conversation with the driver to hear his story and gather tales of the road. I'd looked out the window for hours instead, which was its own reward, or observed my fellow passengers. But now that I couldn't see much of anything I needed an opening to help change my habits, engage the driver's interest in this blindish gray-haired codger who had difficulty talking anyway because of an impediment.

Therefore I'd simply say the name "George Sage," my schoolmate from decades before, whom I'd never seen since, and the driver perked up. Bonanza was headquartered in Providence and ran New Englanders from town to city and back in competition with Trailways and other large lines, and nobody but an insider would have reason to know the owner's name. Then from one driver I would pick up updates on George and his family—the suburban town he lived in, how many kids he had, where they'd gone to college, what they were up to now, how the business was doing, how in midlife he'd invested in a little airline out in Nevada by way of a change from the business he'd started practically in prep school, and eventually been squeezed, but won an out from the Howard Hughes airline that did it to him, which made his losses good—to employ as conversation fodder with the next, when I rode again.

I learned quite a bit about the drivers too—the guys from Vermont, the guys from Massachusetts, each of them above fifty by now, with two or three decades of service to Bonanza, and the inevitable back pains, periodontal problems, heart tremors, asthma, emphysema, or arthritis to contend with. One had developed an allergy to diesel fumes, but it was too late in life for him to find another job with benefits or a decent wage. Four times a week he'd spend some thirteen hours on the road, crossing Massachusetts both ways, stopping at every town he came to, coughing and wheezing all the while, and with kidney troubles to boot, in order to keep his family functioning—though he exacerbated his difficulties by standing outside and smoking at stops and drinking heavily at home. Thanks to the environmentalists, the nuclear power plant near his home was closing down; a lot of jobs had vanished *there.* Maybe a gravedigger's position at the cemetery was going to open up, he thought, if one of the nuclear workers didn't get it. He was worried, although stoic, fatalistic, boisterous, and bluff—a hefty man who loved his CB radio and turned to it for solace on the highway, warning the truck drivers of a rig upended in the westbound lanes by nonchalant lingo: "Yeah, an eighteen-wheeler, and you can see the dirty side."

Another driver, a lifelong Vermonter, made the New York City run from Bennington regularly. He was slim, neat, refined, precise, soft-spoken, happily married, and otherwise with all his ducks in order, only concerned that the yuppie summer people and well-heeled retirees flocking to the lovely scenery around Manchester to buy homes were driving up property values, store prices, taxes, and forcing the regular citizens out. He was self-contained, middle-class in manner, not at all a sort of tethered long-haul trucker like the Boston driver, and his problems related to his budget and style of living or retirement plans, not his job security or

health. The Calcutta carnival of homeless people at the Port
Authority bus terminal near Times Square, where he spent a two-
hour turnaround every weekday afternoon, didn't ruffle his com-
posure. He read a newspaper in the drivers' subterranean lounge
or napped in a cubicle, then would pilot a new batch of passengers back to Vermont. Once you cleared Danbury, Connecticut,
and left the thruway for a two-lane road—old U.S. Route 7 running up the valley of the Housatonic River—it became white clap-
board towns again, almost like home.

Another driver, though, was sometimes rattled by his daily
trips to Eighth Avenue and Fortieth Street in the crazy city. He
was the most traveled of them all, oddly enough, and once or
twice he characterized himself to me as "kind of longhair, a little
bohemian," as if, because I was a college professor, he knew I'd
understand. He was less of a roisterer than the first man but less
white-collar in his body language than the second, and said that
he had been in the air force, stationed in Japan, as a young
man. He had "lost his innocence" there. For a serviceman in
the Far East, the prostitution had been wide open, and what
had gradually happened to him, he said—as we rode for several
hours through the darkening night, the temperature outside falling, Connecticut having given way to Massachusetts, and then
approaching Vermont—was that, with no limits on what you
were enticed and entitled to do, and every temptation available
outside the base on your weekend passes, he had developed a taste
for enjoying small boys. Afterwards, when his hitch in the military was up, he had come home, married, had some children, and
put those experiences forever behind him, he hoped—if not,
unfortunately, the occasional surge of unsettling memories, as
incongruous as those of combat which other veterans were subject to at family picnics, school soccer games, and the like. Yet
these were not of combat; they were unsanctioned, secret, and his
career as a bus driver in rural New England, too, at first had kept
a cap on them, till he was assigned the New York run. Times

Square, with its hungry side street waifs offered for sale, black children or brown and a few white urchins, who could be mauled or sucked for twenty bucks, was like lurid Japan all over again. Eventually he succumbed, and it was souring to his marriage and made him wish that he had never enlisted in the air force and gone abroad in the first place. Yet he had rather a good marriage, it seemed to me. His wife often met our bus, as we passed through their town, and rode with us to the end of the line and drove him home.

I hadn't ridden buses much since the cross-country Grey-hounds of the hobo summers of my youth. They had still been a hardscrabble mainstream means of travel then, but with cheap air travel, that's over. Long-distance buses have become the habitat of busted souls who've lost their cars to the finance company or lost their licenses because of driving drunk; of childless, indigent old people; or frightened new immigrants from Laos or Nigeria or Guatemala, who have too many kids to manage and be able to sleep at the same time; of people who have just been released from an institution; of legally blind people like me. I met several others who couldn't see beyond the end of their nose; and elderly widows who had outlived their money; and frightened children who were being shuttled solo between a terrible-faced mother who stuck them onto the bus at one end and a terrible-faced father who picked them off at the other; and gently retarded individuals who saw the world as cloudily as I did but by a different process— a woman who carried herself like the Queen of England but, always smiling, fell down a lot; a man with stained pants whose feces smelled of whiskey.

On planes out of desperado places such as Alaska I've sat next to haunted-looking people—a young woman crying throughout the flight down to Seattle with absolutely bottomless grief; a man desolately sucking the tail of his two-foot gray beard. But buses are a kind of bottom rung, beneath even the panic of an airport departure lounge, when your life has suffered a tumble. It takes so long to get away from what you're trying to escape and get to where you're trying to go that most of us would much prefer jumping on a plane and arriving in the clean anonymity of the exurbs of our chosen city, with bustly business people all around, renting cars, calling home with credit cards, conferencing here and there, sipping margaritas, snapping the locks of attaché cases, accessing their laptops and PowerBooks. In a gritty bus station, with derelicts on the benches trying to pretend that they are travelers in order to snatch a nap, and the mean streets of an inner-city ghetto just outside, it's not like anesthetically arriving at an airport. I remember once being seated on the Bennington bus next to a tough-faced, diminutive man who looked to be in his sixties and whom I'd first noticed in the New York bus terminal because he had been hobbling about with chest pains, suffering agonies in the queues. He turned out to be a racetrack groom, just cashiered from his pick-up job in Florida because of angina attacks. He spoke in muttered bursts, half-collapsed in his seat as he anticipated the stabbing shafts of pain—although of course he was a lean, fit, hardbitten-looking sort of guy in other respects. Now in desperate straits, he was making his way back to Pittsfield, the Massachusetts town he had left in anger twenty years ago, to throw himself upon the mercy of a son who still lived there, and whom he hadn't seen since then. We arrived in the December chill at ten o'clock at night, but no one met the bus for him.

However, the night was not unlike the day for me, because I couldn't see either the stars or birds, neither a plane's lights nor a fox ranging a roadside field, or even read with my two eyes at once, because I had to hold a book or magazine so near that I was not able to focus both of them upon the words; I'd close one and rest it for a while, while using the other. But my straits weren't desperate. I had a lifetime of preparation for this, in the sense of jiggering my finances into position for long-term survival and remodeling the furniture of my mind for life's later stages. Goodness knows, I hadn't wanted to be blind, but neither had I wanted to be young forever, and some of the changes I was now undergoing were amusing in their way, or curious, and an adventure. When I reached the city on my trips, I couldn't read street signs or numbers, so would have to rely on my memories of its geography and count the blocks I walked from each big two-way cross-street—42nd, 57th, 72nd, 79th, 86th, 96th, or 34th, 23rd, 14th—to find my way, stumbling on the curbs and listening for the lights to change according to the traffic's sound or the lurch of the crowds. Often I took taxis, but even this was complicated because I needed to pretend that I could see the route that we were following in order not to be led round Robin Hood's barn, and also that I could read the meter after we arrived. "What's it say?" I'd casually ask, dropping my eyes to my wallet, as I chose a bill by its placement, then raising them again and gazing at the numerals I couldn't really see about the same time that the cabbie turned toward me and answered.

I couldn't recognize my friends, and when I did know who I was talking to by moving close enough to recognize them by their shape or by the tenor of their body language, I couldn't see if they were attentive or distracted, whether they had had a sleepless night and saddening day or were feeling effervescent and mischievous. The voice alone is not indicative, and by the time I leaned right next to somebody's face to distinguish a smile from a scowl, the play of conversation would have moved on. I remembered that my father, when he was first operated on for cancer, had been insistent, if not even a bit frantic, that nobody in his professional life should know what he had had. He was afraid if word got out he might be written off; that other lawyers would cease to count him as a player or think of him as in the running—as a colleague or an opponent who had any consequence. And similarly if I was now a blind writer I need not be reckoned with. No more essays, or jurying; no more books to come out regularly. I could be politely dismissed—and the good-time Charlies among my friends did depart. With glasses on I was seeing at twenty feet what normal eyes, without eyeglasses, could pick out at four hundred, so the process did resemble being terminally ill, and people came to visit me ritually once and never again.

The platinum light in the early morning, as a gentle rain fell, nearly broke my heart—the tiers of green, each subtle shade different, ash from cedar, spruce and apple, lilac, locust, and dogwood—leaves whose beauty I was losing. I walked through the timothy and orchard grass, the tangles of vetch, the fireweed stalks and raspberry canes, each registering as friends I might not see again, with what was left of my eyesight standing on tiptoe—or dimly perceiving each through my binoculars. Hearing a toad sing, I would visualize him, and a chorus of tree frogs in an alder thicket rejoicing in the rain. My dog I saw because he came to my hands, and birches became my favorite trees (except in July, when the basswoods bloomed with that fetching, incomparable scent that was Thoreau's favorite) because their white bark showed up glowingly.

I bought a telescope to gaze at the rising moon, sometimes following its slow-scudding trajectory through much of an evening, and wore field glasses all day, ready to peer through a window if I heard a car turn into the driveway, or the wind blew and I wanted to see the crowns of the trees bob and interlace. But I was generally too late. By the time I located the car, it would be too close to stare at discreetly through binocs, and a bird—if I heard a bird sing—would have hopped to another branch or taken flight before I got it into focus. Still, just having these eight-power lenses to clap in front of my regular glasses was a comfort, though already I could feel they'd be no help if I went truly blind.

As the curtain drew tighter, closing my horizon from sixty to twenty or thirty feet, I saved my spirits from thoroughly sinking by paying attention to the peculiar details of what was happening to me and how to function. I hitchhiked to my teaching job and home, thumb-up like a boy again—and mapped the seating of my classes, asking the students to sit in the same place each week so I would know who was speaking, and to speak without raising their hands. Walking to town, I focused upon my lungs and legs, and itemized the feel of the weather, or the menu of colors my eyes still took in, after shadings were a blur. I listened to Dickens and Shakespeare on tape, experimented with radio snacking from *Canadien Français,* and when making love to the friend I lived with, I focused in blind obsession upon giving pleasure, on performance, frequency, reliability, as if my existence depended upon it—imagining her a dominatrix who found me of value only as a tongue and dildo and would kick me out into the icy void if I ever failed. It was kinky to be blind.

There are fair-weather friends and foul-weather friends, and we need both kinds in our lives, especially because each is likely to absent himself rather abruptly when the wind shifts. For instance, the drama of an emergency may unsettle a fair-weather specialist, uncorking alarming vibrations in him and causing him to make his excuses and flee. But the same intimations of a catastrophe will give the foul-weather person a bracing sense that life is, indeed, dangerous and interesting. The proverbial social worker who is an ace at her work but only manages to hold her own hangups in check by focusing hard on her clients is an example of this type, but of course it is she who pulls people through their crises, not your sunnier and more politic soul who avoids the taint of misery. On the other hand, when you bask in good news and things are going fine, an ambulance-chaser may not be your best bet for a drinking buddy. He'll remain ambivalent about what it means. He'll be listening for the crump of thunder, the winds of a cyclone, as if your good luck cannot last. You probably want the comradeship of summer soldiers then.

My summer soldiers were now canceling lunch dates with me, quietly dropping me from party lists, and tacitly waiting to see if my eye problems were going to sort themselves out like other difficulties, financial, legal, personal, that sometimes throw a monkey wrench into a person's career and remove him from circulation for a spell. We were at an age when people we knew were beginning to die off anyhow and get dropped from everybody's e-mail. But unlike other paradoxes that plague us, blindness—to be alive yet be denied the chief measure of enjoying life—is studied in Sunday school as a kind of parable. At least it used to be, because even as kids you could approximate the experience just by closing your eyes. We'd do it as a ghoulish game, or maybe a love game—do you trust a girl enough to let her lead you anywhere? You couldn't toy with cancer or other unambiguous disasters. But *why* were people rendered or born blind and squeezed into inhabiting only their fingertips and ears? Though the teacher couldn't answer this, it was an accessible catastrophe and therefore fascinating (one could experiment with how it felt) and age-old (Jesus had concerned himself with blindness)—not one of these dreary, new, overcomplicated geriatric ailments that help to hobble our society now that so many of us live into our nineties.

Jesus, besides his feat of raising Lazarus from the dead and cleansing several lepers, paused more than once by the roadside in the circuit of his travels to quickly heal a blind person with by-the-bye aplomb, applying a paste of spit and soil to the afflicted eyes: or else he just touched them. And as you read the passages in Matthew, Mark, and John, these divine acts of charity seem quite impromptu. Christ has come to earth to offer an eternal afterlife, not succor a few blind people whose privations will soon be dwarfed by the bliss of heaven in any case. It seems not calculated but apparently an accident that one rather than another crippled individual happens to be at hand as, hassled and preoccupied, he passes by. He's nation building, not here to physic the sick, and has an astonishingly short amount of time to do it, though pity for their anguish does mix with his sense of the obvious priority of universal, eternal redemption versus this single sufferer's chagrin, which will soon be at an end, when he stops kindly, almost surreptitiously, so as not to draw a crowd, and asks if they "believe." Presumably, the God who created heaven and earth could cure blindness without "belief"; yet Christ's own powers, swift and serene though they are, might need that extra catalyst. In Mark 8, for example, the miracle requires two applications of his hands. The first only restores the sight of the blind man of Bethsaida to the extent that people look to him "as trees, walking." So, "after that He put his hands again upon his eyes and made him look up and he was restored and saw every man clearly."

In John 9, another incident occurs in which the blind person is not instantly cured, but instead is told that he must go and wash away the clay and spittle in "the pool of Siloam" in order to see. Jesus' disciples had just asked the question that we Sunday schoolers wanted to when we watched a sightless person attempting to navigate the brutal streets, perhaps with the assistance of a slinking dog: "Who did sin, this man, or his parents, that he was born blind?" And Jesus answered famously: "Neither hath this man sinned, nor his parents, but that the works of God should be made manifest in him." Afterward the man, confronted by the exasperating Pharisees, enunciates the crucial line that adorns the hymn "Amazing Grace," I "was blind, but now I see!" This certainly explained that sin was not involved, but not why Christ didn't make more of a dent in the populace of halt and lame in Palestine, circa Zero B.C. What was "made manifest"? I was already more of a pantheist than Christian, intuiting that heaven is on earth, not in the sky, and with my eyes closed I could feel relict senses that are ordinarily blanketed by the gift of sight start to assert themselves. Our Sunday school teacher had quoted blind Milton's line from sixteen centuries later: "They also serve who only stand and waite." And though I understood his meaning, I was unconvinced. The blind underwent no direct pain (pain was after all the real puzzle), but were left suspended as if between life and death while they contended with the arcane, finger-picking language of Braille and an oddly touching dependence upon a trained dog to move around.

The Pharisees were malign, obtuse, sophistical, and eventually they or their like had pursued Christ to his crucifixion. But the softer figure of Doubting Thomas, because of his sincerity and quick repentance, was appealing. Thomas, a disciple, did not repudiate Jesus, as, for instance, Peter briefly did. He only questioned him—asked to "put my finger into the print of the nails and thrust my hand into his side" in order to believe in the truth of the Resurrection. And Christ rebuked him. Thus, perhaps with unshakable regret, Thomas wandered farther than any other of the evangelical Apostles later on, all the way to south India, as legend has it, where on a hill above Madras he himself may have been crucified. I have a special feeling for Thomas because my parents used to call me "Doubting Thomas" when I disagreed with them as a young kid on matters such as Jim Crow laws, anti-Semitism, the right of the rich to be rich, and of America to rule the world. I doubted the established order at thirteen, just as the established order rather doubted me. And although poor Thomas was not the most mesmerizing of all the Christian missionaries who ever came to India (Saint Francis Xavier probably fits that role—who stepped off the caravelle that had brought him to assume Goa's bishopric, circa 1550, and, virtually ignoring the assembled dignitaries, walked straightaway to Goa's leprosarium to begin washing people's sores), Thomas was instead a rebel's rebel, doubting even the consummate revolutionary, Jesus Christ. After I had finally recovered my sight through surgery, I went to India to feast my eyes, and at the end of this trip, feeling twenty thousand miles from home, sick in the belly and very lonely, I found myself standing on the same scenic hill where Thomas is said to have been killed. It was near an airport and my plane had been delayed, but I was aware of the irony of feeling sorry for myself at such a singular spot, while surrounded too by India's present desperation. Poor Thomas, I thought—my dear old cohort from an iconoclastic childhood—how desolate you must have felt, dying in slow agony facing the Bay of Bengal, without the company of Mary or Mary Magdalene and the Disciples, or even the Pharisees, your foes, to spur your spirits a bit by jeering you into the netherworld. Nor the seven-league boots of an airplane.

The ethic of pity was what we were taught to feel with regard to blind people. The taboo against bumping, cheating, or tripping them up was extreme. So wicked a notion could scarcely provoke a titter—it was too terrible; and the story of the boy who'd snuck into the blind man's house and shat in his sink was so wild we couldn't believe it; then couldn't restrain our ugly giggles. To imagine his wail of despair and throttled horror, the disgust and dread for the interminable future he must have felt when he returned, incredulously searched, and finally ran his hand against the turds, or maybe set his dishes down in them all unawares, lay beyond the bounds of civilization. And the perpetrator remained peculiar. The last time I saw him, he was in his fifties and said that he had bought a pair of binoculars to watch a lonesome spinster woman who lived across the road, who he said was "going to hang herself for sure one day." He was waiting for the morning when he would see her skinny body strung from a rafter, her misery having got the best of her—though in fact she has outlived him.

One rarely hears of anybody suffering some variety of biblical self-loathing because of their cruelty to others. Mostly they sit in church, vote, shop, and deal in goods or services like anybody else. They're anesthetized, living well and in denial; and nothing wakes them up. But when I left home for a series of cheap hotels in New York during my twenties, while I was setting my course as a writer, I knew several blind men and women who had been stranded in these bleak establishments by the social agencies and their own lack of money. They'd grope along the walls in the endless shabby corridors or through the lobby, its rug torn, its floor tilting, to get out to the street and feel the sunshine on their faces and buy a can of tuna fish, a quart of orange juice. Though often innocents, they were living like "sinners in the hands of an angry god," squirming upon a griddle of petty fears and pilferage, morning griefs and afternoon humiliations, while the genuine sinners in high-rises along Central Park West a few blocks away lived high off the hog.

Tuna *is* a comfort, if you pay attention to it—tasting of the sea, indeed the very salts of life. And so is orange juice, which opulently personifies the sweet acidity of roots, sunshine, and trees. When I was blind I loved to savor juices—grapefruit, apple cider, and V-8, all of which, considering the pleasure they give, seemed unbelievably available and inexpensive. This was 1990, but I remembered driving across America in 1953 on old Highway 66, two lanes, ten days, and reaching southern California, and suddenly there were orange groves beside the road and canvas stands offering tall glasses of fresh-squeezed juice for the price of a glass of milk back East. Milk has the taste of infancy and is a balm for ulcers, but juice has bite, and tuna, even from a can, has more of the real aroma of sex and life than fowl or pig or steak (though bacon, smoked, comes second).

Corn, potatoes, spinach, toast—I knew from my hotel hot plate in the 1950s that it doesn't take a lot of money to eat with vivid care, and had an impoverished friend one flight down who published cookbooks, using *his*. It was a problem for these blind people just to procure the food, however, or go to the common bathroom at the corner of the hall, with possibly a gauntlet of other souls, less worse off and hanging out, eyeing them with vibrations of satisfaction at their pathetic state. The women sometimes got manhandled in alcoves of the stairs or in the elevator, as they made their way down to the coffee shop, by old men who lay in wait and "copped a feel" under the pretext of assisting them over a set of steps or around a pail blocking the route they had to follow, or by boys out of school. What despair they must have felt as the months and years ground on—the hopeless tar pit they had fallen into!—no end to how precarious their daily position was—and just the jabbering talk-show hosts on the radio for company—except for one tragic and unlucky lady I'd known slightly, who was burned alive when the hotel that the Welfare Department had beached her in caught fire and the crummy sighted men, who'd groped her in the corners of the corridors when she left her room, forgot all about her until the place became an inferno. They remembered her on the sidewalk.

Blindness has many meanings. "Blind" passion or greed, envy or salaciousness; being "blind" to the scams of a crook or the dilemmas of a friend. When blind, I could no longer go to museums: would have had to stand so close my glasses scratched the paintings. Couldn't see butterflies, and realized that, unlike the kingdom of birds, these white admirals and tiger swallowtails were totally lost to me. At least I had tapes of birdcalls, though was soon frustrated to acknowledge I was learning to recognize the calls of little woods warblers that I'd never bothered to track down and actually look at while I'd still had my sight. Blindness, as one feels it from inside, is like a shutdown of the front wall of one's head. The ears—at both sides—are left, but one's eyes, useless now, seem to have constituted one's entire forehead and face, north of one's residual nose. And what wouldn't one sacrifice to get them back! I would have eaten out of garbage cans, gone friendless, given my possessions away, surrendered a leg, to be able to see grass wave in the wind, not just hear it—see whose footsteps were approaching me, not have to wait until they chose to speak. My regret was so comprehensive that I seldom spoke of it, just as when you visit a dying person, only seldom do they blurt out, *Oh god, I'm disappointed! I'm losing everything I've loved and cared for, everything I've paid attention to, and everything important to me!*

Instead I apologized as charmingly as I could when I reached for what I thought was my glass of wine at somebody's dinner party and put my hand into the cranberry sauce, or tripped over a coffee table, spilling the pot and seven people's cups. Reality was hooded for me and, barring such a contretemps, I improvised ways to disguise how sightless I was by keeping my face wisely turned toward whoever was speaking and recognizing my acquaintances by their morphs and stoops, their irascibility or depression, anxiety or kindness. I learned to listen urgently for the click of a stoplight on the street, and to assign my students only books that I had read intensively before, staving off the time when I would be too disabled to teach.

In H. G. Wells's short story "The Country of the Blind," the populace of an isolated Shangri-la in the Andes, who are all congenitally blind, triumph over a sighted wanderer who has slid down a precipitous mountainside into their valley. At first he'd gloated, perceiving that he had stumbled into a cut-off community of handicapped people who lived off only what they grew, and remembered the folk adage that "In the country of the blind the one-eyed man is king." But it turns out not to be that easy. They can trace and chase and capture him by their super-sense of sound, and after they do so and have humored him a bit in his oddities, they decide to "operate" on him for his own good to remove the "growths" in his eyesockets that appear to them to be at the root of his abnormality. Though he has fallen in love with a young woman who often mediates for him, she too wants him normalized. The jelly of his eyes, she realizes, is the source of what she regards as his hallucinations, and therefore of friction between them. Oddity can never reign; and so he flees to freeze in the snows above the valley, alone and in the ecstasy of eyesight, rather than submit to being blinded by them.

Quite so. I discovered that sight was an ecstasy next to which sex, for example, was small potatoes. Watching raindrops running down a windowpane and the gray sky's purplish bellying, the trembling trees davening, I gorged on what I could still manage to see. I studied seedheads through my telescope—and the scrimshaw on the moon—and a balm-of-Gilead's intricacy of boughs. Lying down next to a brook, I watched the amber water ripple, the yellow miracle of moss. I laid my head next to individual rocks, or underneath a pine whose million needles were a sunburst, and above them fishbone clouds. Black crows; the greenish bluish tawny grasses; a red sweatshirt; a white birch's beckoning bark. Nothing else—not speech or smell or hearing—matters like your eyes. I sometimes cried in the city when trying to find an address that I had to get to, but unable to read the numerals on the buildings or the streets, and stuttering so badly that the people whom I asked for help dodged by me as they would a madman.

Walking had always been one of life's centerpieces, especially in the city, where it enabled me to pack in enough joy, sensation, and exercise to make up for the deficits of urban living. Seventy, eighty blocks hadn't seemed a lot, and when younger I had been a whirlwind walker, attentive to developments a hundred yards ahead, which, with my native New Yorker street smarts, had kept me safe for decades. Alertness, speed, good eyes had helped me finesse, too, the more pressing threat of having to speak. My stutter, which extended well past middle age, made me appear not simply importunate like a bum or beggar but disoriented and deranged—my mouth flabbering, my expression wounded, needy, fatalistic. Thus, for any information I needed, it was imperative that in the two seconds I had before a respectable citizen brushed by me, assuming I was homeless and a panhandler, I convince him I was only handicapped, not one of the legion of beseechers inhabiting the street. And it was so searing to be rebuffed—I *did* feel homeless then—that until I had gone semi-blind, I would speedily search and search to almost any lengths to avoid asking directions. But, blind, losing the confident posture and direct, lively eyes of somebody at a peak of life, I really did begin to look like an alcoholic pleading for a quarter or flipping out. The experience of being mistaken for a derelict is only briefly beneficial to the soul; and as a stutterer for more than fifty years, I'd

already been scalded by such episodes enough for them to make
their mark.

My careers as writer and teacher were stalling out. I couldn't
read my students' papers, and had to stop reviewing books for
newspapers. The travel assignments that I coveted dried up because when an editor took me out to lunch he would notice me
bumping into hydrants. I thought of reinventing myself as an
author of children's stories. Like poems, they'd be short enough
to rewrite in my head and dictate later. Otter and muskrat, snake
and frog, fox and woodchuck, owl and squirrel, cowbird and warbler, coyote and rabbit, skunk and deer mouse would be my pairs
of adversaries or characters. But I simply wept at times, disheart-
ened on the darkening streets where my thwarted haste was just a
mote in New York's pariah population—all in need of help—my
badge of misery so commonplace, while in the country the daily
round of radio egos and blurry TV personalities was my company. Friends shrank farther into the haze, as if in a science fiction
novel, though of course it was I who was shrinking. "Good to see
you," I once said in parting, whereupon the childhood doggerel
echoed in my mind: *I see, said the blind man, but he couldn't see
at all.*

Then, curiously, my stutter began to lighten, as if it were at the
far end of a seesaw from this infinitely more serious problem.
Stuttering is probably hereditary, but in degree of severity it is also
the servant of emotions like self-consciousness, embarrassment,
and other low-grade fears and agitations that tend to feed upon
themselves. Yet my mind was now thrown out of its accustomed
tics and potholes. The downward spiral, vicious circle, which had
worn deep ruts in my synapses over the course of half a century,
was broken by the pitch of urgency of this much worse emergency.
Adrenaline, too, always helpful, kicked in, and instead of getting
depressed, I could rise to a challenge with a kind of Battle-of-
Britain exuberance and quit stuttering, crack a joke and ask for
assistance with straightforward good humor. As I saw less, I felt

liberated to chat with strangers because I knew I wouldn't see their silent laughter if my difficulties aroused their *Schaden-freude*. Although I hadn't had a chance to tunnel underneath the wreckage and find the usual detours that blind people use—such as a whetted sense of hearing or aggrandized fingers—curiosity pepped my spirits. Coping, camouflaging is what makes war fun, and thus at parties I could often speak better under the stress of not being able to see. But if you can't make out the mood or identity of the person you are talking to or discern who is across the room, then have to cadge a ride somehow in order to get home, the bravery of blindness remains a small advantage.

Sex was another story. Touch and imagination, being equal legs of a tripod, can fill in splendidly for fading eyes. Sex became an intense focus for me. At fifty-seven, fifty-eight, I was making love as often as ten times a week, both for solace and to insist to my partner, *Don't count me out!* This eyelessly frenetic pace was a survival tactic in every sense—morale, manhood, contact, sanity—and yet, like so much else in life, took a perverse twist. The masochist in me made hay with the fact of my helplessness, and I fantasized during lovemaking that I was becoming a love-slave, employed by my tender friend for no purpose except sensuality, that my existence depended upon getting hard and staying hard morning and night, though I was afraid to confide this to her. Otherwise we seemed an all-American pair, each cozying the other to bandage wounds cut by the recent severance of twenty-five-year marriages. Her husband had been peripatetically unfaithful to her, so my immobility may have attracted her. I'd thought I'd understood masochism psychologically before— babes at the breast are so delightfully helpless, for instance—but had never recognized a Darwinian use for it. We lived together, she now the peripatetic one, and my gratitude to her for taking me in remains immense.

———

"TWILIGHT IS A BLIND MAN'S HOLIDAY" is another well-worn proverb. In Africa and Alaska I had met aging tribesmen with clouded eyes who could still feed themselves despite their cataracts because they knew the animals' trails and haunts, and because the animals emerged to feed at dusk and early dawn, when the sun was not yet glaring above the horizon, glinting off the hunter's milky lenses, effectively blinding him. Every day broad daylight managed to kill whatever vision I had left to the opacity of tapioca; but after sunset I'd go outside again, almost tiptoeing with a tremulous joy, and sit down in the grass, my pupils expanding as dusk fell and as my cataracts lost their blocking power. As if on stolen time, I gazed at the rolling landscape, the profile of the lines of trees, smelling the joe-pye weed, fragrant like vanilla, seeing clouds like lumbering buffaloes pricked by quick winds in the sky. I made a point of being outside at dawn as well, when the tree trunks brownly gleamed with dew, and in the silken demi-light I might see a deer toss up its white tail and hear its pounding narrow feet, its reedy alarm-sneeze, and several birds' chip-calls. The silvery, furry hills lay under bands of salmon red and trout pink, nuanced by a gentle lavender, underneath an ocean blue.

Having perhaps half an hour before the sun got over the horizon and blotted out my acuity, I invested hope and energy in these early mornings, remembering those old Indian hunters on the margins of blind destitution, who might have to make do with the threadlike outline of that deer in order to shoot a month's worth of meals, though the moment could be prolonged by a dark rainstorm, if it was morning, or by the rising of the moon in the dark night. Like a bug's antennae, my hands and ears sought clues, feeling the gusts of wind and hearing them, as I fingered the white flowers of wild carrot, orange hawkweed, tigerish lilies. I couldn't drive a car, hustle a buck, smile at my good buddies, but I still had these sighted interludes, and days full of Chopin and Schubert, Arrau and Rubinstein. Life for a while could continue to be heaven on earth, as I had always believed, enhanced by telepathy as my eyes flagged.

The important thing was to avoid being deranged by talk-radio or TV "hosts" whose egos were like suppurating boils that never popped. Week by week, their garish pleas for applause and rancid false laughter, their acrid logic, their make-nice appeals to the ecumenical piety of chuckling greed or boob-ogling festered like a pus that never seeps away and heals. I knew that the remedy for deep-seated grief is to involve oneself with others, and I was doing a bit of that. I'd always been a listener, even an expert listener, because of how hard it was to talk. But if you have to walk two miles to get to town and can't read people's faces when you get there, you're less convincing than a more self-centered sighted person. Your face goes wooden from the lack of give-and-take with other faces to react to, and your companion, distracted by your blindness, cannot seem to lose himself in talking to you. Also, your limited intake of what is current on the streets and on TV and in the newspapers, your wistful circumference of concerns, your bumbling preoccupation with Memory Lane, makes you a less engrossing listener than somebody whose problem is just that he can't talk.

I was having trouble finding a surgeon who would risk rupturing my retinas while operating on my cataracts. One brightly clever doctor on Park Avenue told me it could be "a Pandora's box" with multiplying disasters; I should wait till I was so old I was "coughing and bent over." Another personable physician with a high reputation, near Fifth Avenue, kept referring to "technical problems" that might blight the prospects for surgery and would venture no prognosis. Maybe it was better to be content with a quarter of a loaf, he suggested. Another only spoke to me with his tape recorder on—he sat by the microphone—though he took painstaking photos of my retinas, perhaps as what is called "defensive medicine." Like many writers, I'm a student of catastrophe and, for example, once turned off the Baton Rouge–New

Orleans highway to visit the National Leprosarium, a languid, breezy institution next to the levee of the Mississippi in the hamlet of Carville, Louisiana, where lepers are warehoused. In the army I had worked in a tuberculosis hospital and one of my fears is of being warehoused (I suppose it always was) in an intolerable family, job, or social situation: not to be free. And here were the patients, dozens of them, not free to leave. "The results of efforts to control leprosy have by no means been brilliant," said my *Encyclopaedia Britannica*. Out back was a desultory-looking lab where armadillos, the only experimental animals that were susceptible to the bacterium, were housed in boxy cages.

But eyelessness is worse than leprosy or the penury of being homeless or my worst experiences when mute for weeks in the vise of a stutter. Hooded like a hostage, I examined my dilemma with a teary nostalgia for lesser troubles, feeling my way along the walls that hemmed me in. Then I heard about a woman surgeon who was said to be both creatively brave and suitably cautious. I called three other doctors to check her reputation, made an appointment, and, dressing carefully in a red turtleneck pullover and blue blazer, practically as if my life depended on it (and carrying my best book along as an offering), I went to see her. By this time I needed to squint in order to look just half a dozen feet ahead.

"You can't see!" she exclaimed immediately, when I sat down and showed her how close I had to hold a magazine. After putting in the drops and situating me in the examining chair, she said, "We ought to operate. How soon can you do it?" Later she explained that eyes with retinas as frail as mine often fooled the ophthalmologists because an early-stage cataract's effect on the patient's already bad vision was cataclysmic, whereas they could still see in and thus assumed that he or she should be able to see out unless retinal deterioration was the real problem.

An active, slim, short-haired woman of medium height and

middling age, she had small confident hands and practical-looking glasses. After my operations, I thought of her romantically as Athena, the rescuer of heroes on the plains of Troy, but at first impression she reminded me of the "A" student at a university who outperforms the males but disarms their customary resentment of a woman of studious appearance who does exceptionally well, by being attentive, perceptive, efficient, unobtrusive, and sympathetic, avoiding any hint of superiority or grandiosity. I trusted her, in other words, and could imagine her diminutive fingers slicing through my corneas and guiding a micro-knife into my eyes.

So, with nothing to lose, I soon found myself lying under a partial anesthetic in a crowded mini-operating room in New York Hospital, hearing conversations but recognizing only light and dark, as various mechanisms and instruments were lowered over me. A nurse said to another that she had "hit the jackpot today, doing all eye operations." I wondered if she was speaking with irony. A surgeon who'd operated on me the year before came in, greeted me courteously, and examined the flawlessly healed incision that he had made in my throat to extract a parathyroid gland. Then my present physician entered, chatting happily with an ophthalmological resident whom she was training. Their bubbling reminded me of sociable hours during my childhood when I'd overheard two women preparing salad for a church supper—except that they were at work on the crux of my being. My surgeon even teased me about not acting macho, knowing I could hear, and when I tried to mumble a protest, she gaily told me to "just lie there and keep quiet." The tactful diplomacy with which she ordinarily negotiated with men evaporated when she had them on the table.

I was naked under a paper sheet, with an anesthetic needle taped to a vein in my wrist and oxygen being piped to my nostrils; and after an interval I heard her interrupt her companionable chatter to the young resident with a pregnant pause, and then the joyous words, almost whispered: "It's *breathtaking,* isn't it, when it goes as perfectly as that? I love it."

"Yes," the student said, having watched her deftly extract the clouded lens from its filmy capsule in my left eye by a new technique called *capsulorhexis,* and now insert a plastic one of sculpted specifications that had been manufactured in Bellevue, Washington, delicately in its place. But a minute later the student added, "Oh, the lens fell on the floor."

"That's the old lens. No harm. We don't need that," my savior answered, mostly for my benefit, as I drifted off to sleep.

Other current methods of operating for cataracts are known as the "can-opener" and the "Christmas tree," according to how they look to the surgeon through the macro-microscope which lowers onto the patient's face from the ceiling. All are outpatient procedures, whereas sixty years ago recovery required lying with one's head between sandbags for several weeks, with no miraculous plastic implants to greatly improve one's vision from the previous status quo.

I woke up in a couple of hours in a chair in a large room full of hernia patients who were also waking up and about to go home. My doctor in her bluestocking street clothes walked through to make sure that I was out of the woods, feeling buoyant because she had performed her morning's string of operations well. She reminded me that she would take the bandage off my eye in her office the next morning. With one eye covered and the other still clouded by its cataract, I was led back to our hotel by Trudy, the lady I live with in Vermont, in a precariously optimistic state of shock.

Next day I was in appropriately groggy pain, half sedated, half elated, at eight o'clock, when the doctor's maid—who was both pitying and accustomed to the sight of early-morning walking wounded—let me into her brownstone. The second floor was for patients, her drawing room the waiting room, with a red-velvet, leathery, sumptuous Persian-rug decor, tall books in a breakfront, silk-screen portraits of falcons, and folding doors and a chandelier, but a properly dim, old-fashioned, functional examining office.

I was early, as usual—another proof to my teasing surgeon of how unmacho I was—and she left her coffee in the dining room downstairs, which was enlivened with an uncaged gray African and a green Amazonian parrot, to come and unbind my wounded eye. My stoicism of the pre-op period had evaporated overnight from the sensation of having run my eye into a stick. I was querulous and flinchy, as my enthusiastic, inspired surgeon mocked and praised me.

"What a fussbudget! But *excellent,* excellent. Your eye is excellent," she exclaimed, peering with her powerful mini-light inside. It was her favorite word to use while patients listened anxiously, as I discovered during the ensuing weeks, hearing many other people being examined, from the sofa in the waiting room.

She prescribed drops to prevent infection or any glaucoma type of damage to the optic nerve, and gave me an eye-guard for sleeping, in case I accidentally socked or rolled over upon the eye. Though most doctors wait at least six months to remove the cataract in the patient's second eye, she decided we were on a roll and let's go ahead again and do it in three weeks. Under my gimpy, grouchy air of extreme infirmity I was swelling with cheerfulness, and so agreed. To amuse me further (knowing my interest in animals), she told me the gelatinous fluid she had injected underneath my cornea to cushion it during the operation was obtained from roosters' combs.

"And no Pandora's box," she added, which became a joke with us. She said her husband was reading my book to her in bed at night.

Before that first operation, she had asked if I would prefer to be 20/20 without glasses when she was finished, or a bit near sighted, as I was used to being, which was better for reading. With the implants, she could choose the result. I naturally answered that I'd like to experience perfection, like an airplane pilot or Ted Williams, in my sixties. But now, Athena-like, she told me casually that she had decided not to give me 20/20 vision; she had sewn in plastic that would assure me only 20/40 without eyeglasses— "better for readers"—because bookish people "feel confused" if in late middle age they are suddenly endowed with pilots' eyes.

This peremptory decision overruling my romantic notion of being gifted with eagle eyes irritated me only slightly because I was so grateful to her and because I remembered with a sort of fond awe the public health nurses I had traveled with as a journalist in Alaska, who often held a life-and-death power in the isolated villages they served. A woman deathly sick was likely to receive urgent sisterly care, but with a man the question was more whimsical. If he was dirty and crude and, whatever his age, had no "cute" aspects, he might languish like a prisoner of war, scarcely attended to until death took him. But if he was appealing in some way, whether by being brave or dignified or funny—if he had either youth or presence—the nurses would exert themselves intensely, even affectionately, to help him, while seldom masking the enjoyment that flexing their power over a man gave them.

When the doctor took off my bandage, there was no *Eureka, I can see,* because I'd never been stone-blind. Instead, just an abrupt, astounding discovery of how bright light actually is. Not at first the beauty of the world, but the *brightness* of the world, as my eye squinted and winced, shutting out most of the sights now hammering at the door. Limping away from her office, I believed her when she said that the vision in my left eye had been restored. Yet the stairs, curbs, cars, and rushing strangers on the sidewalk, and all the lettering or numerals mapping the metropolis, were hardly less of a problem. I reeled and wobbled as I walked. But a bulging though still tentative joy—glimpsing shards of the rich, russet stone of the nearby buildings, and slivers of eggshell blue above that, speared by shafts of sunlight brighter than metal—

more than my staggering gait, threatened to capsize me. I kept the eye four-fifths shut rather fearfully; yet could begin to see fragments of faces, abbreviated as if by a camera's shutter. And even so, many of these first faces were like catching sight of an old friend for only an instant.

I sat recuperating in the darkish two-room apartment on East Nineteenth Street that I'd sublet for the month of November, glad it was both nondescript and dark, and that the month, as well, was a dark one, as I sought to reweave the fabric of my life. White sunshine blazed fitfully through the window bars and venetian slats, utterly delighting me. But I could take only short doses of such splendor. I made impulsive forays into the street at all hours, grabbing a look at random faces; also the scrumptious colors of food on my plate in a restaurant. Yellow squash, green peas, orange sweet potatoes, vivid chicken livers. Ochre or sandstone apartment buildings were underlined by their staccato storefronts, cherry red, beige-and-butter, at street level; and the hauntedly nostalgic neon sign of a bar-and-grill bespoke for me my more than thirty years of lonely, happy scrambling about this and many other New York neighborhoods for love and sex and conversation, for new sensations and friendships. Trudy had had to go back to her job in Vermont now that I was ambulatory. Missing her though I was, I began calling people with real gusto, summoning them to have lunch, supper, coffee, or a drink, like Lazarus, formerly "terminal" but just restored to life. Because I couldn't walk far, they came to me, from several periods of my life—first marriage, second marriage, first bachelorhood, second bachelorhood, old classmates, new writers I admired—and we gabbled keenly in one of half a dozen cozy taverns or Japanese or Italian places. My elation was infectious enough that in one meatloaf-and-gravy establishment that lacked a liquor license, the family kept slipping me complimentary glasses of wine from the kitchen.

I was pleased, too, to come back once or twice a week to have my friend manipulate my pupils with her magic eyedrops—

exclaiming at how "big" they got and how fast they got "big," while gazing in at my retinas and fingering my brows and cheeks—as we talked about our grown children, and her parrots squawked from the floor below. The "crush" or tropism of a patient toward a doctor who has saved that patient's life had occurred in me; and she on her side seemed to indicate that her marriage was in some sort of temporary trouble that agitated her considerably. So we lingered, talking like close pals.

The second operation didn't progress quite as famously. My lens capsule tore, and she had to revert to the "can-opener" technique to slip the natural lens out and the plastic lens in. (This one had been manufactured in Forth Worth, Texas.) The procedure took longer, and I twitched with discomfort, needing extra anesthetic through the needle taped to my fist. Nor was the same note of gaiety present in my surgeon's voice. And the resident apprentice who was observing the operation, a young man this time, sounded sulky in response. She was displeased with her luck at *capsulorhexis*—she told me later that her average success rate at doing it was about 50 percent, which made her performance with my two eyes typical, but that only elegance, not my basic vision, was at stake. The resident, she said, had been sulky because she hadn't allowed him to poke the long main anesthetic needle into the depths of my eye socket after the preliminary fist-stuff had taken effect—as student physicians observing an eye operation are usually permitted, as a matter of politesse, to do. Instead she told him (as I was glad to hear, lying on the table) that "this is a well-known writer." She told me she had finessed the previous resident—the young woman—in this regard by the fact that a charity patient was next in line, whom the resident would have a free hand with. So they'd simply chatted through the moment when my friend did the deep needle-stick behind the eye (patients are completely unaware of it) herself.

My NEIGHBORHOOD at Nineteenth Street, near Gramercy Park, was not a primary part of Manhattan for me. I'd been born in, and till the age of eight lived in, the East Eighties, near my surgeon's office; and certain blocks there still hold a wet-skinned luminosity for me when I pass through on foot or even in a taxi: memories greeny brown, like amphibians, as if linked with my emergence from the sea. Then my parents moved to suburban Connecticut, where I acquired a feeling for the woods. After college I returned to the city to make my way as a writer, married, and migrated between a series of apartments on the Lower East Side or Upper West Side, neighborhoods of pungency, drama, and character. Afterwards when I married my second wife, I lived with her and our daughter for two decades beside the Hudson River in Greenwich Village, an area that will always be my spiritual home, until I felt driven to move to Vermont by our divorce.

So here I was, in digs a friend had managed to find for me on short notice, and sorry at first to be recuperating in a locale that was not piquant with important memories. But I was nearing sixty and, hitting the streets again in this, my natal city, I soon found plenty of personal history near Gramercy Park as well. My daughter's Quaker grammar school was only four blocks off— and therefore bakeries that we'd snacked at after her school plays, corners that we'd met on to walk home, the watering hole where we had had her graduation party. Then of course I remembered that Saint George's, the Episcopal church where I had been christened in 1935, stood across from her school on Stuyvesant Square. I went inside and gazed at the very font—white marble shaped like a seashell—and pictured my parents, both about thirty, standing with their friends, hopes high, in the depths of the Depression. Their hopes for themselves, on balance, had not been steeply disappointed at the time of my father's death in 1967—which reminded me that my mother, who was originally from Aberdeen, Washington, had been courted by him at a residence for young women located right here on Gramercy Park, two blocks from my sublet. He used to deliver her to the door in the evening after supper and come and have breakfast with her early the next morning, as he walked from the apartment that he shared with another man on Forty-fourth Street way downtown to his law firm on Wall Street. A Vassar girl, she had trained a little as a social worker at Columbia and worked in personnel at Macy's.

Looking at *that* building then led me to realize with a start that although my memories of courting my own first wife, Amy, were mostly situated uptown at 242nd Street near Broadway in the Bronx, where she had been living in 1959—or else at 103rd Street and Broadway, where I'd been ensconced—in fact I had proposed to her right in this immediate neighborhood, in a cheap little hotel on Twentieth Street at Third Avenue. I was holed up in a gleeful frenzy to read the proofs of my second novel, *The Circle Home,* and to excerpt fifty pages of it, "The Last Irish Fighter," for what would be my first fiction in a national magazine (or, "The Greatest Boxing Story of Our Time," as *Esquire* billed it), while Amy was working as a statistician at the National Bureau of Economic Research in midtown, and so we had rendezvoused at my fourth-floor room to go out to supper. I may have popped the question in a preliminary way earlier, because we'd already looked at rings, but this was the evening when, in the elevator, we made it official. It was a rope elevator—the relic of a quieter, turn-of-the-century era. You pulled yourself up or down with a simple tug, aided by counterweighted pulleys; and aside from the smooth elegance of propelling oneself with a flick of the wrist, you stopped the conveyance by catching hold of the rope, and thus could do so between floors if you wished—as I did in order to kiss Amy hard and present her with the Tiffany ring that she had picked.

Another precious memory from this neighborhood, dating to the fall of 1966, floated unexpectedly into my mind. I'd lived in another marginal hotel off Third Avenue at Gramercy Park for a few weeks, larger than the one where I had proposed marriage to Amy and which was equipped with a motorized elevator. Seven years had passed and, alas, I was already divorced, but, having just returned to the city from northwestern British Columbia, was engrossed in transcribing the headlong, perfervid, scribbled journal of what became my first travel book. Soon I was going to move to a basement apartment on West Sixty-eighth Street, but in these first weeks had settled here (I went and looked at the old building, now a fancy co-op) to be close to my girlfriend, Leonore, who lived on the eleventh floor of an apartment house at Twenty-first Street and Second Avenue, in the same block as the Police Academy.

I'd arrived sexually hungry from three months in the Canadian wilds, but she was a fastidious woman and was teaching me to make love to her satisfaction, not selfishly, which was a service to me also. I'd never learned to make love to anyone's great satisfaction except sometimes my own. She slowed me down, gave gourmet instructions of specific point and pace, and she, of the women I'd been with, was the most like my own mother—tall, demanding, sumptuously endowed, and rather expansive in her expensive tastes, though more witty, acerbic, and emotive in the Jewish style. She worked for Lilly Daché, the trendy hat designer (later as a customer service executive at the Pierre Hotel and a banquets manager for a lawyers' association), while I was writing excitedly of riverboat and bush plane trips through the wilderness mountains and recapitulating the talks I had had with aged Tahltan, Tsimshian, and Tlingit Indians. But at night we tussled quickly through this incongruity amid her scented sheets. Indeed, we were spurred by it; it was a condiment. My muddy, bloody trappers had tramped through the Canadian bush to catch fur coats for people like Lilly Daché and Leonore.

Leonore had red hair and a perfect complexion. In looks, she resembled the movie star Loretta Young, and had wanted to be a ballet dancer until her teacher told her that her legs were too short. Though never confrontational, she had a duelist's eye for office politics and fed me funny thumbnail sketches of the stratagems and quandaries of her boss and office mates. Totally a city person, she was discerning in every accessory of dress, perfect-postured, wicked-tongued, and usually leeward of change, but lacked the savage instincts or badgery focus that enables somebody without college credentials to seize and hold a bridgehead in New York nowadays. Though she had grown up across the river in the New Jersey suburbs, where her mother had been an almost equally exquisite shopper, she had been told when she was small that her father was dead—when in fact he wasn't; only a humble Grub Street writer—and otherwise had not received much of a welcome in the world or a sense of anchorage. When I knew her, she was thirty-something, also divorced, a vibrant, handsome woman seductive in the manner of my mother, although my mother had derived from quite a firm father-grandfather-great-grandfather line of midwestern businessmen and also a more cultivated mother-grandmother-great-grandmother ensemble from an old upstate New York and New England family that had fallen on hard times. Naturally the two of them became fast friends. My mother's mother had encouraged her to try social work, but neither she nor Leonore were suited for missions to the tenements. Missions of mercy to a young Harvard novelist were more Leonore's style, and my mother developed close pastoral relationships with several Episcopal ministers. Later, as a widow in her seventies, she used Leonore, still fine-looking, to bait younger men to her dinner parties.

So, I was pounding my handwritten Northwest journal into what became in about three years my happiest book and first "essay"; and each night Leonore, while counseling me in a decent delicacy, proper pacing, and the nuances of her anatomy, could tell just how well my day had gone by the strength of my penis. Though I still sometimes came too fast, when I followed her out of the shower, she slipping on a torn nightgown (the only torn garment she ever wore), I could hang our towel on it. Our affair might have ripened into marriage if I'd felt surer that she had a center of gravity to balance my own fractionation. We had each squandered first marriages that left us questioning our conduct. Leonore had thought that her husband was impotent, yet with his new wife he had already managed to have a baby. And my Amy had been a generous, sensitive woman, probably the purest soul I have ever been involved with, so that the marching refrain from army basic training sometimes echoed in my head: *You had a good wife and you left, you left . . . You had a good wife and you left, you left . . .*

Leonore still lived near Gramercy Park, so she and I shared a couple of chastely affectionate evenings. We had kept in touch over the years by telephone, generally on Valentine's Day because of her romantic nature, and had pals in common to catch up on (in fact, in my mind's eye, she herself remains a central friend), and a shared sense of life's fragility. She'd retained her comeliness of face and figure of twenty-five years before, as well as her shrewd, amusing assessments of other people, although her wit's astringence seemed sweeter. She had survived some genuinely shaky years with self-possession and dignity, being competent at her job and secure in the love of a fine old clutch of friends, and her home a proper nest.

I was moved, pleased, wistful, and recognized, indeed, how she resembled my Trudy—her tasteful flair and physicality, her commanding stride and house-proud panache and delight in goodies. I liked her rock-bottom appreciation of the city, both democratic and yet fastidious, and her abhorrence of self-pity and deception. The one thing she told me that did remind me of my earlier fear that she might lack a gravitational focus was about a lawyer who had lived on her floor in the building, whom she'd been rather in love with, but who had then been knifed on the street in the wee hours in Union Square. He died in Bellevue Hospital, where the ambulance took him, but not until a few hours had elapsed and his address was located and the doorman informed, who called Leonore as she was dressing to go to work. She'd rushed to Bellevue and was waved through the emergency room, but at the last instant, in the corridor to the room where he was lying, she turned aside and went directly to work instead. Therefore he died alone.

I don't want to die alone; nor have I necessarily avoided witnessing death when it has brushed close to me; and I suppose this poignant episode represents the frailty or perhaps a brittle squeamishness I had feared in her a quarter-century before: Though you could argue, on the contrary, that the implicit likelihood that her friend had been trying to pick up a boy in Union Square at 2 A.M. to have sex with might help explain it too. We didn't discuss the matter in that context, but one of our homosexual acquaintances told me later with a laugh that Leonore was "in denial" and that the poor man had "asked for it." My guess is that, like several other head-turning women I've known, who were led by a pinched childhood to take their own good looks too seriously (Leonore used to kiss her mirror in the morning before she left for work), she remained excessively perfectionist in judging men. She wanted education, breeding, earning power, humor, integrity, an arresting appearance, savoir faire, and tender intuition—a knight in shining armor—which is not generally a recipe for remarriage. And apart from the fragility in herself that she would have felt, she must have fathomed suddenly that this man also had let her down.

MY WELL-CENTERED, savvy surgeon told me to lift nothing heavier than five pounds lest the pressure spring my retinas, but somehow I assumed that masturbation wouldn't; it was the one "blind" thing I did. Otherwise, *Look at the lights! Look at the sky!* my mind shouted. She had warned me that eventually I was going to lose my sight all over again, but the tiaraed bridges with their lyrelike cables crossing the East River knocked me over—as they had when I'd lain on my back in my parents' sedan at the age of four, going to Oyster Bay on Long Island to visit friends, and treasuring the starry ride. At noontime at Gracie Mansion, near her office, the East River trumpeted, with its blue and pewter sliding water, curling Hell Gate currents, and muscley clouds filling the whole sky, which—when I saw her—upped my exuberance and made us sometimes chatter into her lunch hour after the eye exam was over.

I was now more than usually fearful of being mugged, or of any other violent tumble on the street, because a blow on the head might unstring the back of my eyes: yet forgot this kind of trouble when I looked up to see an aluminum plane banking toward LaGuardia under the ripped, scudding clouds, as dusk began to sparkle. People were suddenly souls, not blurry undersea shapes, and in my gluttonous walking I wandered into a print shop, squinty, stumbly, one rainy day, and saw my first museum art in a year and a half—Titian . . . Tintoretto—as if heaven *was* earth. On Sunday I sang hymns at Saint George's church and sat in various local caravansaries feasting my eyes on the faces, the sunshine spilling over the plane trees outside, a prismatic dry cleaner's sign across the street, the cello curve of a woman's hips. Actual sex, money, fame, advancement meant next to nothing to me compared to what I had gained, and I watched street folk foraging in ash cans with less pity for them just because they could see. The hell with what you had to eat, if you could *see*.

I'M AMUSED if I count back forty years at how many of the central women in my life have been registered nurses (three) or social workers (three, counting one of the nurses), though all moved on to other fields. They were professional caregivers, in other words. Neither of my wives was enrolled in such a category, however, so other affinities, artistic, intellectual, or spiritual, must have appealed more powerfully. Amy's, my first wife's, sterling decency and cleanliness of motive had attracted me strongly. Though she was not a fool, the "holy fool" is among the salient emblems in all of literature for me. I make close friends of such people, and their immediacy, if they'll have me.

My second wife, Marion, was a heavy-duty literary critic and editor who tutored and encouraged me during the first dozen years of our marriage. Marion had an extraordinarily resilient intelligence in sizing up individuals of many varieties, and a quite matchless wit, combined with a kind heart. We of course had a reunion too, gingerly and fond, in our old apartment, chaperoned by our daughter, Molly, who was now twenty-four and a school-teacher herself, and had been stopping by my place solicitously. Marion had just had a cancer operation and was feeling precarious herself. So, mortality made us a foursome. Sadly, Marion died two years later.

But that sure hand and confident eye of a former nurse has been hard for me to resist if we had other things in common. Since I was shy and often clumsy, a woman who had washed and catheterized a hundred penises, slapped babies' bottoms, tickled a smile from Alzheimer's patients, performed the Heimlich maneuver (I had a secret dread that I was going to die by choking on a piece of meat), or called Code Blue and banged her fists on a heart patient's chest to bring him back from the River Styx, then stayed by the bed for many hours while a carcinoma sufferer moaned, vomited, cried, bled, defecated, and died—a woman like that would not find an ugly stutter like mine off-putting, could fix an unreliable erection by simply reaching down, and think no commonplace misfortune insoluble. Men have considered nurses sexy since time began; and belonging to a healing vocation, they were more likely to draw near at a party when they saw me disabled by my stammer than pull away, if that mixture of strength with weakness intrigued them.

Nevertheless, while blind I'd discovered again how few people of either sex will tolerate spending many minutes on the handicapped. They are gripers, needy, self-absorbed, uninformed, living in the past. That child's game where someone pretends to be blind is one of the sexier known and, carried to the teens, you could feel a buttock or breast quite innocently while controlling the girl's progress, making her stumble, then saving her from a fall, until you gave her permission to open her eyes and *you* played being helpless. But, metaphorically, "blind" means to be ignorant of basic facts, a sucker in business, politics, a cuckold in love, the prey of real estate or stock market sharks, a whiner, yet unresponsive to the misery of troubled friends. And in real life it costs jobs, avocations, the very heart's warmth of seeing other people's faces. Now, abruptly, after paying a clever lady $5,200 to stick a knife into my eyes (the hospital and anesthetist tripled the bill), I was liberated. Not just returned to the *status quo ante,* as any heart or cancer sawbones may contrive for you by Roto-Rootering your plumbing, but given plastic eyes that, too good to be true, took in more than ever before. Old body, new orbs: I was ebullient, standing straighter, nervous energy alight, paying intense attention, as if to make up for lost time. The blue dawn, golden noon, funky neon, riveted and bewitched me, and morning, noon, and night I was gazing at dear acquaintances in Irish pubs, Italian and Chinese restaurants, or wooden booths in nosh-and-schmooze joints. I positively loved my white potatoes, earthy meatloaf, red ketchup—the *colors!*—and the foam on the beer, the bubbles in the ale, the checkered tablecloth. And we could go to a movie!

Yet the enigma was that these familiar friends whom I hadn't observed in several years looked not just older, but sadder, pummeled, beat-up. They looked cudgeled, while I in contrast was feasting my eyes. I was supremely happy, while they, who had been window-shopping, movie-going, taking in ten thousand sights during my blind time, seemed tacit testimony that the exuberant evidence of joy I saw in the world was wrong-headed and probably going to be short-lived. Was there something they knew that I didn't; or the other way around? Did the eyes not really matter except as a baseline? Was happiness in the long run entirely internal, grounded in a stew of genes, hormones, childhood "conflict resolution," careerism, and consumerism? Had the visible world, God's greenery, so little to do with it? This sudden elevation of my spirits was obviously because of the freakish salvation I had undergone—but did the eyes have so meager and ambiguous an input for everybody else? Was our fate, as far as happiness was concerned, all just embedded in our foreheads beforehand?

My effervescence was infectious, cheered everybody up for the space of a chat. What they generally wanted, when I asked, was a partner to confide in, grow old with, a nest egg in the bank, and a feeling that their lives had registered on other people affectionately and with a watermark of honor: that they had walked a road, not a treadmill. Okay, amen. But Emerson in *Nature* goes beyond that, speaking of becoming "a transparent eye-ball . . . part and particle of God." I was beginning to be able to read again and kept fattening on friendship as my second eye operation healed—after the famine of my previous isolation—and casting glances up the walls of sunstruck buildings, at stone the color of a pronghorn's skin, or a bloody Mary, at seething leaves, part green, part russet, in a crown of trees.

"In the woods, we return to reason and faith. There I feel that nothing can befall me in life—no disgrace, no calamity [leaving me my eyes], which nature cannot repair," Emerson says in the same essay. I felt almost that way in the city, too, about human nature, but in due course got one of my former students to carry my suitcase to the bus station and put me, still fragile, on Bonanza, where I once again made use of George Sage's name to take me comfortably to Vermont. My vivacious benefactor, the surgeon, had indicated that her marriage was righting itself, and for my part, I had remained faithful to the friend I lived with in Vermont despite the fact that my Lazarus charisma had drawn a few sexual invitations my way. Of the women I have lived with, I have been unfaithful only to my second wife, Marion, and that was a twenty-five-year marriage, in the second half of which I also felt betrayed.

We pulled out of the Port Authority bus terminal onto Tenth Avenue an hour past dusk. Several statuesque black prostitutes were standing shoulder to shoulder in the midst of the stream of traffic like newsboys offering their wares, only in their case they had lowered their dresses to their waists. The driver shook his head as we headed for all-white Vermont. The universal city— Dickens's, Balzac's—lent me its last lurid strings of lights: little clusters of stores, bravely carmine, lavender, sunflower yellow, in a dun stretch of Hell's Kitchen blocks. Then the brief upscale sparkle of Lincoln Center and Amsterdam Avenue; and a spell of visual salsa in Spanish Harlem, jeroboam wine bottles glowing amid orange pumpkins, red peppers, yellow squashes, under green awnings and Christmas-tree lights. Then blitzed central Harlem, the lights self-effacing so as not to draw holdup men, and poverty blinking in the higher windows. The dark funnel of the highway network began just beyond that, sweeping us to Connecticut. The driver told me about another prep-school mate of mine from forty-plus years ago who was now supporting himself by running up bus schedules on his home computer and occasionally doing dispatching in the Port Authority terminal. It was not what he had dreamed of: which led me to remember another friend, now nearly broke, whom I'd visited recently, a peppy guy I'd crossed the country with in 1953, in a 1936 Model A Ford that overheated during the day, so we drove at night. So many who had not foreseen nearing sixty in the particular straits they were in. Or, indeed, nearing sixty at all. In my experience, it was the people who were going to inherit a trust fund and their father's seat on the New York Stock Exchange who thought much in college about getting old, because the relatives they were going to inherit the loot from were constantly talking about old age and making them listen as the price of admission.

I was delighted to reach Vermont's snowy roads, and to see Trudy, at Bennington's bus stop, standing by her car. We bumped bodies a few times before we hugged. She hadn't seen me with my

new eyes before, but they were still so squinty and tentative that
the change wasn't apparent at first. We joked because I was going
to have to go for a follow-up to the local eye doctor, whom she
happened to have had a passionate affair with for several years;
so she was afraid that he might find an excuse to poke my foveae
out. (In the event, he didn't. A husky, playful sort of guy, he was
extremely impressed by what my surgeon had done, which he had
only seen illustrated in medical journals. "So that's how they do it
in the big city," he murmured, peering inside.)

Trudy was naturally alert to learn if I had sought refuge with
her merely while incapacitated, but that was not the case. Nor,
as I'd wondered, had she accepted me because, unlike her errant
husband, I had been immobilized. And now I also groped for a
realignment with Mount Anthony, the little corrugated, wooded,
southerly, cavey, conical limestone peak (alt. 2,346 feet) that over-
looks the town—as with the sensuous roll of the field outside my
window that runs a ways toward it, and the preliminary granite
ridge of the Green Mountains that invigorates my view to the
east. Also the locust, ash, and maple trees, the bluish spruces, slip-
pery elms, white birches, oaks, and red-barked pines, the juncos
wintering in the dogwoods, the hungry possum nibbling seeds
under the birdfeeder, the startling glory of our skunk's white
wedge of fur in a shaft of faint moonlight—plus things that usually had bored me, like moving headlights on the road across
the valley or a tardy fog at 10 A.M., but had become fascinating.
Art books could be mesmerizing—Michelangelo's Moses, or a
Turner—though I still hadn't gotten to a museum because I'd
come home as soon as I was ambulatory enough to risk the jolting
of a bus.

Faces in Bennington seemed new to me. Moving to town when
I'd already been partially blind, I had no memory of them, so
didn't now see them with the perspective of how life might have
battered people, just the novelty of how they looked. A Daughters
of the American Revolution face (whose voice sounded nicer);

another like Mickey Rooney's; and another, W. C. Fields's, or was it slacker, like Charles Laughton's, or maybe Hitchcock's? It was curious to see the layout of the town—the Legion Hall, the Post Office, the taco joint, the rest home, the supermarket mall, all of which I had been driven past a hundred times, blindly. How pretty the old church was where Robert Frost is buried. And down below, the buildings nestled steeply into the hills the way a New England village is supposed to. Only *closer* could you see the boarded-up, red-brick factories and turn-of-the-century, careened-over mills, with peeling, boxy frame houses lined in a dingy cross-grid nearby.

Stumbling with Trudy's two small grandchildren over the snow-drifts on Main Street to get to the Steak House—a town hangout that is also hospitable to family dinners, with coloring books on the table and more fuss made about the kids who come than about the drunks on the other side of the partition—I felt the twin reactions one has to a New England winter. It's awfully repetitive, one snowstorm on the heels of another and nowhere new to go; yet what a delight to hold the children by the hand, with the pink light of the street lamps spilling on the snow, and Trudy's complexity to grip or grapple with. Tall and forceful but also fitful and hysteric, seeming confident yet insecure, fatalistic though energetic, materialistic but idealistic, rather brutal but often tender, she was what's sometimes called a handful. She'd been raised in Great Neck, Long Island, an expensive Jewish suburb of New York City, where her father taught band music in the elementary schools and where some of the parents were paying off the anti-Semitism of other suburbs by giving *goyische* kids a hard time. In high school she had dated the captain of the football team, however, another *goy*, and then down at Duke University, the varsity center. She married a law student, later a Vermont state senator, who had come from a newly rich New York family, his father a petroleum broker. Eventually, one of her sons became a varsity wrestler and then a Navy Seal; the other a logger. Her own parents had leaped to Long Island's suburbia from coal country in the Scranton area of Pennsylvania, where hardscrabble farming or railroad work was the alternative to going into the mines. She'd spent summers and sometimes longer there with a loving but half-crazy aunt, and another year in bed at home because of rheumatic fever—experiences that had marked her. Upscale, upwardly mobile, yet singed by this knowledge of secret skeletons and vulnerabilities, alcoholism and violence in the family's closet, she had become a therapist. Her younger sister had thrust ahead to be a pilot at sixteen, later an astronaut, helping to launch the Venus probe.

Trudy somewhat similarly worked a good deal in the midst of a high-tech, genteel kind of violence. Not the Space Program, but our fancy, avant-garde college where designer drugs were rampant, plus old-fashioned beer and booze to lace it with and four-day weekends that the kids sometimes obliterated. For some of them the whole term was lived in a state of emergency, and she as college therapist was their first handhold if they suddenly panicked and felt as if they might be falling off a cliff. She was energized; she got rolling when somebody's mind went into fibrillation, and prevented a lot of calamities from happening. There was, in addition, a civil war among the faculty at Bennington College at this time, and a third of the teachers were shortly fired. Our president became a sort of Queen of Hearts as time went on, chopping heads off. I needed my eyes to survive, and Trudy her awareness of psychology, and both of us our alliance.

HITTING ONE'S STRIDE

Our parents stand for previous generations until they die, whereupon we have to. Driving down to New York for a holiday, I call and ask my daughter if I can spend the night at her place. She has turned twenty-seven and is a graduate student in history. She says yes as usual, but with a demurral that startles me: "I'm just afraid you won't realize I'm an adult now." Because I fathom what she means, what's startling is that I like the man she has been seeing, have assumed for the past year that they were sharing their lives at his place or hers, and am in favor of postponing such a major event as marriage until one's thirties. Why does she doubt my approval of the firming of the arrangement?

Two by two is a good general rule, more joyful and resilient, I tell her. I've seen solitude in the city begin to lame even people as young as she is insidiously for the future; most grown-ups shouldn't live alone. I thought I'd said this, but we speak to our children so frequently in our imaginations, we seldom know for sure what's said. And maybe she *wants* an old-fashioned dad who will maintain a reassuring cleavage between the generations.

Over supper, I tell them both that at about their age I lived on a Greek island, Samos, for half a year with a lovely Englishwoman. I cared a lot for the women who were kind enough to keep me company before I met my daughter's mother, and want the salient episodes known to her before I die. Since her mother's death three years before, she has been meeting some of the men who preceded me, but tells me with a laugh that she doesn't wish to meet these old girlfriends of mine. Children want their parents' lives to seem pristine before they were born. So did I; but it was easier then. Love and work are what matter, but the density of sensations, the ant-army of information, the pincushion of modes of communication in which we find ourselves embedded make it hard to focus. So many forces try to atomize us that we need our memories ever more. Not provisional or erasable, they don't downsize in a stumbling economy or judder with the collective cacophony from Washington. Dead friends can rise as extra allies, and vanished landscapes are reconstituted; nostalgic cities become fun again. In fact, genealogy—which once struck me as a veiled excuse for snobbery, or a gene bank of angina—is intriguing like a hand of cards. It's a narrative of kindred spirits or flamboyant behavior. I'd been a writer-traveler for umpteen years before I paused to notice that I was not the first. There'd been a pioneering archaeologist in the family who had made forty trips to Mayan sites in Central America, whose voice in his four books sounds a bit like mine. Another voice, still closer in the diaries I have, is a young man's, an aspiring foreign correspondent who was murdered at twenty-nine in Inner Mongolia in 1905.

Insecurity as much as arrogance causes many of us to spurn our family histories until we feel we have defined ourselves. The logs of a cousin who was an R.A.F. pilot in World War II and was shot down over Java, then over France—or the regimental history of the unit my great-grandfather Hoagland served in at eighteen,

when he fought at Shiloh, losing a knuckle and an eardrum—
might have intimidated me until I had done some living myself.
Likewise the harrowing experiences of a missionary cousin who
cared for Armenian and Greek orphans on the Black Sea and in
Beirut and Smyrna, where in 1922 she witnessed the horrific massacres and burning of that city by the Turks.

I have a Michigan businessman's letters from 1865, and a diary
of the preceding year kept by a grocer's wife who crossed Missouri and Kansas while General "Pap" Price's Confederate raid-
ers were trying to intercept the wagon trains. Also the diary of
a cousin who accompanied her husband, a cotton dealer, from
Pittsburgh to New Orleans on a riverboat in 1840 at Mardi Gras.
My mother used to recommend that I pay attention to these; and
probably my daughter will start examining everything after I've
grown too old to urge her on, because that's how it was with me.
My mother had a stroke, and right away I dug out piles of stuff
and pored over it.

Reading letters that my great-grandmother Blendina Hicok
left in a box in 1911, I learned that by sheer coincidence her own
great-grandfather lived right in this town of Bennington more
than two hundred years ago. The local historical society confirmed
it, and I found his marble-topped brick grave in an abandoned
cemetery and laid a flag on it on Memorial Day. (May somebody
do the same for me in the year 2200!) But maybe the most cheerful
omen is that the house he built for his family after the Revolution
is standing, and some of the meadowland he farmed alongside the
Walloomsac River is still open and in the summer full of bobolinks and larks. Locating it and grinning, standing there, I realized
too that when I'd taught in Iowa, hardly ten years before, I could
have driven in a day to visit other ancestors' homesteads, from the
nineteenth century, in Illinois and Kansas—but somehow hadn't
bothered to! Such foolishness, when you feel you need to win your
spurs.

Back in my late thirties, however, I'd hit my stride as a writer, as many do, and caught a second wind. Earlier, I had published three novels, but was stalled on the fourth and in the meantime had discovered essay writing through the vehicle of my journal about the old men of Telegraph Creek, a frontier hamlet on the Stikine River, a hundred sixty-five miles in from the sea and eight hundred miles north of Vancouver. Wilds had intrigued me since my teens, when I had ridden horseback in the Wind River Range in Wyoming, then fought forest fires in the Laguna Mountains in southern California another summer, and joined the Ringling Bros. circus for two spells of caring for the menagerie cats. I'd written a novel about that latter experience; another about New York boxing; and a third, less vivid, about a Pied Piper in a welfare hotel. Though fiction was my first love—I had wanted to be the great American novelist—I lacked the exceptional memory that novelists need. (Montaigne, in his essay "On Liars," says he found "scarcely a trace of it" in himself. "I do not believe there is another man in the world so hideously lacking.") Perhaps as a result, I had focused upon honing a poetic style, which is an inadequate substitute. Still, as Montaigne adds, a weak memory makes you think for yourself. You can't remember what other people have written or said.

Essays, though sprinkled with subordinated memories, are written mostly in the present tense and aren't primarily narratives. The point the essayist is trying to illustrate takes precedence over his story. And the other obvious handicap I'd been laboring under in trying to become a great novelist was my disbelief that life *has* many narratives. I think life seldom works in blocks of related events. Rather, you can break your fingernails trying to undo the causal knots and they stay knots. My sister and her last husband lived next to each other in isolated farmhouses without speaking for years, she with the children and the fields they'd worked, he as a hired man on other people's land. Like any rural residents, they both owned guns, and so if this were fiction their rancid feelings would finally have erupted into gunfire, arson, flight, or nervous collapse. But life is usually stasis, not a narrative; sadness, not a story. Like a car that just won't start, it just won't start.

Yet my main reason for turning into an essayist had less to do with mnemonic deficiencies, or any theory of life as contrasted to the deforming anodynes of fiction, than with the painful fact that I stuttered so badly that writing essays was my best chance to talk. Is *this,* therefore, maybe a story? Well, because it afflicted me so soon—and because it seems to stem from a gene passed down from an uncle of mine who also stuttered, until he died at the age of nine under the wheels of a Kansas City trolley car before my father's eyes—the idea hasn't too much novelistic interest, unless perhaps you count the wringing-out effect of the sight on my father, who later made me suffer: which to me is an essay. Just as I didn't know Blendina Hicok, the great-grandmother on my mother's side from whom I probably inherited my bad eyesight, I never knew that stuttering uncle. I've only seen his photo, where he stands next to my father, both of them in Indian headdresses and buckskin suits.

Their sister had died of blackwater fever at the age of three in a cypress swamp where my grandfather, out of medical school, had taken a job as a contract doctor. Those deep-forest, Spanish-moss swamps of Louisiana (where I've since paddled and camped with Cajun trappers) are spellbinding, larger than life, with alligators, panthers, spoonbills, egrets, and storks, plus legends African, French, Spanish, Choctaw, and Atakapa, but after the death of two of his three children, my grandfather, William Hoagland, forswore further adventures and remained an obstetrician back in Missouri till the First World War. Though he did not see action (his own father and father-in-law had fought on opposite sides of the Civil War), he enjoyed the comradeship of army life so much that he stayed in the reserves for the next twenty years, rising to lieutenant colonel in the medical corps. After his wife's death from colon cancer at fifty-nine, he retired from active practice in Kansas City and quietly managed a rental property that he'd invested in. He was a member of the Ivanhoe Masonic Lodge, the Modern Woodmen of America, and the Sanford Brown post of the American Legion. He sang in the choir of Saint Paul's Reformed Church, took a flier in a few dry-hole West Texas oil leases, and died suddenly of meningitis at sixty-seven in 1940 with an estate of $5,000, which is all the Depression had left him.

My father, though a blue-chip lawyer (in the semi-military phase of his own career, when he worked as a negotiator for the Defense Department in Europe, his rank was the civilian equivalent of major general), shared with my grandfather that ambiguity about their chosen professions and likewise retired early, in his case to try to become a business school professor and memoir writer. But his overly methodical cast of mind did not fit either vocation, and cancer meanly overwhelmed him at sixty-three. His adventuresomeness—instead of heading him from Kansas City to Louisiana, West Texas, and a military uniform—had led him east to Yale, Harvard Law School, Wall Street, Rockefeller Center, and Europe, to explore the museums, restaurants, splendid scenery, the history and social complexity. Berlin, London, the Parthenon, the Grand Canal. We once crossed paths at the Trevi Fountain in Rome and had supper together, and to the pretty music of its plash he told me that "an enemy" of his had lived in this very square during his period as a U.S. negotiator ten years before. But with characteristic discretion, he refused to specify who had won, or whether his adversary had been a personal rival or an outside foe of the United States. Both he and my grandfather were genially clubby, easing their hearts among groups of men more easily than I, though not as inclined to close confidences. Nerdy, squirrelly, yet bold enough within the sphere of a loner, I was leery of the extended compromises membership entails, and maybe too odd to make them. But the professed purpose of my solitude was to speak to loads of people.

MY GREAT-GRANDFATHER Martin Hoagland, 1843–1926, of "Holland Dutch" descent—as it used to be said, to distinguish Dutch from Germans, who were called "Pennsylvania Dutch"—was born on a farm in Bardolph, Illinois, and enlisted as a private in the 57th Illinois Infantry regiment in 1861, mustering out as a lieutenant in 1865 after service at Shiloh under Grant, and in the battles for Atlanta and Savannah and up through both Carolinas under Sherman. At eighteen he had been shipped from Chicago almost straight to Shiloh, where he lost the knuckle (and in Columbia, South Carolina, the eardrum). Soon after his discharge, however, he married Emma Jane McPhey, she being an orphan from Yellow Creek, Ohio, raised by a Bardolph uncle and aunt; and they bought a farm there in Bardolph. But in 1871, with three of what would wind up as seven children, they set out by Conestoga wagon for central Kansas, settling on a soldier's homestead claim on Brandy Lake in the Arkansas River valley, digging a sod house, the westernmost in the area then, said his front-page, banner-headline obituary in the *Hutchinson Herald* fifty-five years later.

There were buffalo and Kaw Indians about, and he built a frame house, then a brick house, and picked up cash by hauling supplies for the Atchison, Topeka & Santa Fe Railway construction crews as they crossed Kansas for the second cross-continental link-up in 1881. But his major enthusiasm was in becoming a Johnny Appleseed to this dry region, bringing in apples and peaches, the first to be grown in central Kansas, and carrying the fruiting branches around to other farms on holidays to show how it could be done. He shipped some fruit to the U.S. Centennial Exposition in Philadelphia in 1876, and became a crop reporter for the U.S.

Department of Agriculture, remaining so for half a century. He learned irrigation techniques with windmill wells, grew the first local sorghum, timothy, and "rice wheat" (the "Turkey Red" wheat that made Kansas famous was introduced by Russian Mennonites at about that time), and brought in Berkshire hogs and Cherokee milk cows. In the 1880s he entered the meat-and-grain business in the new city of Hutchinson, opened a clothing store, and later served as town councilman, street commissioner, police judge. But my grandfather William was born in that sod house, and in my travels over a couple of decades—nine trips to the Yukon, British Columbia, and Alaska—I may have been in search of just this patriarch.

Ah, you might say, a multigenerational novel?—but I don't think so. My father went east to become an attorney for an international oil company, others of his generation ended up with insurance jobs in the suburbs of Los Angeles, and I know of no gunfire, epiphanies, or deathbed conversions among them. To me they illustrate the flattening of the earth more than a story line: the Atchison, Topeka & Santa Fe as a bureaucracy; agribusiness monoculture replacing individual Johnny Appleseeds. John Chapman of the Ohio frontier, the ascetic saint who was the real Johnny Appleseed, is in fact an exemplar of the benign, pacific nature of a majority of the early pioneers.

Indeed, I've really sought frontiersmen in the river drainages of the taiga country—the least accessible country on the continent and thus last to be settled—and these people were growing parsnips and potatoes, keeping bees and chickens, coaxing peas and lettuce, storing carrots and turnips. Their pride was in their carpentry, not gunsmithing; in getting half a dozen Herefords or packhorses through the winter on the resources of a beaver meadow, not in reaming their nearest neighbor out of five hundred bucks. I've stood at so many trail ends and hollered greetings to a rough log cabin set in a stumpy clearing a hundred yards away, lest the person living there be startled by me, that I feel confident I know what pioneers on the earlier frontier were probably like.

These weren't gunslingers or deal hustlers. They were generally peaceable, fairly balanced souls, who liked the sounds of a stream outdoors, and planted flower beds of sweet-william in front and a rhubarb patch behind. If they were placer miners and had found a pocket of gold grains in an old creek bed, instead of going out for a whoopee spree and never coming back, they worked the spot and bought new stuff for the cabin (a zinc sink, an iron stove that didn't have holes in it, a mattress that hadn't yet become a hive for mice) and more hydraulic equipment, and then a truck, a boat, a snowmobile, to haul and float and sled it in. Of course you could say they were throwbacks, not ordinary people, having chosen to leave the loop of cog jobs and suburban malls for a riverbank. But ordinary folk did not leave the loop in Europe and come to America in the first place—or leave the eastern seaboard for unroaded Sioux country, living off the land, not in a money economy. Their guns were like our wallets, having the purpose of procuring food, and not a surrogate penis or Second Amendment fetish.

The people whom I'd sit with for an evening were content to watch the fire flicker in the stove and the flame of a kerosene lamp or miner's candle for entertainment, though they might have a bit of corn whiskey, too, or birch syrup, apple champagne or plum brandy, huckleberry muffins or home-pulled taffy as a treat. Water diverted from a brook ran forever through a food cooler into the sink, and a fire burned continually no matter what the weather was. These were the constants during the summer, when they dressed more warmly, and in the winter, when they dressed more lightly, than me. Their fires of regret were banked, their eyes lacked my squint under the open sky, and they didn't wish for sharp divergences from day to day, as I tend to. They were subjects for an essay, in other words, more than for fiction.

———

MY GRANDMOTHER on my mother's side collected bowlfuls of used tinfoil and balls of broken string, wrote letters to her friends on scraps of paper, and whenever she traveled by ship or train, organized her suitcase so tightly, with her socks and foot medications at one end and her face cream and hair net at the other, that she could unpack in the dark. She would carry a dozen magazines on a trip, with the advertisements already torn out to save on weight—but because she thought that only natural light was good for the eyes, would put her reading material away as soon as night fell. Although she was an enthusiastic walker, the foot medications were necessary to ease her discomfort because her toes had been crushed out of shape by wearing borrowed shoes when she was a child. Her parents were pauperized by the Panic of 1873, when the small-town bank they owned in Homer, New York, failed. Her uncle had been handsomely painted by Abraham Lincoln's principal portraitist, also from Homer, but under the weight of this disgraceful calamity the uncle and her father wasted away, and after the latter's death, she and her sister, brother, and mother were forced to creep to Flint, Michigan, and move in with cousins, whose shoes she wore.

So *here's* a story, you may say. Elizabeth limps on crushed toes in hand-me-down footwear as a poor relation after her father's business failure. Then she becomes a schoolteacher and marries a businessman, A. J. Morley, after his first wife—one of her prosperous cousins, and also a schoolteacher—dies in childbirth. They move first to Chicago, where he manages his family's wholesale saddlery store, and then to Grays Harbor in Washington State, where around 1905 he buys with Morley family money (the family was so conservative that they declined, right there in Flint, to invest in the start-up of General Motors, and later, in Washington State, were to refuse to bet on Boeing) seven thousand acres of old-growth forestland on Delezene Creek and launches a logging and shingle-mill operation in Douglas fir country. For saddlery factory people from Michigan who were expanding into the general hardware business, to participate also in this last hurrah of pioneering in the American Northwest was gambling of an appealingly conservative variety. And, besides, they were chasing bad money with good, because A. J.'s scampish older brother Walter, "overeducated" at Cornell, and later to be dragooned into the ministry as penance, had already gone west to Grays Harbor and fouled up among the con men on F Street and the brothels on Hume Street and Heron Street in the port of Aberdeen.

A. J. was successful; yet my grandmother continued to save slivers of soap and yesterday's bread. You could cast this as a story, certainly, but I wouldn't. To me what's interesting about my grandmother is how, for example, after those virgin hemlocks, firs, and spruces had paid for her to sail to Europe with a grown granddaughter who was honeymooning, and the couple were in Rome and she was up in Florence, and she wished to rejoin them before the plan called for it, she simply entrained for Rome, took a taxi to the Forum, and sat down on a ruin, figuring any tourist, even honeymooners, would soon go there. Sure enough, within an hour they showed up. My mother—whose childhood was sunnier—enjoyed this commanding sort of confidence too.

But Grandfather, as his four children grew up and traveled East to school (he believed, quite sensibly, that eastern children should come out West for summer jobs and western children should travel East for book learning and social skills), took a mistress or two, in the fashion of a logging baron in a salmon-canning and raw tall-timber town of four thousand people on the wild Pacific Ocean in the 1920s—though for this role, as well, he preferred the local schoolteachers to the bar girls who had gotten Walter into trouble. Grandmother's response was to travel extensively, with or without younger companions, on cruise ships and museum tours, or else, less happily, to check into the Aberdeen General Hospital for a week's recuperation. One time, when she returned from abroad, she discovered a red nightgown hanging in her closet, and thought up a better solution. Instead of fleeing to the hospital, she washed the thing and wore it every night thereafter until it was threadbare, never mentioning why to her husband or telling her sons about the incident until they were driving her home from their father's funeral, twenty years later.

Flamboyance, poignancy, oddity, drama, and cause-and-effect are all present in some modest measure, but not, I think, *plot,* in her "story." I do have that other ancestor, Reuben Morley, a "writer/traveler," who was murdered by a French riding companion in Mongolia en route to the Russo-Japanese War in 1905. Two years before that, Benjamin Franklin Morley, a former Union officer, had lost his life in his own gold mine in Buena Vista, Colorado; and in 1942 a close cousin of my mother's named John Morley died as a Japanese prisoner of war, after surviving the Bataan Death March. Reuben had fought in the Spanish-American War, and then lived among the Yaqui Indians of Mexico, and the Igorot tribespeople in the Philippines. Two of my Hicok-Morley relatives and at least one Hoagland fought on the Yankee Doodle side in the American Revolution; and way before that, my Hoagland ancestors had left Dutch New York, post–New Amsterdam, in outrage after the archetype American rebel, Jacob Leisler, had been drawn and quartered by the British colonial authorities, in 1691. But much more often, I see life as being slower, flatter, more draggy and anticlimactic, repetitive and yet random (perhaps briefly staccato but then limpid), than all but a handful of good novels: and these not the best.

I love great fiction. More than even the essays of Montaigne, fiction rivets, inspires, sticks in the mind, makes life seem worth living, if ever it doesn't. Novels, when upliftingly tragic or vivid with verisimilitude, can be unforgettably gripping. And yet I don't find my own life in many of them. That is, for instance, I wouldn't have married Madame Bovary or shipped out with Ahab. My life has *not* been Joseph Andrews's, David Copperfield's, or Ras-kolnikov's. I will always remember such template characters, but my own marital blunders, childhood collisions, career nicks and scrapes, and even my exaltation on certain radiant days when stretching my legs out-of-doors, are not synchronous with those that are plumbed in what we call masterpieces. Like Prince Andrei after the Battle of Austerlitz in *War and Peace,* I've lain on my back gazing into the sky—but not so near death, or to quite the same end. I'm convinced by his feelings and have fitfully known their equivalent after quick bouts with blindness, suicidal im-pulses, and so on. But if mine were really the same, I'd have ceased, with Buddhist resignation, to write books.

Instead of the breakneck conundrums and rapturous gambits of some of the novels I love, it is the business of essays to be more familiar, unassuming, humdrum. The Declaration of Indepen-dence was also an essay, but there aren't many of these; and when I have been miffed with my sister, at sixes and sevens with my mother, groping for an intelligent (as distinct from blind) empa-thy with my daughter, or tangling with Trudy, I'd as soon read a first-rate collection of essays for guidance as *Anna Karenina.* The personal essay is meant to be like a household implement, a frying pan hanging from a punchboard, or a chat at the kitchen table—though it need not remain domestic. It can become an-guished, confessional, iconoclastic, or veer from comfortable wit to mastectomy, chemotherapy, and visions of death, just as the talk in a parlor does. Essayists are ambidextrous, not glamorous; switch-hitters going for the single, not the home run. They're character actors, not superstars. They plug along in a modest manner (if any writer can be called modest), piling up masonry incrementally, not trying for the Taj Mahal like an ambitious novelist.

"Trifles make the sum of life," said David Copperfield; and novelists and essayists share that principle. A book is chambered like a beehive, and prose is like comb honey: honey sweeter (to its devotees) because it has its wax still on. Going the other way, from fifteen years of essay writing to doing a novel again, can be exhilarating, as I later found, because one is inventing, not simply recording, the world. I could myth-make a little, draw things a bit differently from how they were, grab for the brass ring, go larger than life, escape the nitty-gritty of reality for a while. Novelists want the site of their drama to be ground zero, but most of us do not live at ground zero. Most of us live like stand-up comedians on a vaudeville stage—the way an essayist does—by our humble wits, messing up, swallowing an aspirin, knowing Hollywood won't call, thinking nobody we love will die today, just another day of sunshine and rain.

CALLIOPE TIMES

*M*y own launching pad—looking back now fifty years—
seems to have been the day that I joined the circus
in June of 1951 at the age of eighteen. Not that that adventure
fathered my ambition to be a writer, which had turned serious a
couple of years earlier, but it led to my discovering that I could put
my love into the full service of my ambition, making it fun and
worth all of the struggle. Love was the wellspring of work, and
because I loved the circus I wasn't going to stop, no matter how
hard the task became.

I'd jotted a letter ahead for a job from college that spring of
my freshman year, spurred in particular by my fascination with
animals. At home in Connecticut I'd kept dogs, cats, turtles,
snakes, alligators, pigeons, possums, goats, and knew from seeing
Ringling Bros. and Barnum & Bailey perform in Madison Square
Garden as a child that I would have access to bigger critters *there*.
The nightly travel, the exotic crafts and dangerous skills, the association with other handicapped people who had made a go of life

in the big show were more nebulous attractions. Though I don't remember my words to the circus, I believed I had an intuitive understanding of animals and wanted to test it further. And to my surprise a brief note from Winter Quarters in Sarasota, Florida, enclosing a route card, informed me that I could have a job with the "Animal Department" if I showed up when school let out. Luckily, my parents didn't object, it being in both of their families' tradition that young men went out into the world during the summer and worked—my father on a cattle ship from San Francisco to Europe after his sophomore year, my mother's brothers and their friends at logging jobs in the woods. Though I was allergic to hay, I trusted in life and ignored the obvious probability that the only animals a stripling like me might be permitted to touch would be the horses. I'd just have to deal with the scariness of an asthma attack when that eventuality occurred.

My last ride, hitchhiking to the show's one playing date in Connecticut that year, in the town of Plainfield, outside Hartford, was with a middle-aged woman who seemed excited to be helping a boy "run away to join the circus." I thanked her and left the road, surveying and then carefully crossing the intricate tumult of the vast lot and "backyard," clutching my folded letter. Canvas trucks and water trucks roared around. Clowns were changing behind a wagon. A tumbler stood on his hands. Two Caterpillar tractors hitched onto the tongues of a series of other wagons in quick succession and pulled them into the proper position. The immense oval of the billowing big top, ocean blue and about five hundred feet long and two hundred feet wide, had already been erected, with flags flapping from the five center poles. A man, a tiny figure, was adjusting the air vents way up on the ridgeline. And the sideshow and other satellite tops and tents—olive or white or brown—were laid out all around, with personnel exceeding a thousand moving about, and three times that many rubberneckers. The seethe was matter-of-fact and orderly, however. Pole wagons, seat wagons, prop wagons. Performers loafing or dart-ing on errands were dressed like ragamuffins but with astute, daredevil faces. They were Europeans, and looked so, pinched by the hungers of World War II. The roustabouts were less artfully ragged, and slower—gaunt from hard living—but full-faced because they'd been milk-fed, well nourished, in childhood. Several elephants had returned from pulling the quarter poles of the big top up and were being washed and watered.

I would have been awed, except I was doggedly focused on presenting my precious letter; then, step by step, finding out what my job was, and doing what I was told in order to hold on to it. This was not yet a show. This was an itinerant city—everything busy, or people napping, stretched on the ground. Each sector had citizens. Even locating where the horses were, ninety of them, tethered loosely in long rows in two large, low tents with straw scattered on the grass and tack hooked to the side poles, took some looking. But the man in a cowboy hat whom I wordlessly showed my note to waved me on.

"Animal Department, it says here. This is Ringstock, not the Animal Department." He pursed his mouth, spat tobacco juice, and ignored my handicap after a searching glance.

I headed for where the elephants were chained to stakes pounded into the ground in a half-circle under the open sky. Twenty-four elephants, swaying forward and sideways and back, swinging their nimble trunks in idiosyncratic private rhythms: they conveyed the balm of the wild, which had always been such a salve to me, whether watching a salamander swim or climbing a spruce. The men who were idly supervising them carried wooden clubs with an iron hook attached to one end that were long enough to lean on as they stood in the sun but that they swung like a baseball bat if they had to be punitive. These were inevitably big men, compared to the agile, wiry horse hands who ran beside their charges during the performance and rode them back and forth like a rodeo string to the circus lot from the train yards, morning and night. The elephant men rode, too, from the train, in a more august procession, sitting on the elephants' heads, with a leg hanging down on each side of its right eye; and they were slow-fuse types, tall-legged, barrel-bodied. I approached three of them who were guarding the herd to proffer my little note from the front office in Sarasota, although bales of hay were piled about in a quantity that—if this was the job—was going to kill me.

"This ain't the Animal Department. This is Number 12 Wagon," the bulkiest guy told me, pointing at the Elephant Department's wagon nearby, with the number stenciled, and a tent beside it. "You're looking for Number 10 Wagon."

So much for the hay; my life was apparently saved! I nodded my thanks, following where he had pointed, and soon spotted Number 10, a fourteen-foot, red-painted wagon on rubber wheels about fifty yards away. It had a certain air of éclat, having belonged to the Al G. Barnes and Sells-Floto Combined Circus during the 1930s, and the door at the back was open. An old man with white hair, named Blackie Barlow, sat on a folding chair inside, over the four-foot ladder. A tarpaulin had been tied from the roof like a tent fly on one side to cover half a dozen footlockers, or "crumb boxes," as they were called, and a water barrel and buckets stood beside that. A pickup truck was also parked there, from the bed of which a cluster of men had just pulled a dead horse. A Mohawk Indian named Chief, with a dark-red face and large cheekbones, was beginning to chop at the horse to dismember it.

A stunning sight, if I had paused to figure it out or let it rattle me. But I went instead to the white-haired man, who was watching from just inside the wagon with an ironic, not unkind smile. He had a quiet voice, south Florida accent, and looked at my note, observing cursorily that I was unable to answer a question, and pointed without further comment at a better-dressed, huskier, fortyish gentleman in a flannel shirt and chino slacks who was supervising the butchering of the horse. This was the menagerie's head, C. R. Montgomery, who traveled ahead of the show with his wife independently, buying horses from farmers when meat was needed, as well as all other animal food, and dickered with zoo directors in the towns we stopped in, if a trade seemed desirable. (I remember we once sold a gnu in Boston, for instance.) He knew what creatures a dealer like Henry Trefflich had coming in on a ship from Siam or Sumatra to New York or Miami, yet could help Doc Henderson, the circus veterinarian, with basic treatments on the lot, or Josephine, the snake charmer, with her South American red-tailed boas and cream-and-brown Burmese pythons. Like Arkie Scott, the elephant boss, C. R. was an all-around animal man of the sort that circuses used to have. He paused to read my missive, grinned at Blackie with raised eyebrows, and stopped Chief from chopping the horse, to hand the axe to me.

I simply then followed my star. I'd barely fathomed that the "Animal Department" meant where big cats and suchlike were cared for, but I wanted this job, and it was a dead horse lying in front of me, not a sufferer, so I swung and swung at the carcass's hips, my sneakers slipping in the blood, while my future comrades, Ray, Shorty, Chief, and Bible, gathered around laughing. After I had proved that I was willing to try doing what I was told, C. R. took the axe away before I lost my footing and hurt myself.

"I guess we gotta hire him," he said; and Blackie gave me a meal ticket and put me under the wing of Bible, a bespectacled ex-con who took care of Buddy, the baby orangutan, Chester, the big "Nile hippopotamus," Betty Lou, the pygmy hippo from West Africa, Bobby, the "African One-horned Black Rhinoceros," and a chimp, some green and mangabey monkeys, and an Amazonian tapir. Also we helped Ray with his two giraffes, Edith and Boston.

Bible was a reader, a quiet-spoken man, a peacemaker, reasonable and civil, even owlish because of his horn-rims, a sort of oasis of calm, except during the seizures of binge drinking that ripped out the fabric of his life from time to time. He kept his distance from most of the other workhands, perhaps for fear that the more visible alcoholism and other problems, from epilepsy to schizophrenia, that some of them had would capsize his fragile equilibrium. And it did collapse after a few weeks, whether by this contagion or an internally haywire clock. Then, like so many of the men I worked with, he up and disappeared, as abruptly as that—present at teardown but gone by dawn. We woke up on the train in a new town, and he wasn't there.

Ray, on the other hand, lasted. A cynic, a curser, a dirty joke-teller, Ray reminded me of a bus driver I had had in school who was raffish, irreverent, unkempt, and taught little kids to snigger and smoke, or told them how sex was accomplished if they wanted to know, but who was steadier than he looked—always showed up bright and early, drove safely, no matter how loudly he claimed to have been drunk and living scabrously the night before, and discouraged behavior that was mean or cruel. Ray's steadiness was so dependable that he didn't travel two-to-a-bunk, tiered three-bunks-high in the windowless dormitory railroad cars that the rest of us fourteen-dollar-a-week-men were confined to. Instead, the Fat Lady, Baby Irene, took him into her private compartment on a different train, and bought him nicer clothes that (for all of his dirty talk about how Irene complained his cock "couldn't get past the creases") he kept clean and pressed, too. With a weather eye peeled, he took excellent care of the giraffes, and functioned as a number-three man, after C. R. and Blackie, in the department. He'd drink in a beer joint on the nights that it was safe because we were playing a big city and weren't going to travel; the train wouldn't pull out without him. (Irene earned about $100 a week; the Giant, $125; the Fireproof Man, $45.)

We had three trains, seventy railroad cars, forty-one of them flatcars for carrying the wagons in which everything, from the cookhouse to the flyers' aerial rigging, was then hauled to the lot. Chester and Bobby had special twenty-foot cage-wagons, numbers 85 and 82, and the giraffes were in taller, boxy constructions, numbers 83 and 86. Albert Rix's twelve performing bears were crowded into a twenty-two-foot barred wagon, number 93. The menagerie and cookhouse traveled on the first train, called the Flying Squadron, which arrived in the next town around 4:30 A.M. because we could have left the previous town before the actual performance was over, if the hop was long and we needed to. Ringstock and the elephants and the men who handled them traveled on the second train, along with the sideshow, the candy butchers, the ushers, the propmen, the pole wagons, seat wagons, canvas wagons, and the canvas crew who tore down the big top and put it up again next morning. They got in several hours after us; and the performers in sleeper beds or compartments on the third train, after 11 A.M.

But the shrimp-pink dawn was *ours*. And if you'd gone to bed when the crew bus had delivered us to the train the previous night at about nine o'clock, that wasn't so bad. In every town, hundreds and hundreds of small kids had been roused and brought by their conscientious parents to the railroad yard to marvel at our enthralling arrival. They stood overhead on a bridge or on the nearest roofs and lined the service road and vacant lots, waving politely, timidly calling. When we'd been shuttled the few miles to the new circus lot, we would build a bonfire of scrap wood and stand around it or squat on our heels waiting for the cookhouse tent to go up and smoke from the stoves to rise—coffee, oatmeal, toast and eggs—and for our animals to come, while many more local souls wandered near, wanting to speak, or waited to witness whatever we did: blow a harmonica, walk to the river, whittle a stick. There was often a river at hand, Ohio-sized or a little one, because the circus grounds were waste grounds, sparsely used during the rest of the year except for a carnival, a revival meeting, or a county fair. Boosters and businessmen still turned their backs on the riverbank for development in the 1950s until most other land was gone. Rivers had seemed disreputable, like highways now—the haunt of bargemen and tugmen, raftsmen, flatboatmen, keelboatmen, freightmen and drifters, prostitutes, and tramps—a place for fly-by-night people in hobo jungles. The idea that a river is a municipal amenity, a vista of peace and parkland, was decades away.

Bible liked to sleep out next to the wagons on the flatcars in balmy weather, instead of two to a bunk, three-high, inside our rattling, claustrophobic crew cars, having no doubt acquired a love for the open sky in prison. And I sometimes joined him when the moon was out. Crossing Indiana and Iowa, you could hear the lions sniff for the smells of the veldt at their ventilation slats and roar to see if a lion out there on the prairie answered; then thump the walls when they scented the Mississippi; or the forests of Minnesota; or the Platte, in Nebraska. When the train slowed, I was sometimes tempted to open their cages so they could go find a life for themselves in the wild, however abbreviated. These were glory nights, vivid nights. The dreamers dreamed, the drinkers drank; but if your life lay ahead of you, what could be better than the firmament over a moving train?

I don't remember my various bedmates inside the sleeping car, except when they had lots of nightmares, snored badly, or complained of my own nightmares and snoring—or if a man was so husky that he crowded me on the narrow pallet and I had to lie on my side, keeping my arms over my head in order to sleep. Though we lacked windows, the open gratings in the side of the car provided plenty of wind and a loud lullaby of clicketing rails, pistoning wheels, and the occasional wail of the locomotive's long whistle. The swaying, the rocking in rotary motion, the syncopated rumble or snare-drum rat-tat of the hundred steel wheels crossing spurs and section switches, or an abruptly undulant patch of the roadbed, cradled me, as train travel always had when I was a child and still does, even though my first memory is of a Pullman derailment in North Dakota, when I was two years old and traveling with my mother from New York to Washington State to visit her parents. If it was uneven and jerked, so is a womb's progression. The noise was "white noise," and our sixteen-hour workdays, too, encouraged everybody to sleep. When I did have bad dreams, they were very sudden, precipitated by another train on the opposite track roaring past at high speed with a shrieking scream. A circus train might have drunks on the flatcars, riding half-on, half-off; and other freights or express trains were warned to blow, blow, and blow. I would imagine, not the train, but an elephant stampeding, trumpeting, with me in its path—because I *did* like to lie on the ground at high noon next to one of them, Ruth, or Modoc, pretending to nap at a placid moment when the big top was up and the elephant boss was maybe at lunch, and an elephant man let me. The beast's feet and trunk inscribed whimsical circles of her own design in the air not far above my head, like finger painting, dainty and quirky.

If not an elephant's trumpet, my mind might transmute the midnight screaming roar of a passing freight train into a tiger, because I was soon also playing with the big cats. Both Blackie and Chief, their keeper, recognized my interest as useful. Chief showed me how to water them three times a day and scrape dung from their cages with an iron rod that the Ringstock blacksmith had fashioned. Later on, when the circus stayed overnight in a large town—Pittsburgh, Toledo, Detroit, Chicago, Milwaukee, Minneapolis—for extra performances, I slept on the ground under the lions' wagon. Many of us preferred to stay on the lot rather than go back to the railroad yards. The ground was no harder than our wooden-slat beds, and there was a grandeur to the big top, night or day. The sea-colored canvas, eleven hundred fifty feet in circumference, mounted in hammocky waves from a hundred sixteen side poles—each one like a Bactrian hump—toward the sixty-five quarter poles (elephants pulled each of these up), and then higher and higher, with the immensity and serenity of surf, to the bale rings on the center poles, about seventy feet high. The trapeze bars and high-wire rigging glittered up there; and on the ground, perhaps scraps of the jugglers' gear, clown gimmickry, the Liberty-horse ring curbing, and the tigers' round

pedestals in the performance cage. Bible and I had locked ourselves inside Buddy the orangutan's cage, or in one of Ray's giraffe
wagons, earlier in the summer in order to feel protected from the
local muggers that in a city like Albany might roam through during the wee hours. But the farther west I got and the more I knew
about the cats, the better I trusted their protection. No townie
was going to brave the lions' wide forepaws hanging out between
the bars over my head, after I bedded down.

Shorty helped Bible too. He had a cleft palate and was bald
and he may have been a "slave" or a "catcher" in jail, his arm
twisted behind his back when being raped, because he joked
sometimes in the railroad car that "a baldheaded old man" like
him was "nearly as good as a young boy" in the cells: which was
the only open reference to homosexuality I remember hearing in
our collective lives there. The train was a place to sleep, though
people played cards on the tracks in the twilight before we left, sitting on pieces of cardboard, and heated burgers on a kerosene
stove or ate them raw as "cannibal burgers." Bible leafed through
magazines on his bunk when other people were drinking beer;
and Chief would generally show up at the last minute because his
particular friends, a Sioux in Ringstock who was named Little
Chief, and "Navajo Chief," who was an elephant man, took the
later train along with their animals after the show, so he'd stay on
the lot with them as long as he could. He flared into incandes-
cence when he did get loaded, like one of those solitary firecrack-
ers that shoots high and falls without doing harm, but he tried
to stay sober. Like the Mohawks who dominated high-steel sky-
scraper work in New York City at this time, Chief (Ralph Leaf
was his given name) indicated that he had chosen a risky vocation
on purpose, as if to fly the flag of the Indian Nation and thumb
his nose at the pathetic alternatives on the reservation. Rather
similarly, he expected the tigers and lions to maintain their primary dignity and character, although caged—to make a show of
rising, bristling, and roaring at him when challenged to do so. He

stood straight to give them an example, emitting a cheeky, deep hiss and raising an arm, his smile admiringly mimicking their snarls. They appeared to enjoy it, as a substitute for exercise. Most of our animals were confined in eleven-by-eight-foot World War II ordnance wagons that had been bought by Ringling Bros. and converted to carry a couple of lions or tigers, or a mother and three younger leopards, or a jaguar-cheetah-panther combination, partitioned apart. Since they were so cruelly cramped, what you could do for their creature comfort was minimal, apart from being friendly and gentle.

In the circus my enforced silence did not seem especially unusual. Blackie, my boss, himself had a glass eye; and the Devil Liquor reclaimed people from our train every week, if not every night. They vanished into the oubliette of a binge and woke up alone in an alley of a community that was suddenly unfriendly. A circus hand lost his magic when the show scrubbed off its makeup and left town. He was now an object of police suspicion, a hungover, dirty bum. Or if he did manage to scramble onto a rolling flatcar but then lost his hold and tumbled off the train in fifty miles, and was lucky enough to survive, he would have to hobble up to some stranger's door with a broken shoulder, a face full of gravel, torn clothes, smelling of alcohol, and no pedigree at all. Poor Blackie, who became my avuncular pal, eventually died on the shoulder of a highway at Winter Quarters, hit by a car while drunk, I heard. But Shorty lived on. Twenty years later, I met him coincidentally when I visited the circus during its run in Birmingham, Alabama, near his home. He had hitchhiked ninety miles, with his cane and bad eyes, to get there. And Chief had left Ringling Bros. even before I did. Clawed by a tiger in Madison Square Garden, he married his nurse from the hospital and settled in Brooklyn.

A stutter was no big deal if you were a nimble eighteen-year-old, jumping on and off the back of the Caterpillar tractors and scrambling up on top of the menagerie wagons and down, rain or shine, when we set up our part of the show and tore it down again, and genuinely cared for the animals. After all, we had "Sealo," Charles Bavent, whose hands were attached to his shoulders like flippers; and Ted Evans, "The Tallest Man in the World"; and Freda Pushnik, "Our Poor Little Armless and Legless Girl." And the gorillas' caretaker never spoke. Dressed in black, he lived in a compartment of their air-conditioned, glassed-in wagon, next to M'Toto, the celebrated silverback Gargantua's famous "widow," and was nearly as isolated as her. Tenacity in this milieu was better than muscles. Blackie, a trouper for decades, a loner who peppered nuisances with his dry commentary ("Elmer" was what he called all the towners), bestowed his approval on me, and even protection on a few occasions when exceptionally tough guys showed up for a spell, straight from the prison yard—though I was seldom aware of needing it. The turnover was amazing, but my friends were mostly the ones living on borrowed time, before they fell foul of their diabetes or whatever, and giving the big boss, C. R., five or ten dollars a week out of their fourteen to hold for them so that they would have something saved by Thanksgiving to survive on during the winter.

People joined who were simply in flight or had a lot to keep quiet about and were ravenously hungry—wolfing down that first meal at the long plywood table covered with oilcloth—hard home fries and sausage, stewed tomatoes, chicken à la king, Jell-O, bread pudding, lemonade, iced coffee. The experienced hoboes didn't fall into such straits. They knew the Sallies (Salvation Army) or other missions in every large town and how to jump off a freight and negotiate a big switching yard without injury, then maybe coax some coffee and a bun out of the nearest waitress by appealing to her best instincts ("if you're going to throw it away anyway"). But we had people sign on whose roof had just fallen in. Coughing, bloodshot, hunger like a grindstone in the belly: yet they might not stay longer than the Depression-hardened tramps who often vanished without ever quitting—just lingered in a beer joint till our train pulled out and then hopped a freight in the opposite direction. Next morning, we'd look for another smudge-faced drifter to fill in awhile.

You're either "with it" or not, in the world of the circus, much as in a carnival, although carnivals are regarded as a lower order of show business by circus folk, who travel much more than carnies do and perform arcane stunts of scary skill. Carnies, though they are not death-defying, also make this sharp distinction and evince little interest in circuses, nor work in them. They seem more money-focused and predatory, separating the crowds of towners from their dollar bills all day, every day, with little scams and petty games of chance, or frying onion rings and sugared dough, pushing the lever on the Ferris wheel or merry-go-round, living in a house trailer and staying put for a week or two. By comparison, the castes of the circus were byzantine. The star performers, of exact balance and surpassing daring, were supreme. Then the big bosses of the money part, and the performance directors. Then run-of-the-mill, other performers; and the logistics bosses and department heads; and clowns, as a separate class; and sideshow freaks and other attractions; and longtime, senior workhands. Then the come-and-go white roustabouts such as me (eighty-some animal caretakers altogether, for instance, counting the horse grooms and "bull," or elephant, department; and sixty-six men to handle the cookhouse). And finally, last and least, the black workhands, or "jigs," who were paid only twelve dollars a week and limited to the one job of unrolling the big top canvas that would eventually seat eleven thousand spectators, sledgehammering the countless side pole stakes into the ground for an hour or two in synchronized crews of four—chanting slave songs to keep their swings falling in perfect tandem—then getting it all up, gradually guying it all out—and tearing it all down again at eleven at night.

My first contact with blunt Southern racism was here; and although Jim Crow–style bigotry had more complexity and sometimes more "give" than the innuendoes of northern prejudice that I was used to, underneath the South's racism, as late as these 1950s, lay the threat of death. You saw cops—or the elephant men with *their* clubs—chasing a Negro, and knew from how frantically he ran that he might be about to die. No uppityness was tolerated at any time.

As for us white guys, we would have been fired for talking to the performers, though an exception of course was made for the handful of propmen who helped them; and the animal trainers might chat with us about animal handling in passing. The veterinarian's wife, Mrs. Henderson, had raised our four leopards by hand and therefore came by to play with them in jeans and a white blouse or a glittery costume every week, probably to check out the passing parade of cagehands too, lest anybody unkind get hired. Her lacy white blouse set off her wealth of curly black hair, which bounced as she walked. She was an aerialist, a European (in fact, by her former marriage, a Wallenda), with the posture and spring in her step of a star, and—joyfully giving her hands and whole arms to the leopards through the bars, to lick and toy with (as I soon learned to do)—her back arched, as performers' bodies do without their even thinking about it, when life is at a peak for them. I wanted to write a short story about a propman who twice every day in the center ring stood under such a beautiful woman as she gyrated on a trapeze bar, looking upward at her, intent upon breaking her fall if she ever lost her grip: how he would die for her, though they never spoke. I had a crush on Josephine, the Mexican snake charmer, as well, whose hair hung clear to her coccyx, and who hefted those gorgeous boas, and was a waitress in Florida in the off-season, and would talk freely to anybody (being billed with the "freaks"). But Josephine hadn't that slenderness that catches the heart—that aerialist's lilt.

Albert Rix's mixed-bear act, white, black, and brown, had been drawn from the collection of the Hamburg Zoo, and included a couple of polar bears of enormous proportions, galumphing around as fast and yet cryptically as if seals might be on the menu. But Roland Tiebor's half-dozen barking sea lions pirouetted like ballerinas to toss and catch a ball on their noses, then posed like politicians when they had it bagged. In my second year, Oscar Konyot joined up with a pride of German-trained lions: "Man-Eating Comedians in the Most Unusual Wild Animal Exhibition Ever Witnessed. Blood-Thirsty Jungle Demons in Animal Antics That Would Make the Sphinx Rock With Laughter." Konyot was actually a sort of journeyman trainer, a martinet who used to stand and whip a side pole for fifteen minutes after his act was over if it had not gone well. Then, in 1953, we were joined by Trevor Bale, an affable, rather plump, classy Danish headliner from England, a complete and competent showman, whose little son, Elvin, twenty years later, himself became a Ringling Bros. and Barnum & Bailey finale star—hanging by the crook of his heels from a trapeze bar. But Trevor had brought over six Bengal tigers from London, which he worked in the courteous style of other European trainers, from Alfred Court to Dick Chipperfield.

I'd watched Alfred Court, a French leopard-lover and all-time great, with my father in Madison Square Garden in 1939, and later saw Chipperfield perform under a tent in a London suburb in 1964. However, Konyot (who had to roar and whip the walls in order to decompress in Madison Square Garden also) was in the mock-ferocious, American and German, "fighting-act" tradition made famous by Clyde Beatty in large, mixed-cat presentations, one of which I saw in Beatty's own circus under canvas in Phila-delphia in 1956, after Ringling Bros. had folded its tents and tem-porarily closed for reorganization. Later, Wolfgang Holzmair, a contemporary of Elvin Bale's, handled Ringling Bros.' lions with the same Roman-amphitheater Sturm und Drang. And Pat Anthony, though he specialized in movie work, was another "fighting" lion trainer: but a kind man. I knew him briefly in 1953 at the World Jungle Compound in Thousand Oaks, California, when I walked in off the highway—as at the circus two years before—on the strength of a letter from Mabel Stark saying I could have a job if I showed up; and he asked me if I had enough money to eat on.

While I was there in California, Oscar Konyot was clawed by a lion on his right arm in Portland, Maine, requiring twenty-eight stitches; and it did not escape the notice of superstitious show people that *Bangor,* Maine, was where Mabel Stark, the greatest woman tiger trainer of all time, had suffered her worst clawing, in 1928, with the John Robinson Circus, when two tigers named Sheik and Zoo chewed on her, necessitating four hours of sewing. When I knew Mabel, in Thousand Oaks, a series of strokes had crippled her in the quarter-century since those particular injuries. Besides her remaining tigers, all of the official MGM lions were housed there, a row of full-maned retirees, each of whom had reigned for a year as the movie company's trademark on the screen, and whom you can still see emoting before the start of vintage movies—as well as the various "wrestling cats," leopards, tigers, and lions that Tarzan or Mowgli or Victor Mature or Sabu or Flash Gordon had tussled with over the years on jungle sets— plus zebras, camels, monkeys in a colony, emus, kangaroos, and the like, which I took care of, under the supervision of another American Indian. He said he was a "Digger," when I asked his affiliation, using the contemptuous term for himself that white Californians had bestowed on the indigenous tribes, who were often living on roots and nuts in gold rush times.

Mabel could hardly walk. One of her arms hung useless from the strokes (ultimately, she spared herself further debilitation by taking her own life) and the other hand had been bitten again in 1951 to the point of immobility. Yet she still "received" a favorite tigress in the round steel cage every Sunday, for the sake of her pride and a little pocket money from the tiny audience, controlling and directing the huge, lovely animal by her voice alone.

Trevor Bale was not an inspired performer like Mabel, or gracefully, brilliantly intuitive like Gunther Gebel-Williams—

another contemporary of his son, Elvin, in later productions of Ringling Bros., and probably the best animal trainer there ever was, at least in our millennium. Bale was versatile, familial, cheery, and commonsensical instead. He liked animals and enjoyed pitching in at night, for example, to help us herd the giraffes from their outdoor pen into the two traveling-wagons, if they had balked and he was nearby. Circuses roll because people pitch in. So did Gunther, in the 1970s, but Gunther choreographed all of the animals in the three rings, practically at once and mainly by voice command—the entire herd of elephants and all the Liberty horses, with a whip and some body language, plus the covey of tigers that he palled with—"riding" one of them on top of a horse in the center ring, and then on an elephant. He ran about, to up the tempo, gleeful, as most superstars are at work. He was like an Alexander with animals. Trevor Bale was more like that earlier Englishman, Dr. Dolittle, who knew what animals wanted and what people wanted and tried to meld the two.

Pat Valdo was the Performance Director during my stint, and Harold Ronk the stentorian Ringmaster ("Children of All Ages . . ."): both of them circus paragons. Valdo had a mime's face, protean yet self-effacing, a lightness, a quickness, in and out of scenes like Janus in the tragicomedy of what a circus is really all about. The pie in the face, the slipping on a banana skin, yet clockwork horses and obedient elephants; and an ovation for the high-wire man who *doesn't* fall to his death. Ours was Harold Alzana, "Whose Disregard of Danger Has Made Millions Gasp." He began his act by climbing a slanted rigging cable to the wire forty-five feet up, balancing with an absurd-looking parasol that he waved while the clowns gazed up at him, aghast, and his wife, Minnie, and sister, Elsie, having already climbed a rope ladder hand-over-hand to the platform, looked down, plainly worrying. With hip-wriggles, Alzana made the cable wobble dangerously underneath him and once in each performance would step with his heel on a toe, causing himself to stumble, while Harold Ronk, like a royal chamberlain, all presence in resplendent red, ratcheted up the suspense with sorrowful, breathless, trombone tones of voice. Then TRIUMPH! as the climb to the high-wire was boldly consummated, and the bicycle ride began—which was itself quite seriously perilous—with the two women balanced on trapezes hanging from its aluminum frame. The slim, whip-cracking Konyot had a Wehrmacht bearing, but Alzana looked well-fed, uncommonly chunky for what he did.

Emmett Kelly and Otto Griebling were the darkface tramp clowns during my era (Griebling acerbic and Kelly sweet-sad in the humor they projected); and Felix Adler famously wore white-face, using a little terrier and piglets to connect with the crowd's heartstrings, while numerous other "joeys" cavorted around like red-mouthed jumping beans, lending extra leverage to the dare-devil spectacles. Pinito Del Oro, a superb Spanish aerialist who did cloud swings and headstands on the trapeze bar, shared top billing with Harold Alzana, and was also the sultry centerpiece of a thirty-two-girl aerial ballet of "web-sitters" thrusting out their pretty calves from a forest of dangling ropes. And the Flying Concellos, of lengthy renown, wound up the show somersaulting to the catcher over a barge-shaped net. We had foot-jugglers, slack-wire artists, foot-ladder acts, trampoline tumblers, chariot-riders, and a breakaway sway pole—plus a band of thirty or so, which Merle Evans directed while flourishing his sterling cornet. By the close of his fifty-year career, he may have been second only to John Philip Sousa in the pleasure he gave in that line of work.

World War II had ended only six years before my first summer in the show, which was why I could hitchhike so easily anywhere; people were used to picking up servicemen. And we had lots of Europeans performing, needy and pent-up from the privations of the war. Some of the young ones bore that pinch of Occupation hunger. Their faces and frames still hadn't filled out, and they had the exile's air of wistful, agile dexterity—always in transit, never at home. Sirens in bikinis, gamines in tank tops, perch-pole acrobats, Roman riders, slender ethereal pinups, and simple musclemen—more than our hoboes, who at least were roaming their own continent, they looked uncommitted. Whether they had spent the early 1940s in Naples, Marseilles, or Frankfort, it had been a hungry, fearful half-decade for circus people (or "kinkers," or "hulligans," for "hooligans," as we workhands called the foreign performers), with their animals maybe starving, their wives and children huddled in cellars, the husbands in uniform, if not in combat. And this tour they were having of Zanesville and Portsmouth, Ohio; Parkersburg, West Virginia; Battle Creek, Michigan; Mason City, Iowa; Ogden, Utah; and Pocatello, Idaho, surely seemed rather idyllic, painted on top of such scarring memories, however comically unsophisticated they may have thought that Americans were.

A woman's beauty is not necessarily impaired by the mystery, hedonism, and grief of going through a war—the roulette of bombing raids, or making shift during an invasion or in a retreat. We had plenty of seasoned stars who had appeared in peacetime arenas in Bucharest, Budapest, or Berlin, and then done mud shows under canvas through the ravaged countryside for bread and vegetables when anarchy had set in, landing on their feet in a way that not every civilian could have. Wiry, resilient, androgynous, ambiguous, they could sneak or swagger—work hauling trunks and duffel bags and other stuff outdoors through a five-hour rainstorm, and then display their sponged-off, Dietrich-type legs in the limelight of the "spec," alongside the delicate, long-stemmed, heart-faced, honey-blonde Broadway showgirls from Billy Rose's Diamond Horseshoe Club in New York, whom we also had. They could scuttle, dragging heavy rigging through a cloudburst in a hand-me-down Chaplinesque overcoat, but then do front flips on a galloping horse down the hippodrome track, and let an elephant lift them up high by gripping a shapely thigh in its mouth and wrapping its trunk around their midriffs. They could stand on the riverbank, ogling some of us boys swimming nude in the currents (when we stripped off our coveralls for a spell at noontime), but then gaze down enigmatically, vertiginously, during the performance while hanging upside down from a trapeze at another young man in dingy coveralls who was constantly moving underneath them, anticipating on what part of his body he would take the force of the blow if the lady fell, but never otherwise exchanging two words with her.

We menagerie hands seldom watched the show. We hung around at Number 10 Wagon or with our animals to see that no towners hurt them or got hurt trying to fool with them. Meanwhile, the band's selections, like an oft-told tale, kept us exactly informed of what was happening inside the big top—Merle Evans's clarion cornet the leading narrator of a montage of something like sixty snatches from many composers that accompanied each turn of the program. Ever after, that wonderful band became for me the epitome of the circus. As a paying customer later on, I'd sit up high in Madison Square Garden where the music carried best and even close my eyes, lulled and thrilled, knowing what was happening: the lions, the showgirls, the wire-walking, the tumbling and strutting, the human cannon-shots, and diverse buffoonery. Consciously or unconsciously, I took it as a metaphor for how to wake up in the morning and live with stamina and faith and joy—how to pick yourself up when you fall, hide your limp, take a punch, yet drive yourself on, and do what you're best at with verve and panache, being at home anywhere, west or east. I didn't see much Old World black humor among these circus folk. They'd been through a war but believed at least in their work, in children, in craft. I've never blamed God for what people do, and maybe they didn't either. And I've never understood why bond salesmen are paid more than fire-swallowers, slack-wire dancers, and human cannonballs. What *they* accomplish is rarer and gives more pleasure.

The marginal is often what's valued later: whether circus tents, elephants and gorillas, or the composers, painters, and religious dissenters who shoot off energetically from the mainstream. I didn't write down the old slave chants that the Negroes sang to synchronize their sledge-hammer blows in pounding stakes into the ground and tugging the guy lines tight; didn't realize that the Sumatran and Siberian tigers I fed and watered might become extinct in the wild in my own lifetime; and the big top itself a subject for grainy documentaries. Tickets cost from fifty cents to four dollars, depending upon where the spectators sat, and, earning two dollars a day, we didn't feel obliged to answer for the hundredth time a particular question—like what the animals were fed. For Blackie after decades it was almost torture. He probably sat in his wagon all day to escape the crowds asking where they could take a piss. For Chief, it was part of the white man's inanity: *What do you* think *they eat? Where do you* want *to piss!* As a towner myself, I've lingered for days around the mud wrestlers' tent at a carnival, or the jumbo wooden barrel inside which two motorcyclists interlaced in figure eights up and down the curving sides quite endlessly, while their seven-year-old daughter hunted for nickels outside in the midway soil, and a country singer posed with people for three dollars for a Polaroid shot, after her show. But I don't ask questions.

Elmira, Olean, Tonawanda, and Jamestown, New York; Pottsville, Hazelton, Erie, Williamsport, Warren, and Wilkes-Barre, Pennsylvania; Dayton and Lima, Ashtabula and Canton, in Ohio; Charleston, West Virginia; the burned-rubber scent of Akron, Ohio; the sweet-grass banks of the Missouri River at Council Bluffs, Iowa; and of course Chicago, in its spiky grandeur, where I tried and failed to lose my virginity in a whorehouse near Soldier's Field. (As at the Washington-Jefferson Hotel in New York, where I soon tried again, the middle-aged black woman was small and weary, with a cat, incense candles, and colored lights.) But waking up even there in Chicago in the billowing big top under the lions' wagon with dew on my blanket was a delight, and quite as much of a paradigm for the rest of life as Harold Alzana on his high-wire. Jesus, I loved this America. And when I went in the army at twenty-two, there was hardly a recruit whose accent I couldn't place, whose hometown I hadn't been within a hundred miles of. Hitchhiking home from Idaho Falls on old Highway 30, I dawdled along between rides, looking up the cuts and washes, where twisty creeks ran past little cottonwood ranches, seeing antelopes, coyotes, Herefords, till at Ogallala, Nebraska, the road met the Platte River, and I was back in the Midwest again.

Blackie and C. R. by hiring me gave me the chance to scratch inside our hippo's gawping mouth like a Nile tick bird and to donate my tender arms to our milling leopards through the gaps in their bars, thus acquiring my faith in a sixth sense—which is to say, in scientific terms, in "cross-species communication" and understanding—as well as a lifelong belief in clowning, in grace, and in showmanship: to fly, in life, a sort of "banner line," as sideshows do. C. R. ended up broke in a trailer in Florida in his old age, like many an animal man, as I heard from a circus fan who visited him. But Blackie—who had died by the side of the road before that—I was closer to. Blackie was kind to me like another lonely, childless southerner, a Kentucky colonel in the army, Elon B. Tucker, from Lexington. He was a bluegrass blueblood who should have been a civilian but said he had quarreled with his chemistry professor in graduate school and had presumptuously taken "the easy way out." Both Colonel Tucker and Blackie Barlow were dry-witted, observant men with a running commentary on the rest of humanity that was acid but not uncharitable, and my fluttering stutter seemed to chime with some secret wound they each had. So often in hitchhiking, too, I would sense a fluttering wounded-bird in the people who picked me up. My stutter, like a tuning fork, would elicit an answering pain—draw pus from a secret wound.

Because I went into a peacetime army in 1955, I'd already learned more about bravery in the circus, where life was really at risk, and about leadership also. The circus lot supervisor and

first-train superintendent was a beefy showman named Lloyd
Morgan, who would set the whole thing up again on another
vacant lot the next morning. Calm and competent, he laid it out
in his mind's eye at dawn, every iota of canvas and ancillary booth
and wagon. Strolling the stretch of territory allotted to us, he
tossed tall metal pins into the ground to mark the six-hundred-
yard rim of the big top's stake line, and the wardrobe tents, horse
tents, generators, midway, and sideshow. To the sheriff, the fire
chief, sanitation inspector, police superintendent, who might
show up early, he personified the circus. In his oil slicker and rain
boots, or sunny-weather double-breasted brown summer suit and
polished shoes, with an alderman's big pinkie ring, he was unflap-
pably gregarious, yet self-contained and toughly shrewd. Without being at all discourteous, he let everybody know that he had
met about nineteen hundred county sheriffs before, that the circus had a "patch" whose job was to put in the fix with any necessary bribes—not him—and that an awful lot of children were
going to have a splendiferous day if nobody got in the way now
and spoiled it for them. Elephants do shit, derelicts do piss and
spit; yet somehow or other that's how a circus works. The shim-
mying horses, nearly a hundred of them, the legion of wagons,
the hordes of roustabouts, some of them an unknown quantity
undoubtedly ripe for catastrophe, from epilepsy or a diabetic
coma to arson or manslaughter—but not on *this* gala day, not
here: that's how it all goes up, and the greasepaint goes on, and
the band strikes up, and thousands of children every afternoon
depended on it. Cozening, mollifying local officials from Mississippi to Minnesota with decency and equanimity, never flustered
or mussed, Morgan dominated the site rather like a construction
bigwig or mobster honcho might on the docks of New York. But
children's dreams (not police lieutenants, union officers, or plan-
ning boards) were the coin of the realm here. And he had a kind
of subcutaneous flair. The brim of his hat, the glint of his cuff-
links, the twist of his grin were a showman's who would not be in

town tomorrow. If you were in Tucson, he'd be in Seattle and have taken your measure just while passing through. I learned through watching him that improvisation is often prudent as well as spontaneous; that daring comprises a lot of analysis, and you size people up without either wholly condemning or trusting them. You're like an envelope in the mail and in the course of a lifetime, you're going to be in plenty of bundles.

Patricia Zerm was our Sword Swallower, and Betty Broadbent, our Tattooed Lady. Ted Warner, the Human Picture Gallery, had needlework even inside his mouth. Poor Frances O'Conner was our Armless Wonder. Ted Evans, with a cockney accent and dressed in a Buckingham Palace uniform, stood eight feet tall, when his aches and pains permitted him to. Otherwise he sat pinned on exhibit on the stage selling five-cent photos of himself, next to my heartthrob, Josephine, with her Indian and African rock pythons and gaudy boa constrictors. Though I couldn't talk to these people, they understood that. Life was for riding the train, seizing your avenues, and surviving Winter Quarters to see the open road again.

MENTORS AND ROOTS

*I*once asked a middle-aged friend why we WASPs seemed better at infidelity than friendship. In other words, although settled in marriages, our closest friends outside that institution
tended to be girlfriends, either from the past or sub rosa, not
men. Uneasily he pointed out that the cartoon Anglo-Saxon
(nineteenth-century family histories inform us that we are "cousins" from some eighteenth-century intermarriage) is indeed uptight. But if he is so uptight, I asked, how can the guy carry on
passionate affairs, much less illicit, adulterous ones?

Although he didn't answer that particular letter (it's characteristic of our uptightness that we communicate best on significant
matters by letter), I suspect he would have pointed out that a lot
of things are turning upside down nowadays. Illicit is licit; and
furthermore because he married so young, while still in college,
and had his kids pronto, his adventures in experimentation had
to be extramarital. Being a sensible though elusive man, he'd
undoubtedly add, if one could pin him down, that our books indi-

cate that we were each closer to our talkative mothers than our reserved fathers and must have gotten into the habit of chattering more fluently with women early on. Besides, God gave us the ecstasy of ejaculation. Biologically and on the pleasure quotient there's more in it for us. Bantering with women is a kind of dumb show of passing along our genes and Xeroxing ourselves.

Of course when young we're quite bisexual, because on an anthropological level a man's survival presumably also depended on a life-and-death alliance with the other men he hunted or raided with—he wouldn't last a month if he was only a ladies' man—and from puberty to our mid-twenties we're still busily on athletic teams or pouring out our hearts to male "best friends" as much as negotiating with women. I remember another friend, now dead, whom I partly grew up with during my teens, whose friendships later became most intense with women, a webwork of midnight liaisons and dalliances, obviating marriage to the point where I was asked once in middle age by his concerned father whether he was maybe in love with his mom. He may have been; we all loved her—his father, me, and two or three old bachelor hangers-on who were very frequently around. And she schooled us all, holding court with Carolina charm, but also acting with a Miss Havisham streak, I thought, as she used me as a foil to set off her bright and beautiful son, Steele, and watched me fall in love with her eldest daughter, Nell, a lyre-backed, loping walker and dialectician, and, in turn, be the object of a crush by her blonde youngest girl, Lisa, who was dreamy and lovely. I loved them all, in fact, but fleeing my own seductive mother to this household was like going from the frying pan into the fire. Such emotional Sturm und Drang: and the letters I wrote both to Nell and her mother because I was unable to speak!

I profited from all this—the seductive foster mother; the golden-boy friend and rival who would become a brilliant classicist at Columbia and lifelong chum; the ethicist sister who went on to marry Christopher Lasch, a classmate of Steele's and mine and a social historian; the younger sister, as blonde as Goldilocks or Cinderella, who went to Kathmandu and back in a kind of scary fairytale, before marrying a librarian; and their father, Henry Steele Commager, a buoyant, trenchant, prolific Americanist historian, who was my first professional writer: which at sixteen I already knew I wanted to be.

But to have had smothering, seductive mothers is not a condition limited to Anglos like Steele and me. The proverbial Jewish mother is writ large in contemporary literature, not to mention the mothers of Catholic culture; yet I haven't seen as many Jews or Irishmen whose friendships were skewed toward intimacy with past or present lovers to the relative exclusion of other men. Maybe the bursting of Puritanism was what it was about: that after sloughing off our mothers at twenty or so, Steele and I and that novelist "cousin" were *allowed* to have womenfriends, not limited, like our ancestors, to men. What I have seen instead with two or three long-term pals who are Jewish or Irish Americans is quite a different problem—men who have slept with a hundred women but are dying in their seventies almost totally alone, having neglected to win any of them as friends. Apart from these extreme examples, sex can be a cat's cradle of hairpin turns and reversing tangents, cruel and lonely when you either live or lack for it and bewildering in its permutations, though at the same time overwhelmingly logical. Xerox me, Xerox me!

Mr. Commager—"Felix," as his wife called him, meaning "happy" in Latin—was a vital, long-lived, positive man, chunky and indefatigable. He had grown up poor, semi-orphaned, in Chicago and made the best of things with enormous bouts of reading and a clarity at partitioning information and ideas, fountaining energy, writing *The American Mind* and co-authoring textbooks like *The Growth of the American Republic* that nearly everybody read in school. He worked joyfully, plentifully, efficiently. Even as we chatted as a family in a restaurant in the evening, he might move to an empty table and tinker with a review, an introduction, a symposium contribution that was due—delighting in announcing an eccentric detail of Colonial or Reconstruction history he had run across. The primacy of the American experiment was his inspiration, as well as rubbing shoulders with all and sundry on his visiting professorships and tours. Though I didn't aim to be an historian, stamina and versatility, gaiety and independence were going to be a good part of what sustained you, whatever you wrote. I knew I too was wedded to the American attempt to unstring a bunch of Old World miseries, weather the tragedies of democracy, and model a remake of how things might be done. In the fifties this emphasis was not in style among intellectuals or students. It was Gide, Camus, Brecht, Sartre, Kafka, Beckett, Ionesco, and Joyce (whose ebullience and genius I loved)— all valid for the European shipwreck—exalted, wonderful, but mostly voices of a postwar, disillusioned, often cynical or depressive stripe, which I was not. They didn't speak for me as much as the American writers did, or the eighteenth- and nineteenth-century English classics, or *The Iliad*, Cervantes, Chaucer, Rabelais, Montaigne, Tolstoy. I was not a pessimist then. New solutions, Jeffersonian institutions could do it; and here was a historian encyclopedic in his knowledge and exuberance, almost *too* confident, who stood up bravely against the momentary corrosion of McCarthyism, till that strange force slammed against the iceberg of the U.S. Army and shipped water and sank. "Is God dead?" trendy magazines like *Time* were inquiring. But Emerson, Thoreau, Whitman (and I) didn't think so, nor even our contemporary genius, Faulkner. I was a bit like Henry James's Henrietta Stackpole in my nationalism, but genuinely passionate—whereas plays like Ionesco's *Rhinoceros* and Beckett's *Krapp's Last Tape* strike me squarely today.

My college mentor, Archibald MacLeish, a lyric narrative poet and dramatist, was another of Whitman's progeny. Like Commager, he kept calling the country back to its Constitutional values during the fifties with magazine articles and speeches, taking punches from the Left and Right, as an essayist should be prepared to do. He was sixtyish, ten years older than Commager—a Chicago merchant's son with an extraordinary journey behind him—when I came under his wing. A natural leader, he'd been captain of the Yale football team; then an artillery captain seeing action in France during World War I; then a fast-track corporation attorney in Boston after Harvard Law School. In 1923 he quit all that and sailed to Paris to be a Lost Generation poet and friend of Gerald Murphy, Sylvia Beach, Hemingway, Dos Passos, Fitzgerald, Harry Crosby, Malcolm Cowley, and the rest, with his wife and sons. He left that too, marking his homecoming with poems like "You, Andrew Marvell," winging from Persia over to the New World (after his father's death), and *Conquistador,* an epic of Cortez's feats; and then became a New Deal Brain Truster in Franklin D. Roosevelt's administration—assistant secretary of state, and Librarian of Congress—when not working as a journalist for Henry Luce at *Fortune* magazine; and finally the Boyleston Professor at Harvard, where I "had" him. A man of parts, friend of Dean Acheson and Felix Frankfurter, he was supple, resourceful, and widely allied.

As a teacher, MacLeish was generous, paternal, tolerant, not intense, single-minded, and argumentative, like Commager. This was partly because MacLeish was a poet and public official by training, not a lifelong university teacher who had been gearing generations of graduate students to scholarship. But they were both whirlwinds at work—organized, positive-minded, and accustomed to the subtle thrust of Washington politics and a diversity of talent. I learned the importance of self-confidence and the habit of energy from both, plus devotion to the American democratic experiment that had driven so much of the excitement of their careers—to wake up every morning, trust one's genie, and go for it, not befuddled by a bad review, a doubtful publisher, or quarrelsome colleague. Both were rather too fluent, in fact, for original spadework. (Each, though friendly, thought the other "wrote too much.") But they were flagship intellectuals for their time, gaily, gallantly weighing in on the side of the Bill of Rights and other virtues, and flattering me with a temporary membership in the guild of honest-to-goodness writers—just the sort of memory a young writer needs, ten years out of college, to push on with his lagging work when everyone else seems to be installed in a more palpable situation. MacLeish, a proud Scot, was a mellifluous lecturer, velvet-voiced on a stage, a Laureate type of poet ("New Found Land," *America Was Promises*), who could also channel his verse to mark the first spacewalk to a deadline for *Life* magazine. He taught me the usefulness of a façade of guarded dignity, keeping your own counsel, knowing precisely whom you're speaking to, and the importance of fulfilling assignments if you want to get more of them—in short, how to be sane.

This was important because my other poet-teacher at college was John Berryman, who, in a fortunate balance, taught me how to be usefully crazy. Berryman was getting divorced, and so jittery that his hands shook in class from his hangovers until our manuscripts that he was reading from rattled like castanets. He had no faculty protectors at Harvard, as he did at Princeton (R. P. Blackmur) and later at the University of Minnesota (Allen Tate); and this was only a summer-school job, so he cobbled together a social life from the available students—a sulky, zaftig girl he sometimes slept with and a couple of hearty boys who took him to stock-car races on weekends. He and I didn't become friends until later because his drinking at this point alarmed me: that is, for myself. He spoke hurtfully when drunk, though not to me, and I couldn't have answered. He could be a dazzling spieler in a cozy tavern after class (to those whose feelings weren't wounded), about Shakespeare's sonnets, lancing to the heart of the language, or poor, brilliant Stephen Crane, who, much like John, had burned the candle at both ends and whom John had published a book on. During the circus stints I was writing about, I had seen what pathological alcoholism can do—the workhands run over by a truck, or falling off the train, or just disappearing suddenly after a Jekyll/Hyde change of personality—and Berryman seemed more fragile than they. Indeed, he did kill himself in the end, and in between lost a job extravagantly at the University of Iowa after a haywire fracas that finished with him defecating on somebody's front porch, and had begun as an onstage argument with the novelist Marguerite Young about how good or bad my first novel, *Cat Man,* was. In New York, he used to look me up when he blew into town and friends his own age, like Robert Lowell and Elizabeth Hardwick, wouldn't, he said, return his calls because the last time he had broken some of their furniture. Lowell, a bundle of nerves, probably had his own ways of encouraging that, whereas I would just sip a beer with John near the Chelsea Hotel, home to other fractured writing-souls like Brendan Behan, and listen to his caroming soliloquies or pick up scraps of paper with mites of poems on them that drifted out of his pockets when he left the table, then hug him protectively as we moved toward another bar and he would seem to step straight into the traffic to hasten his death. Razzle-dazzle, he'd talk in a marathon of a couple of hours about poetry, with a bit of an audience, while desperately coughing, his voice breaking from compulsive exhaustion, and body tremors, and the liquor he was consuming like extra leg-weights claustrophobically fastened on him: so frail for the engine inside him that his thin frame shook.

He might also go home with young women he stumbled across at readings or publishing parties and enjoy for a few days their full-bosomed (he said) attempts to renovate him; or end hairily at French's or Saint Clare's Hospital for drunks, in the West Fifties, before limping back to his wife in Minneapolis, where he endured more inner detonations and stringent hospitalizations. Repeatedly he asked me out there, but—as when another wildman friend, Edward Abbey, invited me to visit him in Tucson—

I didn't, scared, without admitting it, of being wounded by a tongue I couldn't answer. Berryman, bristly and compelling, was my first genius. (Genius is associations: where your electricity lands you after you leap; and of course he won only one Pulitzer Prize, unlike the more urbane, adjustable MacLeish, kingpost of stability and networking, with three.) He did me the early service of making alcoholism seem unromantic, and lavished invaluable praise on me as I struggled with language and metaphor, which were everything to him—a geyser of half-thwarted imagery— cracked "Henry" and his *Dream Songs,* and *His Thoughts Made Pockets & the Plane Buckt.* When John won belated recognition at an awards ceremony at the Guggenheim Museum, he was frank enough to look out over the well-appointed audience and announce that he saw old enemies there who had "held him up," as well as friends. Then *Life* sent a photographer to do a spread on his work and his jaunty, knightly though untidy air and jutting, grizzled beard. Well-tailored and chivalrous in the sporty-English style of an Oklahoman who'd come East to teach at Princeton, he became famous during a short interval, until his dybbuk re-emerged and the broken veins appeared again around his nose and cheeks, as if a makeup artist had been summoned from the underworld, and his metabolism stalled like a badly fueled propeller blade, and excruciating dreams and centrifugal sieges made existence seem insupportable to him. Even after the *Life* photographer and reporter had finished plying him with whiskey and questions at the Chelsea Hotel and left, and we went to a bar, John looked so shaky he couldn't get served till he showed the saloonkeeper that he had a ten-dollar bill.

RISK IS at the root of the choices we make—in marriage, in what to work on, in money, or what to shoot for—"risk tolerance," as the financial advisors say. I had it for the long haul but not the short. Like other boys, I'd watched my baseball heroes for clues. The pressured grace of Tommy Henrich, Joe DiMaggio, Phil Rizzuto meant a lot to me. I saw a number of home-run hitters at Yankee Stadium—Ted Williams, Hank Greenberg, Charley Keller—and Johnny Mize and Ralph Kiner at the Polo Grounds, and drew the obvious connection that a self-disciplined "Splendid Splinter" like Williams could hit longer balls than bulkier bodies who chewed their lips. Faulkner was another example, in position to ride his surges when they came, as so many lesser writers were not because they hadn't put themselves out on a limb in the first place. Of course I did know lesser writers who *had,* but mostly to their grief, because they didn't ever really have the surges. On the other hand, it's fun to be a big-league ballplayer and it's fun to be a writer even if you don't quite have the right stuff. I've known plenty of writers who got to take themselves more seriously, shooting in their mind's eye for "immortality," than they would have in another line of work.

I never met Faulkner, to my regret, or Hemingway either, though they were still around and about and several of my friends did, because I wanted to earn my invitations to these high-edge parties, not finagle them, much in the same way that I didn't move to Greenwich Village until I'd published several books and felt entitled to call myself a "Villager"—another odd piece of punctilio. And I didn't meet other writers, such as J. D. Salinger and Jean Renoir, whom my father consorted with on the *Queen Mary* or *Queen Elizabeth* when crossing from Europe, but didn't pass on as resources to me lest I be encouraged in my hopes of becoming one too. I still don't know exactly why he objected so much to my going into the arts. He had a pretty fair library, liked the opera, went to the world's great art museums, but said there were only three appropriate avenues for me to follow, "The Law, or Medicine, or The Cloth," which meant the clergy. No business career (or "Trade," as British snobbery had it); and not writing or the arts. Other people could be painters, sculptors, singers, authors, and one enjoyed their efforts, but they were not respectable, and one's family life, besides, was going to become "a goldfish bowl."

This graduate of Kansas City High School must have remained more socially insecure, despite his later Ivy education, than I realized, and it was inevitably infuriating to have a narrow road of professional acceptability so contrary to my own passions laid out for me. MacLeish, being an eminence and also a lawyer, was helpful in talking to my parents; yet my father still took three days to summon himself to telephone me with his congratulations when my first novel was bought by Houghton Mifflin, and then wrote the publisher's lawyer, a legal acquaintance of his, to try to hold up its publication, after I had unwisely shown him the proofs. He and my mother together walked out of early first-run performances of *A Streetcar Named Desire* and *Who's Afraid of Virginia Woolf?* on Broadway, having gone on purpose to "uphold standards" and "make a statement." And he ceased attending the Metropolitan Opera in 1955, after the great contralto Marian Anderson became the first black performer who was allowed to sing there. Yet he once collapsed with emotion in the aisle of our local movie theater when Mario Lanza wound up an aria in *The Great Caruso* in 1951—so he had been going to the opera not merely to wear his tuxedo. As my mother said, they believed art should be "uplifting," like the paintings of Raphael, Michelangelo's sculptures, Bernini's fountains, the music of Verdi, the language of Milton and the King James Bible, the churches of Christopher Wren—not listening to Negroes on the stage of the Met or reading vulgarities like the word "piss" in their son's raw first novel. It was then amazing to them when the book was praised in *Time* and *Newsweek*, and instead of offering snickering condolences about my "dirty book," as they had expected, people were stopping them to praise it or at least to congratulate them.

My father's feelings were naturally complex. A few years later, in fact, he retired from practicing law in order to become a writer himself. Though I was amazed at the reversal, this did not work out and he died, alas, in 1967, from cancer, leaving his big desk empty of papers. No diaries or memoir or fragment of a novel for me to search for clues to what he'd thought. There were half a dozen briefcases that my mother silently disposed of, but I suspect these contained financial records, not his writing, because I don't think he would have showed that to her either. Late in their marriage they were no longer close. He did leave out for me to see a copy of his angry letter of resignation from his oil company (now called Exxon) after being passed over for the number-one job of corporation counsel, which he thought he'd earned. It was a bitter letter, vaguely threatening to divulge to the public the "sinister" information that his immediate supervisor, the number-one attorney, was a secret homosexual and therefore had been a tribulation to work for. I knew, too, that he had applied for a deanship and a professorship at the Stanford and Columbia schools of business administrations, and had been flown out to Palo Alto for an interview, but turned down. So his choice, in his late fifties, of turning to writing as a vocation was not simply a weird response to my publishing a book. Indeed, one of his formative experiences as a lawyer had been when he was turned down, at thirty-seven, for a partnership in the white-shoe Wall Street firm of Davis, Polk, Wardwell, Gardiner & Reed, after having worked there for twelve years. This humiliating event caused him to take the new job at midtown with the Standard Oil Company and move his family out of the city to New Canaan, Connecticut, an hour and a quarter away by train. I was eight at the time, and the change in domicile was crucial for me because it meant I grew up in the woods and fields, not Manhattan, which might have been necessary if my father had stayed in the pressure cooker of Wall Street. Therefore I grew up as a "Nature Boy," in the words of the song our postman used to shout as he drove by me standing by a pond. If my father had "made partner" in 1941, I might be sharply different now.

But these rather straitlaced parents—why did they let me go off and live like a roustabout with Ringling Bros. at eighteen? My mother, although she was more encouraging of my literary career and did not feel as competitive, was after all a woman who had got so excited to go to a Bar Association lawn party at Buckingham Palace that she tipped over backwards in her chair when the Queen walked by. Yet, she was also a Westerner, from Aberdeen, who had made the Daisy Chain at Vassar but been regarded as somewhat hoydenish there, and too effusively free-spoken afterwards at parties in Manhattan, Scarsdale, New Canaan. Spontaneous, impulsive, she aspired to be a socialite, as my father did, but was less accepted by the dowagers on Fifth Avenue whose sons he had known at Yale.

My father, too, had been divided in his reaction to the world of bluebloods that they had tried to navigate during the opening decades of their marriage. He joined organizations such as The Blue Hill Troupe, an amateur singing group that gave parties and performed Gilbert and Sullivan; and Squadron A, an elite polo-playing unit of the National Guard that had originated with a cadre of gentlemen who enlisted in the Spanish American War; and the University Club, a WASP bastion at Fifth Avenue and Fifty-fourth Street. He learned to play passable golf and tennis, mix dry martinis, play adequate bridge, and dance at charity balls. But he also deliberately maintained a trace of his Missouri accent, against my mother's protests, in a few words like "frawg," "hawg," and "dawg," and didn't pretend to posh origins. On his high school bulletin board he had noticed a scholarship to Yale being advertised, competed for it, and then worked his way east that first term on a cattle train, and to England during the summer of 1925 on the cattle boat the *Sagadahock,* from Pier 35 in San Francisco. Not knowing a novel would come out of the circus, he assumed that knocking around would be good for me. Working in an animal hospital and a tuna fish cannery, fighting forest fires, and hitchhiking a lot from the age of thirteen—in that era when people picked you up because they remembered the camaraderie of the Depression or the war years—did lend me an impromptu resilience that handicapped people don't ordinarily have.

It had been a bit of a relief to him, I think, to move from Davis, Polk, Wardwell, in the preppie financial district, up to mid-town New York and colleagues who were midwestern refinery or oil-field engineers, oil marketers or geologists—Oklahomans and Texans from land-grant universities who had risen to the upper echelons. Blunt-speaking Houston and Tulsa people who worked with a level-headed, unpretentious frankness, not intellectual nitpickers, they had more of a drawl than he did and regarded *him* as an Ivy Leaguer. They deployed webbed pipelines and fleets of tankers, and negotiated with the Saudi king, the Iranian shah, the Venezuelan junta, and Whitehall, the Quai d'Orsay, and Foggy Bottom. He liked, then loved, the travel—which in the mid-1950s led to his being loaned to the State and Defense departments for several years as a "dollar-a-year man," under holdover wartime legislation by which his company continued to pay his salary and living expenses during lengthy stays at the Connaught Hotel in London or the Hotel Crillon in Paris, as he negotiated with other NATO powers for the U.S. government.

My father was an agreeable, sympathetic, open-faced man, a nondrinker, with a bit of the Eisenhower style that won Europeans' trust—that Kansan innocence, combined with integrity and competence—which was different from Harry Truman's Missouri-mule, show-me personality (and this was the Eisenhower administration). He'd been born at home, at 920 Woodland Avenue in Kansas City in 1904, his own father the obstetrician, but his father's relatives were indeed Hutchinson, Kansas, people, where his grandfather had homesteaded on Brandy Lake, in Reno

County, near the Arkansas River, in 1871. And in snapshots taken with them from the 1920s, my father looks agile, cocky, upwardly mobile, though not particularly imaginative, next to several lack-luster cousins. Two of his uncles ran a store, the Hoagland Clothing Company, at Second and Main Streets in Hutchinson, till after thirty-five years it went bust in the 1930s. Another—there were twelve children—had gone off at the turn of the century to get in on the Yukon gold rush as a prospector and trapper by way of northern Alberta, and never returned: nor did his partners say why. The contemporary whom my father was closest to, his cousin Arthur, fought in the infantry in Hitler's war and was shot in the back near Omaha Beach in France after D-Day, then spent three months in hospitals having operations, and settled in Los Angeles in the insurance business and never returned to Europe even when he could afford to, having felt "lucky to get out of there alive." My father didn't serve; had been almost thirty-eight, past draft age, when Pearl Harbor occurred. So his war had been a paperwork, phone-wire war that he was glad to make up for with the Defense Department assignments in Rome, Bonn, Paris, London, Athens, and Oslo a decade or so later.

The one Hoagland—in those snapshots from the back porch of the frame house on West Fifth Street in Hutchinson around the time of World War I—who has some real equanimity is the patri-arch, Martin, my great-grandfather. Slim, small, sitting with a calm gaze on the top step, he'd been the rifleman and survivor at Shiloh under Grant, and then in Halleck's and Sherman's fiery campaigns through Mississippi, Alabama, Georgia, and the Caro-linas for the next three years—battles at Fort Donelson, Corinth, Chattanooga, Lookout Mountain, Missionary Ridge, Snake Creek Gap, Resaca, Rome Cross Roads, and the approaches to Atlanta and Savannah. Then north to other battles at Columbia, South Carolina, and Bentonville, North Carolina—and thereafter, Lee's surrender, and the Victory Parade through Washington—Martin having marched in a loop clear from Shiloh. He was equally disciplined as a covered-wagon adventurer and town-founder, married to Emma for sixty years. In the earliest phase, before there was a town of Hutchinson (they didn't move off the buffalo plains until 1886), they kept a candle burning in the window every night for wagon parties that wandered away from the trail and got lost. As many as fourteen strangers might end up sleeping on the floor. There was a kindness to Martin—not merely a veteran's hard-bitten self-sufficiency—as his lavish obituaries make clear, and as I heard from the three of his daughters I met as a child, Nell, Floy, and Olive: who'd all moved to California in middle age during the Depression.

Martin's own great-grandfather, also named Martin, had fought at the Battle of Princeton in New Jersey in 1777, as a captain in command of forty-five neighbors, under George Washington in the Revolution. And *that* Martin's great-grandfather, Christopher, had apparently been a partisan (at least a next-door neighbor) of yet an earlier battler for New World liberty: Jacob Leisler, who was hanged and then cut down half-dead and beheaded for treason to the Crown in embryonic New York, née New Amsterdam, in 1691, after leading an abortive campaign that was successful for a couple of months toward what would have amounted to self-rule. Whereupon a wave of Dutch families angrily left New York for New Jersey, including my primeval Hoaglands.

But Martin—the Shiloh soldier—must have been a hard act to follow. His fifth child was my grandfather, William, known as "Louie," for his middle name, born in 1872 in the sod house on that homestead in Reno County. The first wooden one they built, a story-and-a-half high, and sixteen by twenty-four feet, a cyclone soon blew away (along with "twenty-five dollars in money, six months' provisions and the household goods"). Louie spent a quarter of a century in the army reserve, and was a doctor but not a very chipper one. At least, like my father, he retired early from his profession, and unlike my father, with little money. Yet the army was a good deal of fun and he was a popular man, living on

Prospect Avenue in Kansas City and eating a raw egg for breakfast every morning. My father (now dead for thirty-plus years)—although the photographs of him show the accoutrements of success, such as his Dutch-built sloop, or the living room set—looks more haphazard, as if still wondering *how shall I behave, how shall I live?* He did enjoy much of life—most of his marriage, most of his work—and died lingeringly with some gallantry. But his defeats were often due, I think, to overeagerness. Too driven to please, too zealous to cement his social achievements, he seemed rather isolated and was not taken seriously enough by some of his colleagues; then set in motion an unnecessary degree of estrangement between me and himself. Several of my mother's relatives, although impressed with the wattage of his career, felt a rigidity in him, a coldness or "velvet fist," as they expressed it later. He was extremely ambitious, yet "idealistic," as my mother insisted, which had some truth to it in the sense that he broke off contact with any of their acquaintances who got divorced (which even in the fifties was rather unusual, at least in the Northeast), and didn't like drunks. At Yale, he'd thrown his freshman roommate into a cold shower for coming home drunk, and they had had a fight in which my father's hair got pulled, an ordeal he claimed all of his life might have caused his baldness by "loosening the roots." Also, as an issue of probity, he didn't engage in insider trading in the stocks of companies that he worked with on legal matters, at a time when financial shenanigans of this kind were hardly regulated and many lawyers did. He didn't play the market, just accumulated his stock bonuses and protected the property value of our house with tree surgery and a policy of not hiring "Negro help" because he believed that to have a black person living in the house even in a servant capacity might reduce its resale price. Yet he also sent money to Hutchinson relatives in reduced circumstances to help with trips or a cousin's tuition, and once flew his favorite aunt, Floy, to Florence so that she could savor Europe—though she became so panicked by being in a foreign country that she stayed in her hotel day and night and immediately asked to be put on a plane back home.

His boyhood on Warwick Avenue (where they had moved from Woodland Avenue after the trolley car ran over his younger brother before his eyes, when Dad was eleven) could not have been idyllic. But in his high-school track uniform he looks heads-up and promising: as, again, in a studio photograph taken on Boyleston Street in Boston, when—clean-cut, handsome, with hair parted modishly in the middle—he was a law student. And, as a fifty-year-old commuter in Connecticut, he was sometimes called "Speed" by the other men on the train, when he would hold them all up by refusing to run from his car to get on, if he had pulled into the parking lot a little late. Walking with deliberation, he simply counted on his presence to persuade the conductors to hold up their departure. The dowagers on Fifth Avenue—whose sons were his classmates and brought him home on weekends from Yale—had thought him "fresh blood," a good influence, and introduced him advantageously around. He probably could have married an heiress, he said, instead of my mother for love. But we did watch the motorcades of Winston Churchill, Ike Eisenhower, King George VI, Queen Mary, and the like, from the big bay windows of their brownstones during my childhood. And we kept seeing some of the scions of these families, when visiting their summer homes on Chesapeake Bay or Martha's Vineyard, as they squandered their patrimonies, or matrimonies, or whatever. One man I last saw frantically polishing the brasswork on a huge mahogany motor yacht that he had inherited and was trying to sell: his one tangible asset. Another died on the street from a blow to the head, after trying to pick up some rough trade. Another ended in a walkup apartment in Brooklyn, dying of gangrene because he hadn't gotten a leg injury treated. With his family broke, he had been working as a leasing agent for gas-station sites on vacant lots for a wholesaler, where his plummy accent was about as useful as a wooden nickel. Another man—nursing along the Main Street brick house on Nantucket that had passed to him but that he couldn't afford on a retired schoolmaster's pension—died in his studio apartment in New York City all alone, after having just had tea in a restaurant with my eighty-year-old widowed mother, because she didn't think it proper to walk home with him, although he had told her that he felt sick and was her lifelong bachelor-suitor, since even before she had met my father.

MORE THAN MERE "FLAPPER," there is a wanton look in some of my mother's photos from the early 1920s, sitting on her uncle Paul's knee, as a college girl too big to be there. They are at his fishing lodge on the Au Sable River in northern Michigan, but he is wearing a white shirt, lounging jacket, and tie, near forty, with a mustache and pince nez, and would die "of a broken heart" at forty-six, as my mother said. Paul's wife had been committed for life to a mental hospital, and one of his two daughters would finish up that way too. A son, Paul Jr., crippled with polio—forced to hang for an hour from a frame hooked to the ceiling of the sitting room every day, on the theory that this might help to straighten his back—would kill himself at thirty-three. Another son, Albert, was institutionalized as "retarded," and Paul's third son, Chuck, diagnosed as oversexed or hyperactive, had been surgically castrated in his middle teens, under the supposition that it might "calm him down." So Paul *needed* to borrow his brother A. J.'s daughter during her summer vacations, first from a boarding school in Maryland and then from Vassar. Indeed, she eventually married my father in the Music Room—with an Aeolian-Skinner pipe organ—of the four-story house, with five German servants, of her other Saginaw uncle, Ralph Morley, on South Jefferson Avenue, but wearing Paul Morley's mad, rich wife's lovely wedding gown, which had been sent to New York from Michigan to be made over for her at Saks Fifth Avenue and shipped back again. Ralph's wife was the daughter of a timber baron who left each of his five daughters a million dollars; and Paul's wife was nearly as rich from timber money, though in her case the bargain wasn't as good. The adage then was that you could make more money in five minutes by marrying it than in a lifetime of earning it, but that if you did, you'd spend the rest of your life paying it back.

My mother, for her part, was glad to escape her bleak logging-camp of a hometown, Aberdeen, for Saginaw (though to other Vassar girls even Saginaw might have seemed the end of the world). Every troupe of classical or cabaret musicians or stage actors—from Eugene Ormandy and Enrico Caruso to Eleonora Duse, Anna Pavlova, Sarah Bernhardt, and John Barrymore—who toured through Saginaw came to Ralph and Paul's after-performance parties in that Music Room (not to mention Amelia Earhart), till Ralph also died and, by the terms of his will, the whole house was bulldozed, lest it become a funeral parlor for the black neighbor-hoods that block by block were creeping near. General Motors (it is still proclaimed at the Saginaw Country Club) "ruined" Sagi-naw during World War II by bringing in southern Negroes for the hot toilsome foundry jobs at its local chassis plant—and by set-ting up such a plant in Saginaw, in the first place—instead of pre-serving the city for skilled workers immigrating from Europe, as it had in the past.

So my mother, Helen Kelley Morley, was something of a queen in Saginaw, as well as Aberdeen. Her brothers called her "Circle H," she was such a center of attention. Morley Brothers, started in 1865 by her grandfather and great-uncle, Edward and George, had become for a while one of the largest wholesale hardware businesses in the country; also a major manufacturer of har-nesses, especially for the logging industry, because Saginaw was a supply point for timber-cutting. Salt mines had been the bonanza when the Morleys had first arrived; then some oil wells were dis-covered; and then the sugar-beet industry started up, for which refineries had to be built. They'd participated in these entrepre-neurial adventures or observed them closely, and helped found a well-managed bank, which, a century later, remains a solid enterprise. Their pulling-horse harnesses were shipped all over, and the general-hardware store backed onto the Saginaw River (you "could spear bullfrogs and shoot wild ducks" off the dock at first), at the head of deep-draft navigation. Boats from Lake Huron brought in merchandise that could be sold and loaded back onto the logging-company barges that shuttled from upriver for supplies—axes, saws, caulked logging boots, blankets, rain-coats, peaveys, pots, wood stoves, whatever. This emphasis on timber helps explain why the Morleys turned down both Henry Ford when he was starting his motorcar company in Detroit, and W. C. Durant, who asked them to invest in the start-up of General Motors, nearby in Flint. Another reason is that twenty separate varieties of patented automobile were also in development right in Saginaw: we forget what a mob of patented inventions vie in the opening rounds of a convulsive revolution in technology, whether motor vehicles or cyberspace. Instead, Walter, the college graduate among Edward's sons, was sent west at the turn of the century to invest in what was going to be a new Michigan—the uncut Big Woods of the Northwest—and then my mother's father, after him, when he messed up.

The Morleys were not particularly bold with their money, but married plenty of it: into the families of lumber barons, ore mag-nates who owned Mesabi ironlands in Minnesota and a railroad bridge across the Niagara River to Canada, or had invested in Montgomery Ward, the department store, or with George East-man in the Eastman Kodak Company. The clan had originated in Bottesford, Lincolnshire, England, from which a Thomas Morley emigrated to Braintree, Massachusetts, where he is recorded as having married in 1681. They spread to central Massachusetts, Connecticut, and upstate New York, eventually establishing in 1837 a sort of a family seat in Painesville, Ohio, where the public library still bears the name Morley Library, endowed with money from an early paint, or "white-lead," manufacturing facility. The patriarch there, Albert, was a fiery Abolitionist, sheltering parties of escaping blacks in his barn, preparatory to their moonless boat trips across Lake Erie to Canada. His descendants gradually moved to Cleveland, twenty miles away, to become lawyers, or to Chicago, to wheel and deal in coal. But Edward, my grandfather's father, first went west to Hannibal, Missouri, at seventeen with his brother Thomas, fifteen years older, and helped him set up a store, Morley Brothers, Wholesale Grocers, during the scary time from 1856 till Mark Twain, too, quit Hannibal and the river and skipped the brewing war. It was especially dangerous for Thomas's family because he, like his father, was a public Abolitionist, openly subscribing to William Lloyd Garrison's newspaper, *The Liberator*, there in Hannibal. So they cut their losses and moved north to Davenport, Iowa, to start a grocery business— but in the middle of the war left Davenport for Fort Scott, Kansas, crossing that troubled state during a series of guerrilla raids by the Confederates, under General "Pap" Price. I have the diary of Thomas's wife Emma describing these events. Another of Thomas's brothers captained a Mississippi River Union gunboat, being a riverman, which may be why Thomas had tried Hannibal in the first place. A cousin died in the Confederate prison at Andersonville; and another cousin headed a military academy in Pennsylvania after the war; then went to Colorado to prospect, but his gold mine collapsed on him in 1903. His son, also adventurous, Sylvanus Griswold Morley, became that pioneering archaeologist in Central America.

The Morleys display this bifurcation, when you look back. Two in the twentieth century, for instance, fell to their deaths off mountains (Fred Morley, off Cathedral Peak, in 1921, in Yosemite, and Bill Morley, off Mount Jefferson, in Oregon, in 1954). Adventurousness alternates with the mercenary conservative bent. Edward, my great-grandfather and namesake, had seen Hannibal and Fort Scott in hectic times; and although his brother and later partner, George, went west by ship around Cape Horn to California, to sell supplies in the gold camps, and even up into the Cariboo gold country on the Fraser River in British Columbia, they both bought their way out of service in the Civil War and soon became businessmen in Michigan. Their letters to each other on trips from Saginaw were all couched in terms of dollars and cents and deliveries of leather, hardware, and glass, except that Edward once writes to George, "Saw a Nigger show last night"—meaning minstrels—having probably had quite enough radical politics back in Painesville, Hannibal, and Fort Scott.

Edward, though he is said to have had trouble reading, married an Armour meat-packing and Otis Elevator Company heiress who had been to Vassar for two years (remarkable in 1871)—Helen Kelley, my mother's namesake—and did very well. He then established a trust fund whose interest was dispersed each year to the one of his five children with the lowest income. This eventually set off some squabbling between poor Walter—the Cornell Phi Beta Kappa ne'er-do-well and would-be lawyer-playwright whom my grandfather had had to rescue from his business troubles in Aberdeen—and Walter's sister, who had married an apple farmer and photographer in upstate New York. When Walter won the toss, he would take his wife and kids on a penzione tour of Europe the following year, which inevitably qualified him for yet another low-income prize. He died "of a nose infection," family records say, just short of sixty, in southern Wisconsin, where he had become an Episcopal minister, in his son's footsteps.

But then there was Ralph—the uncle in whose Music Room my mother was married—who closed the harness factory and created Saginaw's principal department store, and still had enough company money in the depths of the Depression to guarantee the city's $500,000 payroll one time, when the municipal government went broke and otherwise couldn't have paid anyone. However, a couple of decades after Ralph died, Morley Brothers finally did have to close, with its stock certificates virtually worthless, the many employees who had invested in it hurt, and one of Ralph's sons getting penile implants to improve his performance with the prostitutes he brought home to relieve his beery solitude. The Morley womenfolk had been staging private showings of each fall's collection of frocks that came into the store, choosing what they wanted with their "stockholders' discounts" and sending back the duplicate gowns so that no other woman in town could buy one. The sales clerks weren't trusted with cash registers, but had to shoot the customers' payments upstairs in pneumatic tubes, where change was made and returned to them. Ralph was not easily amazed, but he might have been. Money and family were important to him. He had carried his flamboyant, tragic brother Paul as nominal treasurer of the company, though Paul was there only irregularly and often wore a cape and monocle, fancying himself an artiste. And when his sister Abby's daughter married a war hero in the 1940s who deserted her, he made a concerted effort to mentor the kids ever after: play with them, take them places, teach them to drive, and insist that they be included in all the family festivities they would have been invited to if they hadn't been poor relations from a "broken home."

Ralph had no hobbies, as such, except for the partisanship of Family and following the manifold fortunes of first and second cousins. I remember Ralph's last visit with my father, in Ralph's room at the Biltmore Hotel next to Grand Central Station. He favored the Biltmore because he could come into New York from Detroit in a Pullman compartment on the *Wolverine* and be in his hotel room—his bags trundling behind him, first pushed by a porter, then a bellhop—and on the phone to a banker, a broker, a ticket-scalper, a maître-d', a travel agent, in fifteen minutes. After passing the helm of the big store to his three sons (the third set of "Morley Brothers," and the ones who ran it into the ground), he often liked to go on from the Biltmore and sail to Europe for the fellowship of the First Class public rooms on a Cunard steamer (like the bar car on his Pullman train), look around London for a bit, and enjoy the five-day sail back to New York from Southampton. It was his escape from a marriage that chafed: just as my grandmother, Elizabeth Morley, Ralph's sister-in-law, also made quite a number of ocean crossings when her husband was unfaithful and her family responsibilities had loosened; and Ralph's brother Paul's surviving daughter escaped the tragedies of *her* family by going to Europe twelve times. (This daughter of Paul's, whose name was Abby, had been in love with her cousin John Morley, who died in Japanese captivity after surviving the Bataan Death March, much as Paul's sister, also named Abby, had been in love with her cousin Reuben Morley, the aspiring foreign correspondent murdered in Inner Mongolia on his way to the Russo-Japanese War.)

But at Ralph's last meeting with my father, his niece Helen's husband—who was consulted occasionally in the family because he was a financial lawyer—Ralph surprised my father by spending their little private time together showing him the notebook that he always carried in which were jotted his current securities portfolio holdings. He didn't quote aloud any valuations, or the prices paid, just turned over each page and pointed, looking at my father like the cat that swallowed the canary and smiling. My father, who was a buy-and-hold-come-hell-or-high-water man, expressed courteous approval for several minutes, until the waiters arrived, as well as the "difficult" cousins, for this banquet of the eastern branch of the Morleys: in particular, a woman from Bucks County, Pennsylvania, famous for her school board and zoning board fights, whose approach I dreaded because she always used these public occasions to try to cure my stutter.

"Don't be self-conscious!" she exclaimed, as I blocked on my first word to her, and then also embarrassed my parents by announcing to everybody that stuttering was caused by problems with one's parents. She and her husband had deployed their inheritances into an egg farm in the country, but soon afterwards tragedy struck, when their beloved son, after being a frogman in the navy, died precipitously of leukemia.

So many deaths since then! My favorite cousin, Nancy's, I didn't even hear about until three years after it happened because everybody in that crowd out in Oregon assumed somebody else had told me. And the divorces—Nancy's own, her sister Elizabeth's, our cousin Anne's, not to mention mine! Nancy was the most open-hearted of us all yet seemed to have the worst "luck" with her children: one boy a suicide, another child, a girl, hitting the hippie road and never surfacing again. Inexplicable, if you think life is logical, that it would happen to her.

Saginaw was of course the boyhood home of Theodore Roethke, as Aberdeen was Robert Motherwell's. The mother of two of my cousins in Saginaw burned Roethke's love letters to her, and my own mother invited Motherwell to supper with my father and her in New York in the late 1930s (his father, a banker, did business with hers), but then never bought any paintings. Worldliness had dissipated a good deal of the romantic streak that also animated the family. And Ralph, mercenary, aloof, with a stoop-shouldered, hardbitten energy, and family loyalty his paramount virtue, was the flagship figure. Albert, or "A. J.," my grandfather, on the wild, far-west coast, was less sedentary than Ralph because dealing with a payroll of a hundred-sixty loggers required somewhat different skills than managing a bunch of department-store clerks. He was financed by the Saginaw crew, and though not quite a bottom-line master like Ralph, A. J. was tough. His company was known as "Dirty Old Saginaw" in Aberdeen among the logging community. He, too, had three sons, Dave, Bill, and Ed, who worked for him as heirs apparent, as Ralph's Ted, Buzz, and Ginger did for *him*. Bill was best at handling the books and negotiating with the mill owners to whom logs were delivered, or the shippers who sold whole freighter loads to Japan, and the landowners A. J. contracted with, as well as executives at a rival timber company, such as Weyerhaeuser, whom A. J. had quarreled

with. Fortunately, the leading Weyerhaeuser son had been a classmate of Bill's at Yale, so they could go around their fathers' suspi-
cions and work something out. Ed, on the other hand, was a
"people person" who wrestled with the personal problems of the
men and their many families, and bunkhouse disputes, cookhouse complaints, pay arguments, and union demands. He picked
the crew chiefs and department heads—from the fallers and buck-
ers to the donkey engine and railroadmen—and the two made a
wonderful team, outlasting my grandfather's reign much better
than Ralph's sons did with the family's Michigan business interests, until Bill suddenly dropped dead in church of a heart attack
at fifty.

Dave, of A. J.'s three sons, was the square peg, the individual-
ist, the difficult one, and the eldest. He was also my mother's
favorite, though she deeply loved generous Ed, the youngest, as
well, who was so sympathetic and adjustable to everyone. Dave
was moody, argumentative, independent-minded, until his death
at thirty-nine; and because I was sometimes compared to him, I
tried to find out what he was like. What did he argue about? Was
he a socialist like me, for example? Did he and his father fight
about the bitter and violent IWW strikes, brutally busted with
clubs in Aberdeen in 1911–17 (though their aim was only to
obtain an eight-hour workday), or just logging techniques? "He
had his own ideas about everything" and was stubborn, I was told
by Ed and my mother and Dave's two sisters-in-law, but not what
those ideas were. Nobody seemed to remember whether they were
about New Deal politics or how to cut and drag trees off a hill—
nor to have taken them very seriously, to begin with. Anyway,
Dave had been firm enough about whatever he believed that he
quit his father's company and started his own little "gyppo" out-
fit, with five or six men working for him, cutting by contract on
other people's parcels of land: whereupon the stub of a "widow-
maker" tree broke off overhead, dropped down, and killed him.
There seemed to be no record of his thoughts and actions to con-

sult. I was simply told, when I asked inconvenient questions or wanted to stay outdoors an extra while or was ethically disputatious, that I was "like Dave."

Then I did stumble on a piece of evidence, a single long letter that he'd written home from Cambridge, Massachusetts, where he had gotten a most enterprising job, after graduating from the University of Pennsylvania, in Philadelphia. My mother must have saved it from her own mother's papers. Dave said he was waking up very early to go to Boston's first airport every morning, where he sold tickets for the little plane providing air service to New York and handled the baggage, then took that flight himself, and sold and took tickets and tussled bags at the other end—then flew with the next set of passengers back to Boston, and so on and so forth for a tiring but fascinating twelve-hour day. He was so exultant and detailed in this letter to his parents—so wholly absorbed and competent and normal-sounding—one wonders why he didn't stay with the infant aviation industry through the 1920s, instead of going back to Aberdeen to work for a father who could be dictatorial, and why he had acquired a reputation within the family for being maladjusted. The dynamics of families can squeeze a curve of one's character into a bend or a bend into a crook; but he may not have been so very odd. My mother, tacitly, seemed to think it was more a question of male conflict—the two brothers younger than Dave and herself siding with their father in questions of business and marriage, and Dave then, single, trying to find his own way: as she also was doing, first in Michigan with her uncle Paul (who people now think was "gay," despite the fact that he brought back a French mistress after driving an ambulance in the First World War and his wife tried to stab him), and then in New York City. The fragility she had seen in Paul's family made her sympathize more with Dave, I suspect—as certainly the six months of exile they had shared in the Far East must have done. She had come home at twenty-six from Manhattan, telling her father that she had fallen in love with a divorced

man and wanted to marry him. And A. J. took her right down to
the docks and put her on a Japanese timber boat that was about
to sail, with her brother—also home from his job in Boston by
now—as chaperone, to "get over it."

My mother often told me when I was small how she had stuck
secret notes to her best girlfriend in a crevice in a stone wall while
walking the mile downhill to school in the rain and back. And
how in her teens she and her roommate had been expelled from a
boarding school in San Francisco, accused unjustly of smoking
because they'd had a ground-floor room and some sailors from a
naval base had come and flirted with them from the sidewalk,
blowing the telltale smoke through the window. Although the
Morleys tended not to send their daughters to college, believing
that higher education was unnecessary for them, my mother's
mother, a Hicok—a family that had fallen into bankruptcy but
was "distinguished" in its history—intervened, pointing out to
her husband that his own mother, Helen Kelley, had been allowed
to go to Vassar for a couple of years. So she went too, majoring in
English. (When she told her teacher she would like to write a
novel, he asked if she could summon the patience to copy *War and
Peace* word for word by hand, "because that is what it would feel
like.") Afterwards she took some courses at Columbia's School of
Social Work and handled several cases in an Italian neighborhood, which she found grueling. She took a job as a receptionist in
a psychiatrist's office instead; and then moved up to become office
manager at a pioneering industrial psychiatric clinic at Macy's
department store, where, under Dr. V. V. Johnson, employees
could come for very brief periods of assessment and counseling at
company expense. Dr. Johnson's books of case studies, when read
nowadays, appear harsh and wholly geared to company interests:
whether a salesgirl's desperate personal dilemma was going to
incapacitate her, or her good intentions might still surmount her
neuroses if Macy's exercised some patience and allowed her a

second chance. It was quite revolutionary at the time, however, and did provide a check on a supervisor's snap judgment—an informed hearing, in fairness if not mercy, so ahead of its time in the 1920s that it did not survive long. One of the two Straus family sons who were being groomed to take over Macy's supported the experiment, but the other thought the idea was fashionable nonsense, a trendy waste of money. Eventually he won, but not before my mother had lost her job for her passionate partisanship, clashing cheekily with him on his skeptical visits.

Headstrong—she didn't marry till 1931, six years after she'd graduated from college—she may never have had a real boss before or lived in a city where the Morleys were not a power (or, indeed, where Jews had power), and she treated Jack Straus like a dolt threatening social progress. As a puzzle and a setback, it ranked with being kicked out of boarding school after the headmistress had smelled smoke in her room. Just as her heart was touched by the counter clerks who showed up for solace at Macy's mental-health clinic, she had democratically regarded the sailors as human beings who were worth flirting with. (Maybe the headmistress knew she hadn't smoked, but kicked her out anyway for doing that.) And not having established herself in a career during those six years of bachelorhood, in such a difficult era to be a woman, she was liberated but shaky, too—giving up the divorced suitor, then retreating from Aberdeen to Saginaw after the Oriental trip, and marrying my father after losing the Macy's job. To the end of her life, she would drop her eyes when arguing with a man, and, in a sort of Chaplinesque pantomime, mouth or inaudibly mutter, but not speak, her objections and counterobjections, thereby relieving some of the frustration she felt without voicing them.

My father was an agnostic, though he did go to Episcopal services during the years when he was working on Wall Street, and tried Unitarianism as well, after having grown up in the Dutch

Reformed fold. No church attendance after about forty, however; and even my christening had been delayed until I was three. During my teens he encouraged me to believe that the outdoors was a better place for worship. But organized religion, high-church ritual, was important to Mother throughout. She went alone—genuinely disturbed that he and I didn't—and apart from the factor of faith, found release in the social interplay and the minister's ministrations. Prayer mattered, and the benediction of someone who had taken vows to a vocation. Yet those pictures in Michigan show her at seventeen as head-and-shoulders more sensual-looking and prettier than the rest of the girls in their frumpy frocks who had been assembled by her uncle Paul to come north from Saginaw and do amateur theatricals at The Lodge on the North Branch of the Au Sable (Henry Ford's family and the Dow Chemical clan had fishing camps upstream).

Sprawled loosely on Paul's lap, forcing him into a stiff posture to provide her with secure seating yet not touch her, she looks like the ruler of all she surveys—the cousin with polio, later a suicide, and the other boy, soon to be castrated, nearby. She seems already bored, gazing beyond these paltry Michigan conquests toward Vassar and New York. And my father in his late teens, photographed in Hutchinson or Kansas City family assemblages, looks similarly alert, "finer," and poised to fly away from the Midwest and hazard eastern challenges at Yale or wherever. Society women must have liked my parents in their early years better than their children did. My father's too-tense striving for blue-ribbon acceptance, my mother's tinge of hysteria under that fresh-spirited, Washington State spontaneity, would not have overly alarmed an experienced hostess, because their intentions were good. Though so eager to please, neither in the end did marry for money or hurry into a marriage before the pivotal age of thirty.

Eager beavers! I remember that ambitious energy from when I was old enough to be aware of other people's preoccupations and was taken to birthday parties of other well-provided-for little kids at the St. Regis Hotel on Fifth Avenue or a Sunday outing at an estate on Long Island Sound. City clubs, well-picked foursomes on golf courses in the country, access to the concentric circles of trust-fund wealth and power downtown or the nation's capital. Fame wasn't the aim: in fact you kept your name out of the papers. Fame was for trial lawyers, those flossy self-dramatists without real clout. To be noteworthy was to operate backstage and keep your corporate clients out of trouble, so there would be no need for trial lawyers and public relations experts. My parents' interest in money was its intangible accoutrements, not just cars, furniture, and a green lawn, but the stream of retinal images that money bought, whether at one's leisure in the great museums of Europe or sailing in the Gulf of Maine. I suppose many people's is rather the same—a life punctuated by frequent travel and grand scenery—with the extra fantasy that not only won't they "starve" when they are old and feeble, but money will add years to their lives. We lived at first on Sixty-sixth Street, but they baptized me fifty blocks downtown at J. P. Morgan's old church, Saint George's. Their friends included a Quaker who had worked with the American Field Service in Europe after the First World War, and a woman who had gone to India in the thirties to sit at the feet of Rabindranath Tagore and work for him for a decade there. Besides inviting Motherwell to dinner when he moved to New York, and the prominent publisher Mitchell Kennerly, who had married a Morley, my father bought *The Poems of Oscar Wilde,* perhaps as a youthful declaration of separateness from Wall Street's mores, and copies of H. G. Wells's *Outline of History,* Havelock Ellis's *Dance of Life,* and *Selections from Johnson,* plus calf-bound, multivolume, pocket-sized editions of Kipling, Byron, Shakespeare, and Shaw that I still have. He told me how several men, stockbrokers he sat next to regularly on the commuter train, would express their regrets for how they had spent their lives "just on money." On the other hand, so many artists "lived below the belt," while creating their stuff. He didn't believe in Christ's divinity or a likely afterlife, but in optimism as a matter of temperament and in Christianity's domestic ethics, and when he learned that he was soon to die, tried to perpetuate his name by endowing a professorship for studying cancer, but the late-life care of my mother used up a lot of that.

It's touching, dropping in on clusters of relatives after a patriarch is gone. Uncle Ralph, for instance, who had his house bulldozed lest it fall into the hands of the Negroes who were already buying property in the next block, would be surprised to find that two of his grandnieces have since married African-Americans; and the male who physically most resembles Ralph—burly and stooped—had been living as an out-of-work semi-recluse up in the north woods for umpteen years, very likably, when I met him. A majority of A. J.'s grandchildren were likewise spraddled out into various woodsy retreats in Oregon, New Mexico, Hawaii, on the mists of the Internet, eking out a scrap of left-over inheritance, with most of their childhood assurance gone. A world of paid therapists, free crisis centers, twelve-step addiction groups, and television figures who simper and wink at you in the afternoon as if they are "friends," would have amazed the old guard. I've always had a sense of friendship as being a potential alliance for emergencies, yet I've never experienced an emergency where friendship actually saved me. In risky situations in Africa, I was traveling with strangers, not old friends, and my life was protected by them for reasons of policy and decency, not loyalty and affection. Or, when suicidal, I have found my footing alone, as we all must do. Fidelity, in any case, has blurred as an ideal, erasable like e-mail. With so much else in flux, that is too, and people tend not to see life as a trajectory anymore—just avoiding breast or lung cancer or down-sizing or money loss. Believing in next-to-nothing, we live merely preventively, absorbing garage sales of information and trying to wedge some extra space for it in our flea-market minds.

I was the New Yorker in the family. Born there in 1932, I returned for the key decades of my adulthood, age twenty-five to fifty-five, when you do whatever you're really going to do. The piano lessons at Mrs. Holcombe's house on God's Acre (where three of New Canaan's churches surrounded a traffic triangle), and the ice-skating on Mud Pond, the good English and biology classes with Mr. Swallow and Mrs. Morris at New Canaan Country Day School—that's all behind you now, you think; you're on your own. Of course not quite. And in my case in the metropolis, my new friends who weren't Jewish were mostly Irish lapsed Catholics, the other ethnic group that had been looked at queerly in the suburb where I'd lived from eight to eighteen: which cut both ways. There was a certain resentment of me as a WASP, as well as the necessity for me to make my own mental readjustments. I'd recognized and hated hometown anti-Semitism from the age of twelve, but to try to correct parental indoctrination in one's unconscious mind is a complicated process, whereas the New Canaan (ironic name for an anti-Semitic town) boys of my generation who hadn't bothered themselves about it at all remained in orbits throughout the nineteen-fifties and even sixties and seventies paralleling their parents', where Jews were not permitted to function, and scarcely afterwards.

Maintaining a Protestant mien of reserve and understatement was okay (under the rubric of eccentricity) in my Irish saloon on Christopher Street, The Lion's Head, because I did love storytelling, although I couldn't do much of it, and laughed immoderately at blarney, knew poverty—even though my novitiate had been voluntary—and understood from the exigencies of my handicap the basic imperatives of the Irish virtue of loyalty. Photographers, sportswriters, carpenters, seamen, firemen, screenwriters, celebrity chasers, a bank branch manager, a

Transit Authority bureaucrat, a marijuana dealer, union officials, police-beat reporters, publicity flacks, salesmen, agents, accountants: for Manhattan it was a reasonably polyglot hangout, and there were also chummy women bellying up to the bar—painters, teachers, editors, credit-checkers, secretaries—who were for the most part middle-aged, buxom, and maybe remembered sleeping with Jimmy Dean or Norman Mailer or Marlon Brando, and who drank a bit too much, though not as much as the men, who, they claimed, seldom performed more than limply if you softened to their pleas and brought them on home. Later in the evening the atmosphere turned mildly rancid, as the people with structured lives left and the souls newly alone after a split-up faced the rows of bottles against the mirror across the bar. We had waitresses such as Jessica Lange, who were on their way up, to stare at, and others on the way down, but scarcely less haunting.

Wes Joyce, The Lion's Head co-owner, had been a gloomy cop and flounder-dragger on Cape Cod before he'd invested in this rather theatrical project, moving it from Hudson Street over to Sheridan Square in the center of Greenwich Village. The other owner, Al Koblin, was saturnine more than gloomy, distrustful but merciful, and formerly the manager of the Figaro coffeehouse on Bleecker Street throughout the Beatnik epoch. Tommy Sugar, the night bartender, had quit construction work in the Bronx after an accident and before it got to him. Shaped like a heavy crate, he could block a door, return a punch, pick up the phone and deal with the Mafia jukebox guys when needed. His partner, Mike Reardon, an actor, was matinee-handsome and smooth, a ladies' man. The day bartenders were Don Schlenk, who had cultivated a contemptuously snappish temper that went with the chip-on-the-shoulder aspects of the place, and Paul Schiffman, a retired ship's captain, who lived with his mother uptown and preferred a persona that was uncommunicative and sulky, though he wrote poetry. Three lawyers, a speechwriter, a bookie, an adman, an ambulance attendant, and an apartment house owner might face

Paul, each with an amputated marriage or an undertow of the fatalism of the lapsed Catholic or kicked-out Jew, but demonstrating an elaborate patience with each other that helped keep despair at bay. Virtuoso conversationalists like the Clancy Brothers, Tom and Liam, or Frank and Malachy McCourt were not daily visitors, yet faith in friendship can be almost as brave a leap for some people as conversation or religious belief, with everybody glancing sideways as they gimp along, through a magnetic field that galls them but that they depend on.

At The Lion's Head I needed some schooling because of my fastidious physical offishness, verbal reserve, and ignorance of many customs. For example, when I spilled coins on the floor I'd stoop to pick them up instead of leaving them "for the sweeper." I thought struggling artists were supposed to be frugal and my tips were mathematical, not flamboyant. Nor did I get drunk and run up a tab, like some of my neighbors who had already skipped through a bankruptcy. And my sense of public gesture was paltry, though I soon grew to appreciate other people's shticks, and saloon talk, if nothing else, improved my teaching. The slightly stinging atmosphere in which the evening peters out in watering holes where people have nowhere else they want to go and hope that they sleep late tomorrow to cut short tomorrow's disappointments, was a small price to pay; and you escaped it entirely if you left early. Soon, however, I was an honorary Irishman; and a longshoreman blacklisted for being a Communist was bear-hugging me until my bones cracked; a wizened TV documentary cameraman was telling me about the upper Orinoco River; and a tabloid writer trying to transplant himself to Hollywood was arguing the merits of a Philadelphia light-heavyweight whom he thought I'd overpraised. The derailed sea captain behind the bar was praising my tugboat essays; the Clancy Brothers liked the frontier stuff I'd done; and, as a foreign bird of passage, I roused myself, when kidded, to defend American and British WASPs as having introduced free speech and parliamentary democracy to national governance.

These Irish American guys had "cheatin' hearts" like me when their marriages went sour, and I saw with a bit of surprise that in some cases they abandoned or betrayed their male friends, too, just as readily as a Protestant might have, all the blather about Emerald Isle loyalty notwithstanding. The behind-hand snickering at blacks was no better and no worse than what I had grown up with, but I was startled by how cavalierly the bar talk applauded the blood-oath bombings that were rocking Belfast at this time, and the exploits of the silencer-and-trench-coat hit men, though I did sympathize politically with the Catholic cause.

Joe Flaherty, whose father had been a longshoreman murdered and dumped off a Brooklyn wharf into the harbor for challenging the power of the Mafia (his mother then worked in the lunch line of his grammar school), found crossing the East River to marry, then getting divorced—with the anguish of suffering kids—and becoming a newspaper columnist in Manhattan plenty jam-packed with risk. But he may have died because, loyal to his roots, he kept using chiropractors, not doctors, for his aches and pains. Around fifty, he discovered that advanced prostate cancer was the cause of the discomfort he had thought was from "throwing out" his back. Lying in his hospital bed, he remarried the night before the operation which castrated him: timing it for the insurance. And because of how authentic his affections were, he was as beloved as any man I've ever known, but both his wives were dumped by his many friends as soon as Joe was off the scene.

There was drama to these Irishers—Pete Hamill caroming between streetwise opining in the *New York Post* or *Daily News* and dashing off movie scripts in Hollywood (an "Irish Ben Hecht," he called himself), while squiring screen stars like Shirley MacLaine and Mary Tyler Moore, and Puerto Rican or Japanese-American wives. He lived a good, generous, voluble, energetic life, though without the literary acclaim that his honest but more astringent friends William Kennedy and Frank McCourt won— just as Pete himself had more success than Joe Flaherty did, who seemed to me still more a prince among men. I haven't found, over the half-century that I've been observing the literati (since, let's say, meeting John Steinbeck in 1950), that "nice guys finish last." They tend to finish in the middle—Steinbeck a nicer guy than Hemingway and not as good a writer, though better than many; Bernard Malamud a nicer guy than Norman Mailer and not as talented, yet more so than many. Frank McCourt suffered a harder-scrabble, back-street misery between his marriages than Hamill. His travels, his interests, his outlets were fewer, his anger more confusedly diffuse, his pen coagulated, and he had less energy and money. But Frank's wounds obsessed him in a way that eventually hemorrhaged like a burst blood vessel into brighter colors than most newspapermen can muster; their vociferousness, if not their cynicism, defeats them.

However, bar-drinkers aren't risk takers, as a rule. They fence-sit on a stool, contemplate the options, comment if a parade goes by. I'd hear the banker confess to having fired a man that afternoon for "sexual harassment" who was probably too old to find another job. He was fifty-plus himself; his brandy shook in his hand. And Marty, the real estate man on the other side of me, who called himself Vox Populi and spoke as if his marriage were a wound, responded to my kidding that he must sometimes accept sex in lieu of rent by saying, "No, sir. Rent is a religious experience. Better to take the rent and pay for sex." My friend Joel Oppenheimer had grown up in Yonkers but gone to Black Mountain College in North Carolina to study with Robert Creeley and Robert Duncan, then been a printer's devil, while writing slews of poetry. He was a romantic, a lyricist with a sweet sense of line right out of William Carlos Williams—a thorough night person and downtown habitué, yet loved such tokens of the Old West as the buffalo rifle that an astute girlfriend had given him, and poured his heart into a book about baseball, then ended his life by leaving the city with lung cancer to teach at a little college in Henniker, New Hampshire. Like many of us, his writing lent him a sense of mission and importance that civilians with just a day job never have. Also it provided him with a considerable love life, even though he bathed irregularly, and even after he had lost his teeth. Hirsute, lurching, doggish-headed, Joel cultivated the suffering aura of the quintessential Greenwich Village poet after the death of Maxwell Bodenheim, which indicated that in spite or because of his muddled drinking and querulous indiscipline, it might become important to have known him. Maybe he'd break through! He was endearingly jittery, shaggy, in earnest, and looked the part. I never had that specific sort of confidence in him, but, like my other favorite Village friend, Ross Wetzsteon, who edited twenty of my essays at the *Village Voice* before he died, Joel's picture remains on my wall: along with my dairy-farmer sister, Mary, now fifty-eight, whom I love, of course, and who was adopted at three months old but often appeared beleaguered by a sense that only her mother, of her parents, had truly wanted her. And still another teacher, Alfred Kazin, is on the side of my refrigerator, for his essays and memoirs, like *A Walker in the City*, his comprehensive intellect, and his personal courage. "Edward, my son," he sometimes said, when we stumbled on each other at a literary party. Once, he asked me to edit his journals if he died before he had a chance to. Though I knew him in college, he ended up influencing me most during my forties and fifties—as MacLeish and Commager had in my teens and twenties. He was the best of critics and best Americanist.

THERE SHOULD BE A MUSEUM of writers' shoes. Charles Dickens's, Jack London's, Dostoyevsky's, Defoe's, Twain's, Turgenev's, Stephen Crane's, Dreiser's, Sherwood Anderson's, George Orwell's, James Baldwin's—on and on, city or country, pick your own particular crew of walkers. More than first editions, their shoes would be a memorial. And in my humbler way I'd breezed the sidewalks of Boston, Philadelphia, San Francisco, and New

York; then, in my thirties, traveled in British Columbia; in my forties, more exhaustingly in Africa; in my fifties, around Alaska; in my sixties, to India and Antarctica, as well as back to Africa. Though far from the only path to being a writer, this suited me. A writer's work is to witness things, indoors, outdoors, wherever.

The wars I've seen, to me, don't prove the case for atheism. Yet now, as living nature shrinks, my faith *is* shrinking a bit, almost in proportion to the fewer birds, the skimpier trees. A roaring ocean climbing a beach (all over the world you still see it) reassures me that at least inanimate nature remains imperial. But just as Saul Bellow has written that God may simply be light, I think She/He may be life itself, and have always thought so, from childhood on, without articulating it: the stream or pulse of life, and not differentiated as much as Christianity or evolutionary science would have it seem. Religion is spirit, life is spirit—living electricity, conducted on and on—and people who know how to live wholeheartedly manage to ride that current without cringing or resisting it. They work with a deft kind of curiosity, a regular appetite, as if for food, yet rest with equal splurges of pleasure, throwing themselves into a chair with almost the same absorption as taking up a piece of work, as well as an open flow of love when appropriate—not thought out, just brimming up, an electric current of engagement.

I did leave New York for Vermont in my middle fifties to escape the scorched earth of a divorce. Yet it was a reluctant departure, by no means a case of Vermont supplanting Manhattan in my affections (it never has), whereas my parents had left New York for Connecticut in their late thirties with pleasure and, I think, some relief, never feeling easy in such "multicultural" complexity. Though blundering at first, I had delighted in New York, after the monochrome of suburbia. To me, great cities are as Emersonian as the country and feel as natural too. Whitman made that view respectable, as Thoreau made independence intellectually respectable in America also. My trips were far-flung but had an orbit around Manhattan or New England, to which I always returned. And although I had wanted to be classless as a young man, I moved rather sideways in that respect, not down or up—finding my work, plunging into that, maintaining a negligently convenient status. I was not a self-sacrificing socialist. I wanted America to be classless, as I thought a democracy should be, but since no utopia was in the offing, I put my energy into books, not changing things. As in a marathon, everyone hits a wall at some point, and you want to reach where you hoped to wind up at that time of life: to "have written your books," as writers say, and done what you could, when the stroke hits or you simply run dry.

Fires and Fights

*F*ires are another natural force. Fighting them awhile with a Forest Service "Hotshot" crew in the Laguna Mountains behind San Diego during the summer of 1953 gave me a second opportunity, after the circus, to learn whether my Connecticut woods had instilled in me enough equilibrium with wild things, enough intuition to go much of anywhere. A fire, though not playful or loving, is of the earth and does act with about as much rhythm and logic as a big cat, given the wind, humidity, and ground cover as defining factors. It certainly knows what it has already burned. "Run into the black, not into the green" if you are trapped was almost the first thing our instructors taught us, or (as with an angry bear) downhill, not up, where the fire tirelessly leaps. But better not to have to run. That's what our mattocks, brush hooks, shovels, and Pulaskis were for: cutting siege lines down to bare mineral sand, rock, or soil which contained nothing organic to burn.

Like many little kids in New York, I'd wanted to be a fireman.

Their daring and flair in swerving those big red, two-section, unmuffled ladder rigs around the crosstown corners with sirens wailing—and wearing black rubber slickers and high boots with the tops folded dashingly down, plus rakish helmets, brimmed front and back to deflect a shower of sparks or a cascade of water—pierced the aplomb of an eight-year-old who wanted to ride on a running board, as they did, anyway. When they reached the tumult of the blaze, they would hustle to unspool their jumbo hoses and tap into the bottled-up pressure of the nearest hydrant, while a white-helmeted captain directed the operation. He superseded any police officer (who seemed a mere martinet by comparison), or even the ambulance team, because it was the firemen who ran up the extendable ladder to get to the giddy height of the rooftop or darted inside the burning building and hauled out panicky people, using the Fireman's Carry. We tried it at recess ourselves, slinging a lighter child over one shoulder like a victim who had passed out.

These were forest fires, however—nature as physics—and ordinarily no human lives besides ours were at risk, so we weren't expected to be preternaturally brave. Instead, equanimity was needed in the face of a conflagration, though I did see an occasional eight-year-old boy gazing with rapturous admiration out the window of some rubbernecker's car, as we hiked off the road into a fire zone. Our camp was up in the pines just below the spine of the Coast Range that caught the cloud banks blowing off the Pacific and wrung the last wet mists and rains out of them before a stingy remnant blew east over the sudden desert and the saline Salton Sea, thirty miles long, glittering and evaporating far below us in the direction of Arizona. In the evening I liked to climb up to this knife-edge watershed, marveling at how pine-needle soil changed to desiccated sand just over the hump, in a matter of a few hundred yards, and on my days off would hike for many miles down canyon tracks below the forest out toward the Pacific side, talking a little to ranchers and hermits and looking for mountain lion sign. We were a miscellaneous crew of older dropouts and kids from Escondido or El Cajon, riding around to lightning strikes in a stake-sided truck and trained by a couple of clean-cut young Forest Service pros, who were pleasingly cautious about endangering our lives.

The fires crawled through the manzanita and chaparral in hundred-degree heat, nourished by every fitful breeze and patch of tinder. We'd have a bulldozer to help us after the first few hours, like a tank leading a platoon of infantry, but still needed to kill sparks with our shovels and bang at the hot spots spontaneously regenerating behind it. Tanker planes flew over, dropping water on some of the worst flare-ups to flatten them. We wore bandannas over our noses like bandits in the smoke, and watched the fire rear in a creeping wall thirty feet high, then grow arms like an octopus when the wind whooshed through a gap. It roared, crackled, and pawed, mastering the terrain.

A big fire was divided into sectors. State crews and prison crews fought it along with us. And there were stages to an aggressive blaze—the campfire that had got out of hand as a tentative beginning, modestly clothing itself in brush until an explosion of fuel gave it red legs. You drove toward it on a radio report from the man or woman in a tower on a mountaintop, finally spotting a spiral of gray smoke, faint and slow. What sort of country was it in? How to get there from the truck? Then the spiral plumed, widened, and darkened. A snaky flame climbing a dry copse of trees looked almost ornamental at first, as though decorating them with red flowers, oddly festive and ribbony as you wound toward where it was. A primitive part of you maybe rooted for it, grasping for food and footing, at the same time that you wanted to get there quicker to put it out. Gray smoke, blackening, kindling, hid the reds and yellows, as though they weren't getting brighter. You wanted to hurry; you wanted to come in on a forward side, not be left behind, fighting to save vegetation that had already been mostly abandoned by the fire unscathed, but not right to its leeward where the wind might burn you up, or cut the calculation too thin.

Because our bunkhouse was on the heights, we generally approached these fires from above, though after an hour's drive we might have to climb up from a dry creekbed again on foot, depending on how close the truck could get. The smoke smudged wider than we could keep a picture of in our mind's eye as the fire grew businesslike, not flickering as much as grim, and wrapped itself in the trappings of a natural disaster—the freight-train roar when the prevailing wind gusted as fast as a horse for a couple of minutes, and the cruel-sounding crunch as shrubs and thickets died and hardpan trees were scorched. When the destruction became wholesale—though we were only chopping at a corner of the flank—our young foreman got on his radio to coordinate a line of attack with a prospective path of flight if the wind spun partway around unexpectedly to menace us. We focused on the immediate theater of fire that was in sight (it *was* a theater), and paced our endurance to the labor of chopping brush and throwing it aside, as well as the furnace heat, breathing carefully in the smoke and hoarding a reserve of energy for moving fast, if we needed to. We drew some confidence from each other's stolid alacrity, and the cage that the wind built to herd as well as speed the fire, muzzling, steering it. Its noise absorbed our nervous impulse to make conversation. And fighting the flames, one ceased to notice their beauty. They were instead a chaos of incineration, sometimes fluctuating as red striations in the smoke, but grinding on. Your canvas-covered, one-gallon canteen, indented to fit across a hip, was what your thoughts strayed to, plus the eating-oranges stowed in your pack for a last supply of fluid.

I don't remember the men I worked with in any detail because I never was especially interested in this job and didn't stay too long, but hitchhiked up the coast to visit relatives in Oregon, then briefly rejoined the circus in Salt Lake City, knowing by now that *that* was what my first book was going to be about. But we were all good soldiers, stretching our strength, taking the endeavor very seriously. At night we'd camp on a gravelly river bottom, eat steak, tank up on cowboy coffee and soda, and watch the fire burn up-slope from where we were, although slowing as the evening cooled. The California forestry crews, and the state prisoners and federal trusties, both guarded, were camped separately within sight of us but at a remove. In a national forest, we didn't have the anguish of people's houses burning up, and it was a dryish place so we didn't see a lot of trapped wildlife. Hawks swooped to grab the woodrats and ground squirrels in front of the grassier conflagrations, and vultures sailed into the blackened area after the fire passed. We felt considerable comradeship—as in my army training at Fort Dix two years later; you don't dump a friend or scant an officer's judgment lightly after that. But to defeat a forest fire is not like George Patton against Erwin Rommel. It's nature reenacting an ancient form of physics that you employ a sort of jiujitsu to cut short. Feed it bare ground; chop and scrape a fire line: minerals against fire. Then we might sit whole days, each of us in a scrap of shade under a boulder, watching for breakouts after the blaze was supine. The sun in August seemed in cahoots with the fire, however, enabling it to flicker and flare up or fingeringly smoke at twenty points again. And we would check the whimsy of the wind as often as any primeval hunter. Nature might slip its collar and make a run for it—new smoke could put us flat on our stomachs on the ground, sucking air.

The wind could kill or save us, and the heat reminded us that the earth is molten inside anyway if you dig far enough. Leaping the crackling treetops, masticating branches at an acre a minute, a fire is like a hurricane, and you can't stop it by meticulously depriving it of food, deflating it like a dragon, if the wind doesn't consent, but gooses it right past the skirmish line. The air is acrid, the flames gain territory, presenting a new reality as you duck for cover to windward, and will burn up yet another slope all night long, before a rain squall from the ocean finally hits them on the crest and the bulldozers and a couple of tanker planes come in again, until at last they gutter out.

I WENT BACK to college for my senior year and upped my writing schedule to fifty hours a week, from forty as a junior, thirty as a sophomore, and twenty hours when I had been a freshman. The concentration did pay off: a combination of love for my materials and frustration at not being able to speak. By that spring I'd sold my circus novel to Houghton Mifflin, with MacLeish's help, and *Life* magazine said they were interested in an excerpt. While waiting to be drafted, I moved to a six-dollar-a-week room on Pinckney Street in Boston to finish it. But the bulk of the novel had been drafted through eight versions in pencil on green, lined, "Eye-ease," three-ring-binder paper, in the sprawling "C," or third, (sub)basement of Widener Library, where I could pace long solitary distances between the stacks during the course of the day. It was ideal, though you might think that to be surrounded by hundreds of thousands of unread books would discourage a budding author. Somehow, no. They were dead, these writers, but at least *here*. Obscurity, loneliness, dissent, and nimble roaming were how the mind best worked to break the mold, I thought: as in Thoreau's emphasis on "Sauntering," *à la Sainte Terre*, "to the Holy Land," as he defined it, or *sans terre*, "at home everywhere"—or Melville's edgy walk to the oceanfront that opens *Moby Dick*. But now I was out of the classroom, out of the university's great library, and out of the dorm, living on Beacon Hill, with the world mine to crack. When not writing or wandering, I hung out on the sofa of a homey little gallery nearby, owned by Art Wood. I remember his kindness not only to me but to his stroke-struck father and a generous, needy friend of mine named Ethel Vodisch, as well as to a white-haired, impoverished sculptor who was said to be the best in Boston in the 1950s (though I've forgotten his name), and who reminded me of Joyce Cary's randy, marvelous hero, Gulley Jimson, in a favorite lark of mine, *The Horse's Mouth*.

I mostly chummed with Liz Thomas, who lived three blocks downhill and was engaged, like me, in a happy pitch of composition, writing her first book, *The Harmless People,* which came out in 1959 and was still in print forty years later. It's about the Bushmen of the Kalahari Desert in Bechuanaland, and has the transparent purity of genuine wonder, the fluid immediacy of mimicry, by which the author herself became a Bushman. She had lived for a year or two with her parents and brother John in the Kalahari, acquiring an arresting self-assurance, and she also possessed a quick smile, a lyre-shaped back, limber body, seductive openness, a cap of shortish hair, and that air of practical otherworldliness some artists have when they're onto something. Our classmate John Updike had had a crush on Liz too, and one of my roommates soon wound up marrying her. But for that interlude we walked, gabbed, experimented with frottage, and went to her family's place in New Hampshire, under Thoreau's old haunts on North and South Pack Mountain, and ran through the woods; or at the breakwatered beaches at Cape Ann, soaking our ears in the ocean's roar, pretended to be mating lions—she having known gangs of lions close up, as well—under the moon, in the extravaganza of the sky.

The arts are mostly celebratory. We pour our proteins into what we love, although of course there are invaluable satirists who do the opposite. But we have the world's ear so briefly that we had better make it count, and in art museums with more than just our hapless century displayed, the preponderance of expression is praise. My own belief is that whatever heaven exists is here on earth and if you can't be jubilant while you're alive, when do you plan to? The deaths of people I've been close to and the manmade atrocities I have witnessed during several trips to Africa have not shaken this view; and Liz and I as twenty-one-year-old kids already shared a commitment to ebullience, wearing grins as if engaged in the Lord's work—as, indeed, so many so-called nature writers do.

Gaiety and glee are usually twinned with misery, however, which sneaks up on you like an ocean wave, filling your mouth with seawater, and can almost take you under, like a nether beast risen from below. My dreams are generally uneasy, not transcendental, and my brain chemistry can turn topsy-turvy, a little like Anna Karenina's, who when she is abandoned by her lover, starts for the railroad station to catch a train and ends up underneath it. Like the sea's own sibilant rumble, so soothing and yet menacing, rasping a beach, one's head can become a maelstrom. Though mine never has, I've never felt sure that it wouldn't. Part of the risk we run when going out on a limb is falling off. I've just trusted life, trusted my intuitions, and even trusted death in the sense that it would be no worse than life switched off.

IN THE ARMY, after basic infantry drilling at Fort Dix, New Jersey, and medical aidman training at Fort Sam Houston in Texas (how to drag and bandage a battlefield casualty, stop his bleeding, administer morphine, apply a splint), I was classified as a lab technician and sent to Valley Forge Army Hospital in Phoenixville, Pennsylvania. There I did urinalysis, read tuberculosis sputum slides for the acid-stained, red, bar-shaped bacteria on a blue background, did photo development, and cared for the pregnancy-test frogs and TB guinea pigs. I also helped the pathologist do autopsies, which brought me in weekly touch with the dead. I was his "diener," as the official term is, cutting open skulls with an electric saw, draining blood, sewing up the cadavers afterwards, most of whom appeared relieved. In fact, many of them had smiled slightly in their final moments. Worn and careworn from the ordeals of cancer or emphysema, they looked more enigmatic than beamish, but it was not merely that the muscles of the mouth had relaxed—and you never knew if they had been cut off just before they could start to beam. No terror ever showed, except for the surprised and lunky privates who had crashed, drunk, on the Pennsylvania Turnpike, or struck a match to see whether their gas tank was empty, or done something else of the sort that privates are known to do.

I was a private first class myself, having told the examining psychiatrist before my induction that I wanted to serve and was only stuttering because I was nervous talking with him. When I'd considered another course, both that and my asthma had clamped a vise on me: *you want to see what guilt will do?* This was still the Just War era of the 1950s, before Vietnam (where I would have refused to serve; as it was, I tore my registration card in half in 1967 and mailed it to Lyndon Johnson). But even so, after seeing the psychiatrist, I had to perjure myself on a loyalty-oath form, avowing that I hadn't attended any meetings of any organizations on a "subversive" list they had. The hazing, or harassment, as it's called during training, extended to our having to polish the backs of our belt buckles and shine the insteps of our shoes. Yet under that veneer reason prevailed, and the firing range (like any naturalist, I shot well), tent life, and field maneuvers were fun. We had able, forceful black sergeants, and for almost everybody, including them, it was a first experience of real integration, the military being the initial location in American life where that occurred. But when I asked another private, from Jim Crow Georgia, if the experience was going to change his attitudes, he just asked me without laughing if I was going to shine my shoes every day when I got home.

I'd sought to be assigned to the Medical Service Corps because war has never greatly interested me and I wanted to use my stint to learn about other universal facets of experience. But politics is also universal, and once I was stationed at a hospital near Philadelphia and New York, where I could go on weekend passes to research my second novel—set in a boxing gym—I pulled strings to avoid later reassignment, even to places such as Europe and

Alaska, where I traveled eagerly when the time was ripe, in five or six years. In the privacy of the morgue (the only privacy a private could obtain) I was working three hours a night on this new, boxing book, and also, in Philadelphia on many a Saturday, cinching the belated loss of my exasperating virginity. A fellow soldier had introduced me to his sister, Barbara, a social worker with a little house on Twelfth Street near Pine, who had now become a precious friend. Barbara was four years older than me, more experienced sexually, and empathetic (indeed, she was a professional playground director), as well as a walker and savvy comrade, extending past my army years.

There was an inconsistency in my love of boxing, yet sheering off from much interest in warfare in favor of the Medical Corps. But that's how I was; even later, I didn't choose to go to Vietnam as a war correspondent, but saw war only in Africa during my forties and sixties. Though boxing is the purest sport and closer to war than basketball or chess, it isn't really that. It's a test of craft and guts and need-to-win, raw and gaudy but wrapped in ritual, as war is not. And Philadelphia's prizefighters were of such feisty caliber that there was a special name for them in New York. A "Philadelphia fighter" was a guy so tough at punching and with such heart yet so out of the swim that he was always denied a decent shot by the matchmakers for fear that he'd upset some mobster's applecart. I was in the local gyms on weekends when not with Barbara, and this was the right place for me, I was sure. The circus novel had come out (officers stopped me on the post to ask if I knew that my picture was in *Newsweek* or the *Times,* and I said no, which was the truth), and I wanted now to get a head start on the next. I wanted to stay where I was, but suddenly needed to fend off my father's attempt to get me transferred—one of those comical episodes in retrospect that infuriate you at the time. He had not wanted me to be a writer; then after I made the mistake of proudly showing him the proofs of my first book, had written to Houghton Mifflin's attorney, Charles Curtis, without my knowledge to stop its publication because it was obscene. He feared (he told me after the attorney turned him down) that it would damage his own legal career, my mother's social life, and my sister's marriage prospects, if I didn't hold it up myself, or at least use a pen name. And when none of these consequences happened—instead he was congratulated in the corridors of Rockefeller Center by Frank Abrams, CEO of what is now Exxon—he had a change of heart. Not about what constituted obscenity, but his own life.

In the meantime, though, midway through my service an order came to Phoenixville directly from the Pentagon transferring me to SHAPE, "Supreme Headquarters Allied Powers, Europe," in Paris. My parents were living there, and it was a plum, yet had an agenda, I thought, rather like when he had gone to Harvard's Dean of Freshmen, after I had been admitted but unbeknownst to me, to choose my roommates lest they be "literary," since I had chosen a college he didn't want, and before that, when he had asked my prep school headmaster to hold me for a postgraduate year at Deerfield in hopes my tastes would mature to resemble his. Fortunately the headmaster—like Mr. Curtis later on—hadn't agreed. And when my fascination with the circus became too plainly clear, my father said he wouldn't send me back to college if I joined up for a summer again. But by then I'd got enough material to do my book. Art should be inspiring, like Leonardo, Botticelli, whereas the underlife of the circus or Stillman's famous boxing gym on Eighth Avenue demeaned you, smeared you in its degradation. So I figured that this military summons to Paris was another attempt to abort a novel-in-progress.

Grandson of a sodbuster, my father wanted to be five thousand miles away from Hutchinson and pull me too. After finishing that first book, while awaiting the draft, I'd hitchhiked to Saint Louis to scout for a new one along the Mississippi. I was motivated more by reading Twain, Faulkner, Cather, and other heartland writers than the thought of my Great-grandpa Hoagland maybe coming past here in his covered wagon on the way to homestead on the Arkansas, or Great-grandpa Morley spending part of his boyhood in Hannibal. Unfortunately, my efforts to chart an independent course did not include visiting my surviving Kansas or, for that matter, Michigan relatives, so I missed meeting many of them. But I was excited by the westward impetus, and here I was, on the riverboat wharves, sniffing for a tale to tell. (I *did* come back to the big river twenty years later to write some essays.)

But Houghton Mifflin telephoned my hotel at this point to ask me to fly east for a talk before *Cat Man* went to press. Alarmed, I found a huddle, rather friendly, awaiting me in Boston. I was, after all, only twenty-two, publishing a heartfelt, hundred-and-ten-thousand-word, youthfully graphic novel written entirely in iambic meter—I couldn't have been more sincere. Two editors, Paul Brooks and Craig Wylie, were there, as well as Mr. Curtis, though I still didn't know about my father's letter. They had one question, on a passage where my circus character Fiddler was hunkered down next to a townie girl behind a wagon off the midway. "What's he doing there?" Charley Curtis asked.

"What do you mean?" I said.

"What's he doing? Why is he crouched there by her knees?"

I said he just *was*. Being myself still a virgin, I had no idea what the man was talking about. I'd never heard of or even imagined cunnilingus. The girl was pretty and cleanly dressed and had a house and home, whereas Fiddler was a roustabout, a stranger, a cagehand wearing coveralls, who washed out of a bucket. Yet he liked her looks. Once they got beyond the smallest pleasantries, wouldn't he be likely to sort of crouch down inoffensively so as not to alarm her by his physical presence and hope that she would linger and ask him about the animals?

"But what is he doing?" Mr. Wylie and Mr. Curtis wanted to know.

I didn't know how to talk to girls unless I was in love with them, since I couldn't talk casually to men or women, boys or girls, without severe impediment, and had twice been impotent in bed with prostitutes. So what else *would* you do, trying to pick up a pretty girl off the midway, except try to ingratiate yourself by wordlessly hunkering down close to her knees?

They looked at each other—Messrs. Brooks, Wylie, and Curtis—and Mr. Curtis laughed and said, "I think we may be inserting ideas in his mind that weren't there. He doesn't know what we're talking about."

I shrugged, not wanting to expose my innocence but not denying my ignorance. The interview was over. They shook my hand. The book came out.

I'D TAKEN A BUS DOWN to New York, thereafter, to wait the two months until induction—my momentum on the Mississippi having been broken—and moved into a sublet on East Seventeenth Street near Union Square, which at that period was the Hyde Park of New York, a place of soap-box speeches, especially from the rear of the plinth of George Washington's equestrian statue—"Under the Horse's Ass"—on the Fourteenth Street side. I often went to those in the evening, or the arraignments downtown at Night Court, next to The Tombs on Centre Street, if my ramblings took me that far, or to gaze at the night lights on the ships, over on the Hudson. In the *Daily Mirror* I read a piece about Stillman's boxing emporium, near the old Madison Square Garden on Eighth Avenue in the fifties, where I was at home anyway from working in the circus. And so I went, and went (you paid a quarter to get in to watch), gradually choosing this new form of risky showmanship as the setting for my second novel. But again I focused on a loser, not a champ. My fighter was overmatched by his manager, deliberately manipulated in the gym as a kind of unpaid sparring partner against opponents who were too strong for him. I rather liked the trainers that I saw, in fact, but did despise most of the managers, although it took hundreds of hours of observation over the next three years to put this all together. As a choice of subject matter, the gym was too close to my first novel, for somebody who aspired perhaps to be a great novelist, and played too much to my previous strengths in style and observation. But I was instead in embryo an essayist—a witness and describer—and boxing was good early training for that. Right and wrong, mixed motives and irrational punishment, honorable defeat and corrupt victory, brute suffering and innate equilibrium. Grace and coordination: yet the resilience to take a punch. All the misery, cruelty, humiliation of such a sport: and yet delight.

I was living in this high-ceilinged apartment off Irving Place with two young women, also just out of college. Gina, a friend of friends, was petite, black-haired, pallid in complexion, and smoked Gauloise cigarettes, being Gallic in her intellectual enthusiasms as well. Audrey was a fresh-faced smoky-blonde, more showbiz-oriented. She later won a spot for herself in upscale New York under the wing of the television maven David Susskind, producing public-interest shows for him. Audrey was full-figured and outwardly cheerful but had a vaguely Marilyn Monroeish aura of doom and sometimes reminded me of Pinocchio and Jay Gatsby, too. The entrepreneur she was infatuated with she used to describe as mean and slightly sinister, but he got rich and sailed off on a racing schooner. Eventually she married the gangster-chronicler Peter Maas (Gina went to Paris, then married a professor at MIT) and seemed happier, till she died of a head injury in the aftermath of an auto accident out in the Hamptons on Long Island, about twenty years after we'd shared that apartment near Union Square.

I had run into her occasionally in the meantime at well-coiffed parties where literary people intersected with television folk and we would sidle into a corner and hold hands wordlessly on a couch for a few minutes, while her blow-dried escorts, delayed from moving on to the next event, puzzled over who I was. My stutter touched Audrey; she even seemed to think it connoted innocence. Though I didn't go that far (realizing that the pain and frustration of a stutter can engender sadism, for example, and that my attraction to circus tigers and New York prizefighters was not so different from her affinity for traveling with an entourage of brutal-looking celebrity-handlers), I did sometimes want to cling to her hand as you might have to Pinocchio's when he got caught up in bad company. And we differed in that I was more drawn to losers in my life and work, and she to winners, which turned out to be, I think, less germane and more dangerous.

Lovely Audrey, her blonde hair finger-combed, brewing coffee in her nightgown in the morning in those brownstone digs, talked of how men must mistreat her a little to gel her interest—a new concept to me, though I've heard it a hundred times since—and it *did* remind me of my one glimpse of Marilyn Monroe, on the neck of Ruth, the best circus elephant, posing for a publicity shoot in the basement of Madison Square Garden that same spring of 1955. The cavernous menagerie and sideshow area was empty because the performance she would be in was in progress upstairs. And, what with all the bowing and scraping Ruth was being made to do, one of Marilyn's breasts had fallen out while she bent forward to display her décolletage for the crowd of news-paper photographers from the *Daily News, Daily Mirror, World Telegram, New York Post,* and *Journal American,* to give them what she could. They politely lowered their cameras because the picture would have been unsalable in that era (though glancing at one another to make sure nobody snuck a shot). And Marilyn walked up the center of the ramp in her high heels, when they were finished, to get to the hippodrome, with her makeup man mincing backwards, touching up her bee-stung lips, plus a hair-dresser following closely, primping at that end. Then suddenly the floor shook, and a whole horse herd came thundering down the ramp at a rodeo gallop, with their act just over, careening like chariot war horses. And all the publicity flacks, the retinue of newsmen, chivalrous paparazzi, the hairdresser, makeup artist (plus yours truly) promptly ducked against the wall for cover aghast at what was just about to happen. Marilyn stood stunned, frozen in the path of twenty hell-bent horses too massed together to be able to dodge her or stop. She would have been trampled, if a circus straw boss hadn't also been walking up the ramp on his own business, keeping to the side. He saw her danger and flung himself across the runway with a shout like a red-dog tackler, arms spread, upright, body to body, and swept her clear, gently knocking her against the wall. And like a trouper, Marilyn collected herself, shook off a spate of tears, and went upstairs to do her stunt, "riding a pink elephant" in the center ring for a "party of the century." She was a good, long-striding sport, but it was not nice guys like Joe DiMaggio and Arthur Miller she was really looking for. Nor, probably, was my young friend Audrey, verging close to the celebrity flame.

Meanwhile, a couple of blocks east of our apartment, old Wobblies, Anarchists, Trotskyists, Stalinists, and Socialists were haranguing large crowds of unsettled men from George Washington's equestrian plinth. They divided the time that was available into blocks, but spoke of each other with as much disdain as for the bankers, capitalists, big corporations, and McCarthyism they were attacking. This one public spot where dissent could be amplified drew a lot of wistful, knotty men who had been labor organizers during the thirties, or remembered the Red Scare of the early twenties, and were ready to fly off the handle all over again if a bunch of Blue Suits set a bunch of Blue Coats with billy clubs after them. They'd been thrown into a drunk tank for weeks for exercising what they thought were constitutional rights of free assembly, or beat up on the road by railroad bulls and industry goons. Now they were beached in the Bronx or on the Lower East Side, arthritic, hard of hearing, living penuriously with a long-suffering sister, girlfriend, or wife (if they'd got lucky), and these free-speech fests were rousing events for an hour or two, as the rallies for the Lincoln Brigade, and then debating the Hitler-Stalin pact, had once been. It is poignant when you see back into a person's lifelong passion, whether that's a romantic love or utopian Marxism. These gimpy merchant seamen whose ships happened to be in port, or copper miners from Butte, steelworkers, radical garment workers, house painters from Brooklyn, mingling on the pavement under the sparse streetlights, were revisiting old loves. Not precisely the same ones—perhaps Earl Browder, Big Bill Haywood, Henry Wallace, Norman Thomas—and there were plenty of FBI agents in mufti chatting people up and monitoring the speakers, trolling for information and an invitation to further meetings. I was touched more by the listeners than the speakers, however, wondering how these faces had been scored with suffering. Was it the System or the individuals' fault? Obviously a bit of both—but what was the mix?

I was a throwback among young writers in caring much about this, and glad to be vanishing into the army as my book came out, not tempted to hustle it. Publicity was for writers whose aim was publicity; mine was to write as well as I could, and generally since then also I've left town when a book of mine came out. You have the Admiral Peary versus the T. E. Lawrence pattern of explorer, or Henry Stanley versus David Livingstone—self-advertisers vs. self-effacers—and the Vladimir Nabokov and Isaac Bashevis Singer type of author versus the Norman Mailer breast-beaters. But the boxers I was watching sure wanted fame: the klieg lights, cameras, the roped-in ring. Not Thoreauvian, they fought for money and wanted the front table, plush clothing, camp followers, low-slung cars, and pushbutton houses that might assuage whatever deprivation had made them want to punch so hard in the first place. Each bout was a night's supreme effort for them, not the daily but dilatory nine hours or so that I enjoyed putting in. Their emphasis was on the quick kill of a knockout, not four years of ten-words-per-hour pacing for a single novel. Fame alone was not a fair price for such a drawn-out endeavor as writing, you had to love the procedures, whereas for a boxer, whose job was to simulate killing an adversary he didn't even know—leave him for dead on the floor after a fight-for-life—fame may have been the only adequate reward.

Contenders like Joey Giardello and Isaac Logart trained at Stillman's Gym for a chance at a title while I was haunting the place. Logart was a fancy dan, a lithe, bolo-punching welterweight, one of a series of whizzing Cubans who came to America to find their fortunes. Kid Gavilan and Emile Griffith were others, and were better. Though Logart was very stylish, his punches were weak. He never got above number four in the world ratings, but coincided with the time that I was paying attention, and I liked his peppy grace.

Joey Giardello was a slugger, all heart and swarming arms and slurpy mouthpiece. Briefly, he became the Middleweight Champion, in 1963, after he had changed managers and got connected to Frankie Carbo, the Mafia don who ran all big-time boxing in this era for the mob. Giardello was a Philadelphia fighter who soon moved north to New York and to my 1960s neighborhood, around Tenth Street and First Avenue, when he began to be allowed to have some money bouts. "Philadelphia" was such a synonym for heartbreak in boxing because fighters like George Benton and Harold Johnson, no matter how good they were (and Johnson—whom I watched train in a hole-in-the-wall down there—like Benton, was far better than any fighter at Stillman's), so often were only matched with journeymen, or else with spoilers, who hopelessly beat on them. Joey, too, had been shut out because he might endanger the trajectory of the Cosa Nostra boxers, but now with his new sponsors could see light at the end of the tunnel. He was exuberant, and clusters of well-wishers accompanied him to the speed bag and heavy bag for his sessions at punching, and then watched the couple of rounds that he sparred with a paid opponent in the practice ring in Lou

Stillman's loftlike walkup room. Joey was white, which already was unusual, and not stuck-up—a good, brave, slouching, street-fight brawler who punched through the other guy's attack and defenses. He didn't bother much with a strategy or parrying anything. Somebody more vital could beat him, but he would have to knock Joey silly to do it, and at that happy point in his life, he didn't think anyone could.

The managers connived at the row of pay phones on the back wall while their fighters trained. A suit-jacket pocket for phone numbers might be all the office that they had, and Lou Stillman, spitting on the floor when he yelled at them—the most sardonic, eruptive man there, tougher than any *fighter*—ruled the place with his sneers and kicks-in-the-pants and threats of exile. But my favorites were also his, I think: the cornermen and cutmen, like Whitey Bimstein and Chickie Ferrara, Charlie Goldman, Freddie Brown, and Dan Florio. They were the good guys who saw each fighter through his bout, win or lose. Nobody was a "bum" to them. Whitey and Charlie were teeny, wizened family men, veterans of the ring, whose own noses had been rearranged in their previous careers. Chickie, Freddie, and Dan were more mundane in height and build, but Chickie was high-strung and snappish, whereas Freddie and Dan had a calming, fatalistic, even avuncular air. Hundreds and hundreds of passionately hopeful, macho souls had flailed through their patient hands, but by and by had been smashed.

I was a baseball fan, for entertainment. Its multiple heroes, complex rituals, and intricate elegance can't be topped. But boxing is the ultimate sport, where you leave your unconscious opponent for dead if you win, and next month may be derided as a broken-down pug yourself. It's combat, not diffused into a team sport such as football where the officiating is more solicitous and the pain is blurred, or gentrified like tennis or golf. It is conflict with no drinks together afterwards. I never thought boxing entertaining, and stopped following it when I had finished my book, in contrast to other subjects—such as my beloved Alaskan-Canadian wilderness, or Ringling Bros., or central Africa—which I've done books on. And, while I rooted for home-run hitters like DiMaggio, Williams, and Hank Greenberg, in Yankee Stadium, and Stan Musial, Johnny Mize, and Ralph Kiner, at the Giants' Polo Grounds, I didn't go to championship boxing bouts at all, and never saw Rocky Marciano, Ezzard Charles, or Jersey Joe Walcott, who were the reigning heavyweights in this period. Instead of Madison Square Garden, I went to club fights, as they were called, the minor leagues of boxing, at the St. Nicholas Arena on Manhattan's Upper West Side, or at the Sunnyside Garden in Queens, where young fighters fought old fighters to make a name by tearing apart a faltering head, torso, and reputation. *My* heavyweight was poor Hurricane Jackson, a Stillman's fighter who trained endlessly, skipping rope, punching the light and heavy bags, but was treated as a sort of inside joke—somebody's cash machine. He seemed to function as a clumsy punching bag for favored heavyweights who needed a winning payday on TV, yet brought in money for his owners in the match and was named "Hurricane" for how he windmilled, as part of the hype.

Prizefighters brutalized themselves for cash, like an extravagant paradigm of what warehousemen hefting hundred-pound loads all day, steel puddlers, hod carriers, and stoop laborers did for no glory and less pay. Like a male equivalent of the strippers I'd watched on the vaudeville stage at the Old Howard Theater in Scollay Square in Boston, they displayed their topless chests as public bodies (with the extra titillation of bleeding). And from my viewpoint, the grungy club boxer or workaday stripper was more affecting and representative than movie stars and headline athletes who take off their clothes for the crowd for lots more bucks. I'd learned on the highway and in the circus, in the army, and at boxing gyms that even if you have a cutman in your corner to stanch the blood, it doesn't obviate the need for stamina, self-reliance, and keeping oriented to what I think of as the earth's magnetic field. You can have allies, mentors, be married, but still you're going to be alone most of your life and, if you run off the rails, you had better be good company for yourself. You've got to be able to take a punch and get up after you're knocked down— the cutman doesn't do that for you—not feel sorry to be alive and mark time, nor accept the idea that only the rich can be mobile. Though the circus taught me *that,* I've also been on the faculty of ten colleges in the past thirty-eight years, for instance, and prize those several climates, milieus, and sets of friends.

CARDINAL POINTS

*A*part from "falling in" at reveille at sunrise, with a survivor of the Bataan Death March disdainfully calling our roll, my army posting was easy duty. I enjoyed barracks life, too, for the first year, but by the time my seven hundred thirtieth day in the service rolled around, I was teary at the prospect of release. I'd hung out with two pharmacists, Jerry Davis from Brooklyn and Larry Abrams from Baltimore; Dick Hitt from Dallas, the post newspaperman; Burrell Crohn, a hip student of jazz from New York City; and Pierre, an aspiring painter from Philadelphia. Pierre (named for the capital of South Dakota) was sincere, intelligent, and gloomy. He worked in the linens department of the hospital, and now that I think of it, resembled my best friend in prep school, an aspiring poet named Eddy, in his fragile sensitivity—even to the nervous breakdowns they both suffered a few years after leaving the institutions where our friendships were close.

I witnessed part of Pierre's, when his spirit was smothering, like the goldfish in choked tanks in his vegetating apartment, and he took me on a terrifying spin in his car, spurting forward, jerking back. Eddy's mad epiphany happened cross-country, as he slept under the tables of hotel ballrooms, whenever his hitchhiking brought him to a city (once waking up in the middle of a banquet in Denver, seeing hordes of feet surrounding him), or in a meadow with the deer. In supermarkets, he would get into fracases with the employees because they were dressed in brown, a color that mysteriously alarmed him. But then if the police were called, he would turn into the politest person because a uniform benignly blue somehow lulled him. By the greatest stroke of luck, he had his culminating episode while wandering east again from the Pacific's beaches, on the highway in Kansas that runs past the Menninger Clinic, where he was taken and received enlightened care.

Our hospital specialized in tuberculosis and mental patients, though neither wing was fun to be sequestered in. Radical surgery was the recommended treatment for bad TB, in the absence of effective drugs in the 1950s, plus a year or two of isolation from one's family; and still some of the people wasted away and died. Electric shock was the primary course of therapy for our mental patients, which resulted in some horrible scenes that corpsmen retold in the barracks. The "nuts" in specially marked pajamas who later tried to escape were chased down in the woods by MPs and clubbed for their pains. We had starchy, gung-ho MPs because a military madhouse does pose risks. Their crisp stockade was near our barracks, and I also dealt with them whenever I released an eviscerated body to an undertaker—helping him tote the stretcher to his hearse, then carrying the two bucketloads of organs that the pathologist had removed to the incinerator, under MP escort, where I dumped them directly down into a leaping fire.

I'd enjoyed drilling at Fort Dix and Fort Sam Houston; and here our laboratory disciplinarian, Sergeant Strickler, kept my effusive friend Jerry, and lawyerly Larry, and elusive Pfc. Hoagland sufficiently aware that we were in the army. He'd known the clamp of poverty as a miner's child in Appalachia and functioned avuncularly with some of the privates who weren't college graduates, however—even to the extent of turning one of them in for a court martial for stealing his camera, but then inviting the boy home for dinner on the first night that he got out of the stockade. In prep school I'd first learned to pay attention to the wishes of those in authority. You could object a little, but not neglect to notice. And I was circumspect enough that Colonel Tucker, my own protector, didn't have to intervene to pull me out of trouble (as he *did* in the short story I wrote about our relationship ten years later, called "The Colonel's Power"). Yet in observing the avalanche of institutional cruelty that could descend on soldiers whose façade of military obedience cracked and who then ran afoul of him or any other officer or senior sergeant, I learned a lot for future reference about talking to supervisors. Even the Colonel's incendiary tiff with his chemistry professor at Tulane, which he said had buried him here in the Bachelor Officers' Quarters on this lonely post, was an object lesson—like watching "uncrowned champions" like George Benton and Harold Johnson, Philadelphia fighters rapping a speed bag with fearsome power alone in a room with just the outline of a ring chalked on the floor, compared to punch-drunk "Hurricane," getting TV matches with rent-a-title, mob-connected figures in New York. And so were the men in Union Square, "under the Horse's Ass," who had been betrayed by their leaders in the Lincoln Brigade in 1938 in the Spanish Civil War, yet were idealists still.

Larger and seedier than Boston, Philadelphia had a scent-rich southward sprawl from Market Street, where black and Italian neighborhoods interlaced. My friend Barbara and I walked for miles along the Schuylkill River, or the bigger Delaware River, as Liz Thomas and I had done in Massachusetts, and made love in her three-story house, one-room-wide. She was the first of several generous nurses or social workers I was destined to be enamored of in the next forty years, and we parted only temporarily when I left the army. We enjoyed the art museum, orchestra, Connie Mack's Athletics, and the Strates Show carnival midway, plus my first consummated domesticity. I can't ascribe my sexual dunderheadedness solely to my handicap. I was gullible in many ways—can remember putting my finger not once but *twice,* at thirteen, into the spark-plug hole of a jalopy that some of my friends were working on, when they promised that the shock I'd got the first time had been a mistake and wouldn't happen again. Similarly, I believed that "no" really meant no, not yes, and that genital sex meant a lifelong serious connection. I knew plenty of "ass-men," as womanizers used to be called, who would solemnly promise anything to get inside some lady's pants—but imagined that the women were fooled, not that they might be playing along with the charade. It had been intimidating to be at close quarters with girls—the price exacted by a seductive mother (and I still have a weird phobia about handling buttons, no doubt from some forgotten bosomy incident sixty years ago). Going to an all-male secondary school instead of a coed public school hadn't made it easier. Only now was I learning that to pour out one's heart to the opposite sex was part of what having two sexes was *for.* The disequilibrium lent a special dimension—the mystery a shamanistic excitement—and at the end, the lubricant of jizzim.

On weekend passes when I went to New York, not Philly, I'd pay some gas money and catch a ride to the Holland Tunnel on Friday night with three Brooklyn-bound barracks mates who soon fell deep into the opaque, arcane argot of the Italianate *omerta* of their other lives. About 10 P.M., I'd find myself standing like Rastignac on big, hollow Canal Street, with two days in this supremely laddered metropolis to accomplish whatever I could think of. Writers serve an apprenticeship in shoe leather; they lope along, Balzacian (there *should* be a museum of authors' shoes), and I did the fumbly best I could, although punctilious about making my own way in the world. I regret now not deploying my connections to win invitations to parties where I might have met Tennessee Williams or Faulkner, as I'm also sorry I didn't go to Fifty-second Street to hear some great vintage jazz. The fans, or at least the white-Negro phoniness of some of the crowd, put me off; yet it shouldn't have, just as I didn't want to brown-nose among the literary hangers-on who were wangling an exchange of words with Faulkner or Williams, but would happily do so if I could now. We define an outline of ourselves by punctiliousness when we're young, then get more comfortable and don't feel a need to walk such a fine line.

What I did do in New York, besides look up friends and watch boxing, was often stay in sailors' hotels on the waterfront, downtown near West Street and Morton, where the floorboards slanted over foundering joists and the desk clerk might be wearing only her brassiere and the bar on the corner bled a lemony-raspberry neon light into the sorrowful night. I wasn't sorrowful, however. The wide Adirondack-fed Hudson rustled by exhilaratingly, not far beyond the street lamps. And though people do fetch up on the waterfront after a disaster—Alger Hiss, the perjured State Department Communist just out of jail, was living nearby, for example—it's also your landfall just off a ship, with a seabag and the clothes on your back and whatever wits you happen to possess, to scout about, rest up a bit, and ship out all over again. I wanted to start from scratch, not as a Morley or Hoagland or Ivy League man, but delineated by my native wits and whatever I'd manage to see for myself. Melville, Twain, Conrad, Jack London, as embryo novelists, had got started on big outbound waters like this.

Hiss had been a law school classmate of my father's, and his rise in the New Deal at the opposite political pole must have been nettling for two decades, until his giddy fall from grace became a cause for conscience-searching for many high-profile people, like Acheson and Frankfurter. In Boston in 1953, I'd gone experimentally to a few meetings of a Trotskyist cell with a fellow student whose parents were old-time radicals down in New York. We were the only young people in the small group sitting on folding chairs in a dusty rented hall up some stairs in a commercial building near the Skid Row district (where I was also writing a thesis for my geography course about Boston's homeless). In that blacklist era, it was mildly risky for me to do this, but unlike Union Square two years later, the proceedings seemed airless, cultish, as well as dogmatic and hair-splitting. These were not social democrats arguing against the Soviets' dictatorship, but for a different dictatorship, and they lost the thread in ancient personal antagonisms toward one another's lack of purity or dim intelligence. Like persecuted churchmen arguing doctrine in a forgotten catacomb, they were pasty-faced, whereas the merchant mariners in Union Square had salt crust in their hair, and the labor organizers castigating Jim Crow had been in jail in Birmingham.

I had classmates who stayed out of the army by getting graduate school deferments for several years, or marrying earlier than they might have otherwise, or by signing up with the CIA. One guy went over to Tehran and hung out with university students there, then fingered them for torture to the shah's secret police, according to a friend of mine who was living in the country on a Fulbright fellowship at the same time. He had practiced for this duty without realizing it, I suppose, by the sex contests that he had set up with a couple of pals while in college. As Harvard dandies with plush clothes and plummy accents, they would go to Boston Common on a weekday afternoon, then each pick out a different office building on the skyline, name a certain floor, and see—scout's honor—who could bed a secretary from that designated floor the earliest that evening. He was a would-be writer and probably thought the stunt was Hemingwayesque, but it turned out to be less like the Lost Generation than practice for winning the confidence of young Third World idealists and marking them for destruction in the classic manner of such Agency work.

To be light-footed, do no harm, yet get the good of an experience, in the army as in prep school, and emerge unscathed was my
aim. My intimacy with my good friends Jerry and Larry, the two
pharmacists, snagged beyond a certain point, however, because,
as Jerry finally told me with a laugh one day, I wasn't an "MOT."
"Member of the Tribe," Larry elaborated when I said I didn't
know what that was. "You're not a Jew." I was startled because I
had naively assumed that people who have been victimized by
prejudice want fewer barriers, but was so happy with Barbara it
hardly mattered, particularly after I caught hepatitis from a corpse
and won a three-week sick leave that I spent with her. Gentle-
handed, long-striding, efficient, frugal, a Scottish doctor's daughter, she perhaps understood me better than I did her, or was
exceptionally generous.

AFTER MY RELEASE from the army, I moved to a ground-floor
room on Stuyvesant Street, which runs catty-corner between
Ninth and Eleventh Streets and Second and Third Avenues in New
York. It cost fifty dollars a month, but I had to leave when my
landlady, chancing to stand on the sidewalk outside, saw me pissing into my sink to save a trip to the communal bathroom
upstairs. "Oh, he's pissing in his sink!" she yelled to everybody. So
I moved then to the Endicott Hotel, on Columbus Avenue at
Eighty-first Street, which later became the setting for a novel. Yet
there was as much stasis in these rooming houses and welfare
hotels as in the army. (Indeed, we'd had a sergeant on our post
who had risen to the rank of lieutenant colonel during World War II,
been downsized afterwards, but stayed in for the pension.) Stasis
was not for me, and I fell in and out of love with a woman who
soon married and divorced a friend of mine. I was vomiting from
the roller coaster of that experience, not doing too well, when
Barbara showed up from Philadelphia, pregnant by another man.
    We mulled it over and decided to go to California so she

wouldn't have to undergo the abortion that her parents were pressing on her. Barbara owned an old brown-and-white Chevrolet and a cocker spaniel of the same color, so we swung past my family's place to collect my English setter, whereupon, it being early winter, 1958, we turned south through Georgia, Alabama, Mississippi, Louisiana, and Texas, to cross by the beautiful Dixie loop. In 1955, hitchhiking to St. Louis, I'd gotten a ride with a soldier who was returning to Fort Leonard Wood, Missouri, from Providence, Rhode Island, drunk, nonstop. And in 1953, I'd driven to Mabel Stark's World Jungle Compound in Thousand Oaks, California, with a friend from upstate New York in a seventeen-year-old Model A Ford that boiled over unless we drove all during the night through Oklahoma and the Texas Panhandle, onto the Staked Plain, and finally the real desert—two-lane Highway 66, with broad-spreading gory sunsets, then a million stars and the white sheen of the moon, till the puce, early-June dawn and energetic sunrise—and slept in the day.

But this journey with Barbara, traversing the Deep South, was different. We could stay overnight in a candlelit inn on some Main Street under live oak trees, enjoying coition after a leisurely dinner of red shrimp, warm bread, and blackened catfish, or in a scruffy, homey "Guest Cabin," as those preliminary motels were called. The jagged underjaw of cozy Dixie hospitality was of course the chain gangs in striped suits whom we saw chopping brush and cane beside the blacktop, and the jeering columns of "Colored News" that decorated the back page of the local newspapers, telling who had "snuck through" what window—and the sidelong self-effacement of so many black people we took note of everywhere, their faces furnace-seared before they were middle-aged, who stood as silent advertisements for what the situation was. Once, I was yelling at Barbara's dog for being slow to get back into the car, when a young Negro woman who was walking by turned quite naturally toward me to learn what she had done wrong. Her passivity, or impassivity, said it all.

But such a lovely land: the Blue Ridge Mountains and the Pied-mont, the Black Belt and Delta, and Creole and Cajun country. And I remember how wide Texas was—three days' worth. Fifteen years later, I came back to Louisiana and southeast Texas for essays like "Lament the Red Wolf" and "Virginie and the Slaves," as well as to go out in a pirogue for weeks with French-speaking trappers in the salt marshes south of Lake Charles. But this trip with Barbara—my hand on her neck for hundreds of miles—was a swift drive, simply an enticing glimpse of the succulent com-plexities of the great South that have obsessed so many writers. It gave me, too, some juice for my boxing novel, which went cross-country in order to "circle home." We felt as exuberant as we were apprehensive, because our goal was to save this fetal life. (The child is now forty-something, herself a mother, living in Florida near the Everglades.)

New Mexico and Arizona were grandly painted in geologic colorations, a primeval palette until it bleached, past Phoenix, and eventually we crossed the San Bernadino Mountains and slid down the slope of the Coast Range to palms and eucalyptus, amid bungalows, and then the first luxuriant round orange trees next to the highway—green, green groves of them, groves and groves (the tree crowns round as oranges), washed in January sunshine, with fresh-squeezed-juice stands alongside. We skirted Los Ange-les and swung north up the lush coast through Pasadena, Santa Monica, Santa Barbara, Big Sur, Santa Cruz. Beautiful names, creamy surf, stiff personable cliffs, a landscape of lavish spectacle. We turned off the road at last in San Francisco and rented a dou-ble room by the week downtown, on a slant near Kearney Street. The gusty fog, the zany pitches of the up-and-down city with comely houses in pastel or clamshell shades, the amazing blue-water bay and magnificent bridges, all seemed exhilarating. A new ocean, new coast, new culture so happy and hopeful and con-fident about itself surely would spring us free of our tangles and help us both.

Barbara's parents had given her money to live on, relieved that the baby at least would be born out of sight of their social circle and perhaps given up for adoption. And I had signed a $3,500 second-book contract and, more significantly, had inherited $20,000 from my grandmother Morley, which I intended to eke out for five or six years while confirming that I was a writer. She was my bookish grandparent, and her money was crucial in this first push, since I still couldn't speak and therefore couldn't teach, and since my parents still hoped I would change course. I sensed and later saw how many aspiring novelists vitiated their energies by playing it safe in those first years out of college or the army, going to work for a magazine or getting jobs in public relations or digging footnotes for a Ph.D. for an academic sinecure. Then, after a decade or two, they'd return to the novel in the drawer and find it unwieldy and blurred and give it up.

After a few weeks downtown, Barbara and I settled on Oak Street, half an hour's walk from Nob Hill or Russian Hill but on another breezy rise, renting separate furnished apartments; and when the father of her forthcoming child showed up, he took yet another place, tacitly dividing the task of chaperoning her pregnancy with me. Unwed motherhood was a tough act in the 1950s; and Barbara did marry him (a chef, a programmer, math teacher, nice guy) a year later, and after him, another high school teacher. But in the meantime we took turns squiring her around, and I sought no other romantic involvement.

The Beats held sway in the literary life of the Bay Area in 1958, eclipsing by their pizzazz other figures like Wallace Stegner and Ivor Winters, whom I also looked up. I brought Barbara to meet the poet Kenneth Rexroth, who lived near us and was riding a wave of ancillary popularity as father figure to the Beats (the father figure who, unlike William Burroughs, had *not* shot his wife). Rexroth was genuinely learned, a translator of Japanese, Chinese, and some French poetry, winner the previous year of the Shelley Memorial Award, and able to compare, say, Horace to

Dylan Thomas. I'd read his article "Disengagement: the Art of the Beat Generation," in *New World Writing*, which was as lively as it was partisan. (He preferred a writer named Ward Moore to Eudora Welty, and a writer named Ernest Haycox to William Faulkner.) This was just two years after Lawrence Ferlinghetti's City Lights Books had published Allen Ginsberg's *Howl* as its Pocket Poets Series #4, and all sorts of people were declaiming frenetic verse in nightclubs, accompanied by a drum, a sax, and a slide trombone. Rexroth, at fifty-three, did too, and like the leaner, more perfervid, hirsute Ferlinghetti, was dismissive of products of Harvard and New York, taught by establishmentarians such as Berryman and MacLeish, like me. But he was polite to us.

I did like Ferlinghetti's *Coney Island of the Mind* and loved Jack Kerouac's *On the Road,* having been there myself. Both caught the spirit of the decade that followed, and maybe millennial Brownian motion as well. Yet being partisan too, I took a while to respond with honest admiration to *Howl* and to the brilliance of another friend of mine in after-years, Gary Snyder. The snappish split in poetry circles between the "A's" and "B's", "Academics" versus Beats (who trumpeted the name), made for plenty of intramural silliness. For instance, Ferlinghetti, though a Beat, had a Ph.D. from the Sorbonne, whereas the arch-"Academic" Berryman had no advanced degree and surely took as many wild risks in his personal life as any avatar of the Beats, dying a suicide. "Academic" meant reworking your poetry painstakingly, not going with the flow of improvisation; and San Francisco, all float and improvisation, was exciting. These writers thought they might be forging literary history—a new Left Bank—being stoned enough anyhow. Genius was so spontaneous, berserk, chemical, and cryptic that who knew? I went with several Beat friends to high-pitched warehouse parties put on by a guy with a trust fund, where a certain anorexic blind girl was always lying among the coats in the bedroom waiting to be screwed, while on the rooftop clusters of artists and their guests tripped on acid. Shortly after I left one night, a painter, imagining that he could fly, flipped out and "flew" off, temporarily shutting down that particular singular scene.

Having a baby is a serious business, however, and the cheeriness of our arrival in Baghdad by the Bay inevitably succumbed to the undertow of the supposed illegitimacy of our errand. Barbara's mother flew out for a visit, and Barbara entered a Florence Crittenden Home for Unwed Mothers, where she could receive more support. I drove out to Stinson Beach, on the ocean to the north, and stayed three months in a two-room cottage, working on my new novel and giving the father a clear field for himself. It was lonely, yet one of my life's minor idylls, smothered in sumo surf and spindrift weather, scudding birds and seething stars. A couple of retired sergeants lived over the general store, and there was other driftwood, though my immediate neighbor, with a baby and a beautiful wife, worked as a guard at San Quentin prison. The second-most beautiful woman in this transient hamlet ran the coin Laundromat for her parents, and, of high school age, was so desperate to get away to the big city that she wanted me to take her with me. Having a prison guard eyeing me uneasily anyway was a useful reminder.

But these weeks, steeped in husky winds and burly sea-sound, were all the corrective I needed. When Barbara left the Home to live in her apartment again and escape the wholesale weeping and in-house pressure to give up her child when it was born, I came back to help her through the endgame. She and the father had found that their problems did not relate to my presence, and her morale had strengthened. I was peppier after walking the thunderous beach, and we were in daily touch until she woke me with a phone call the morning the contractions started. I drove her to the hospital and sat with her in the labor room for eight hours (hers was worse pain than when my wife had Molly a decade later). The baby was fine, but I was shaken by the gravity of those hours. Life was serious, not just sitting on a rock watching the surf roll in. Surf was a metaphor only if you recognized that it was going to hit you. I went to a church with a black congregation that Sunday and bathed in soul music. In a couple of weeks we drove east. Oakland, Sacramento, Reno, Salt Lake City, Denver . . . California has perpetual allure; and we each came back more than thirty years later—me to teach at a university near Sacramento, Barbara to visit grandchildren not far north of Stinson Beach. I'd decided during our sojourn to remain an easterner, figuring that I might write twice as many books in a lifetime spent as a New Yorker, rather than in laid-back, noncompetitive San Francisco: which was a better place for late starts, last acts, honey hopes. And Barbara reconciled with her family and had more children, near home in Philadelphia. I missed her soft melodious voice and the way her mind would triangulate on a middle course of action. Decency was her watchword.

OH, FAMILY

I moved into the Alexandria Hotel on 103rd Street, off Broadway, and began pushing to finish my second novel. The previous tenant in my room had been a prostitute, so her customers kept knocking loudly on the door, and there were needles under the bed. The Alexandria was also a center for Haitian revolutionaries, huddling excitedly together and printing pamphlets, though it was a calmer sort of place than the Endicott had been because the Haitians wanted no trouble with the New York police, and was more integrated, with elderly whites who were living on government checks, and fewer kids. The Endicott had had shoals of ragged kids, a yelling whirligig running up and down the mineshaft stairwells and maze of ten-watt corridors, terrifying the aghast old people living in encysted isolation on bread and canned tuna fish, on public assistance: so much grief, despair, and rageful agitation amidst the smells of pot, spaghetti, semen, spilled potato chips, and rancid beer.

But the Alexandria Hotel, owned by two Holocaust survivors,

was quieter. The kids actually seemed to have some chance of doing their homework, for example, and the halls were cleaner. Once, a maid even brought a girl of eighteen or so to me who had been beaten up overnight by her boyfriend or whomever. Her light-colored face was bruised and swollen, and she was wearing a nightgown. This wouldn't have happened in the Endicott because there were no maids and beatings were more commonplace. *Now,* I would give her a hundred dollars and some phone numbers, or put her in a car and get her out of town, if that's what it took, having gained confidence on the Lower East Side during the 1960s that you could interfere in that way almost safely if a woman was being beaten; the street code permitted it. But this was 1959, and she was offering herself to me in her pink nightgown and slippers—perhaps the only means of escape she knew—as the maid told her in English and Spanish that I was a "gentleman." So I expressed sympathy but offered, I'm sorry to say, no protection.

Riverside Park was two blocks away. I walked there daily or on Broadway, till after a few months my life changed. I met Amy, my first wife, at the apartment of a friend who was married to a classmate of hers, and I liked the immediacy of her reactions, an honesty which was innately married to kindness. Soon she seemed to me to have the clearest spirit I'd ever encountered. Although she laughed a lot, no witty hesitancy or ambivalence bespoke a hint of New York *Schadenfreude.* She was open-hearted, yet reserved, sentimental but seldom hoodwinked, and not money- or especially advancement-oriented. A former math major at Bennington College, she was living in the Bronx at the end of the Broadway subway line, near Sugar Ray Robinson's house and Van Cortlandt Park, and worked in midtown at the National Bureau of Economic Research. Though less down-to-earth than Barbara, she lived closer to the wellsprings, maybe because she was still somewhat childlike—still just a bit as if she were looking out a window for her father to come back. He had split up with her mother when she was thirteen, and Amy's fragile edge was partly the result, I thought. My own mother had been as brittle, though less self-sufficient and idealistic. Amy's was the fragility of virtue, as I continue to think forty years later, having seen so many high idealists not compromise as much as simply crumple under the pressure of things—like Eddy, my Deerfield chum, mustering the courage in Night Court to finally tell the judge, as he sank from view, "Judge not, lest ye be judged," and Pierre, my best friend during our army stint, fugueing unfathomably in his apartment next to a tankful of asphyxiating fish in a water-jungle of dying plants. So many perky intellectuals turned into patio professors as the decades ground on. Writers and lawyers lost their zest to try doing good; publishers and doctors settled for less.

I've always been attracted to people of uncommon generosity or a stripped-bare, Tolstoyan sort of idealism, though such folk are rare, to begin with, and often stumble into trouble, as Tolstoy himself did. In fact, you seldom meet them after early middle age because life has mauled the few candidates so badly along the way. It may signify my own deficiencies that these qualities of decency were so important to me, but I *did* want to see the world change for the better in my own lifetime; could hardly believe at first that it wouldn't. And not just, for instance, that ours and other nations would allow other holocausts to occur in Cambodia and Africa within a few decades of witnessing what the Nazis did. But the mundane inequity I saw as a child—the scabbed Harlem streets the Connecticut commuter trains rolled through so sleekly and obliviously, morning and night, to and from grandiose sub-urban avenues like mine, full of money-making-money trust funds and snickering snobbery—could at least be adjusted. Yet of course it wasn't. There are just more trophy houses and "starter man-sions" now, and I've seen worse poverty in the wider world than Harlem's ever was, yet heard the people in the trophy mansions boast at cocktail parties of having made a bunch of millions speculating in Third World junk bonds.

I didn't think my generation was going to leave the world so

shamefully unchanged: that new technology was all we would provide, plus a few switchovers in how consensual conduct is regarded
and some constitutional reinterpretations of discrimination—but
not ethical changes which go beyond legalisms or personal conve-
nience. One doesn't see a less selfish society in the year 2000 than
we had in 1950. The blip of activism of the 1960s, like that of the
1930s, has left a legislative legacy, but no significant change of
heart, and the churchy preaching and bully-pulpit orations from
politicians in the other decades has only served for us to tread
water. The 1930s and 1960s influenced me politically and bene-
fited me personally—the sixties by liberating me sexually and the
thirties by facilitating my wanderings across America, because it
was veterans of the Depression who picked up hitchhikers. And at
the end of the century, both Barbara and Amy were engaged in
idealistic work—Amy at a cancer hospice, Barbara taking battered women into her home through an Episcopalian group. But
they, and I in my environmental passions, perhaps weren't typical.

Amy was a peach, heartfelt in her responses. We traveled with
panache through northern British Columbia for six months during our honeymoon in 1960—living in log cabins in a series of
pioneer towns up spindly dirt roads, like Clearwater, McBride,
Barkerville, and Hazelton, and listening to first-settler stories,
venturing onto wild trails while watching apprehensively for
moose, because the cows with calves could be dangerous. Once a
grizzly's tracks in the mud were still filling with water as we came
onto them. Amy was invaluable, and not only because she could
talk winningly and bake bread with our neighbors, but wasn't
clumsily blunt and "fierce" in pursuit of the seeds of a story, as I
soon started to be. On the other hand, I could keep up with and
shoot as well as some of the off-duty hunting guides we lived near,
and I was to come back alone to northwestern British Columbia
again and again, and half a dozen times to Alaska during the
1980s. But this half-year sojourn with Amy, delving into a wilderness that had scarcely been broached, built a foundation for all

that. (My father, to give him credit, had laid it earlier by bringing me into the Alberta Rockies in 1952, and probably my uncles Ed and Bill, on our family's trips to the Morley logging camps in Oregon and Washington, even before.)

After this, we lived in a ground-floor apartment on East Fifth Street between Avenues A and B for a year. It was the benign early sixties, not much violence outside; and a whole murmuring community of homeless folk, both men and women, slept on a row of mattresses on the floor beside the furnace in the basement underneath us, courtesy of the super, who took a dollar apiece when he let them in at the cellar door through the sidewalk each night. No loud drunks or fights. It worked well, and we were glad to keep mum about it. When we had a party, we'd dump all the leftover glasses into a jug, the wines and liquor together, and pass it downstairs. No problems until the super himself, alas, suffered a nervous breakdown and ran through the tenement with a knife in his hand, in fear for his life from a phantasm no one else saw who was chasing him.

New York is perennially a tale of two cities, and Amy's impulses, when she saw coughing bag ladies uptown next to jeweled women in limousines, were those of a fabulist more than a social worker. Parables in the making: the Ferris wheel where maybe the seats don't rotate and those who go to the top, totally to their surprise, fall out, if they have ignored their kith and kin. She was not political so much as inclined to give her lunch money to a street person, and her employer eventually became the United Nations. First, though, we sailed to Europe on the USS *Independence* for a year and a half, landing at Palermo, Sicily, where we stayed for three months in a village under Mount Etna. Then on the Janiculum Hill in Rome for about as long. And the Alpes-Maritimes in the south of France for five months. And the rue du Sabot and Place Saint-Sulpice in Paris. And the Sierra Nevada in the south of Spain. I loved it all as a traveler—climbing up an ottery valley full of cataracts within walking distance of the Matisse Chapel in

Vence—or a valley stippled with almond and fig farms that wolves from the mountains sometimes visited at night, north of Motril on the Costa del Sol. Rome was my greatest delight, to wander its pitches and colors early and late. Yet no stories sprouted from this feast of months. Though visually more splendid than America, Europe wasn't my home or my subject matter, as New York, New England, the West, and then Africa, too, became. The beauty of Venice, the zest of Paris, the perspectives of Rome were sheer happiness to sample and savor, but were not my work.

Again, as translator, Amy made our trips easy in Paris, Rome, and the villages, she was so genuine amid the passing stream of tourists less authentically interested. In Sicily, we saw our first hunger—cats hanging in the butcher shops of Acireale for people who could afford them, and bread that, crumb by crumb, was crucial to the souls who ate it—under the fountaining eruptions of the red-topped volcano. The classic puppeteer, Signore Emanuele Macri, worked here, a broke, devoted artist, effusive, who recapitulated the feats of the Chanson de Roland (Orlando Furioso) onstage, and tried to sell us some of his puppets, he was so poor. Our own little town and its lemon groves were owned by an insufferable nobleman who woke up all of the inhabitants at 3 A.M., driving back from his parties or liaisons and honking the horn of his sports car down the entire length of the main street, so that the gate to his estate would be opened before he got there and he wouldn't have to slow down. (The little boys used to retaliate by breaking off whole boughs of his lemon trees to flavor Amy's breakfast tea.) Yet the poverty in Spain was even grimmer because of the *Guardia Civil,* Franco's fascist police, who were more severe, unbending, and sadistic than Palermo's Mafia. The Spanish temperament, too—while the Puritan in me responded to it primevally—seemed implacably fierce, by comparison with Sicilian flexibility, and the gaunt women and ragged bony children we saw in country towns in Andalusia were pinioned in a crueler, more claustrophobic thralldom than mere feudalism and criminality. I never saw Italy under Mussolini, only Spain under Franco, but Rome's spiritual base was so much broader than Madrid's that that protean resourcefulness had perhaps spread southward through Naples from the capital, like Italian common sense.

Wild places in Europe have a phenomenal human reverberation because outlaws and guerrilla fighters have held out in them, as well as ibex, wolves, imperial eagles, lynx, and bears. On the Greek island of Samos—as in Sicily and Andalusia—I climbed into high country where dirty civil wars had petered out in thirst, hypothermia, and sniper fire. Yet up there, you didn't just find the skeletons of those irregulars and partisans who had lost, but a solitary shepherd in the prime of life lying unexpectedly with a few goats in a hidden col, where you'd think that only birds of prey would fly. Like an ancient city whose individual neighborhoods have been put to many different uses over the course of centuries and epochs, a wilderness in Europe was not virginally tooth-and-nail. It might be layered with vultures, goatherds, wolves, royalist or revolutionary guerrillas, and Muslims fighting Christians, Fascists fighting democrats, or Capitalists versus Communists. Yet, always, money was crawling up the slopes: new chalets, hotels, and getaway resort developments creeping toward the avalanche or lava zones, trying to squeeze out of nature's disaster-odds another ten or twenty million bucks worth of scenery. *First just let me make my little pile,* each landowner says—and sets a forest fire vindictively (as happened wholesale to Samos's breathtaking pine woods) if he is prevented.

Decades of greed and triumphalism were to follow, but in the sixties, when I spent two-and-a-half years in Europe, the anarchy of World War I and the villainy of World War II still had reach. People had learned first-hand in Italy, Greece, and France and Spain that the possession of money and power did not signify goodness, but perhaps quite the opposite. The Nazis had had money and good folk had been destitute. And there was so much building and rebuilding to be done that paving over wild country was not yet scheduled. Almost as in America, you could go out into it and no one cared what was there. The springs in the cliffs watered a congeries of songbirds, running foxes, and three-foot snakes, instead of strings of cement swimming pools landscaped between trophy vacation houses. Travelers didn't need to block out with their hands what they didn't want to see. Behind Vence or Granada or Syracusa, you could just walk and look. Plenty of land spread out in a natural state.

I'M RELUCTANT to confess that when I returned to Europe for another year, in the fall of 1964, I was alone: not with Amy. My second divorce, thirty years later, doesn't embarrass me as much. I don't mean that I didn't share the blame then, but it doesn't seem as frivolous in retrospect. It was more of a 1990s type of split-up, made necessary by bitterness, betrayal, and social change. By contrast, I'm at a loss to explain the breakup of my 1960s marriage coherently. Infidelity or other excesses had no part in it. I thought fooling around was wrong. Nor were drugs the way to go, if you wanted to be a writer; drugs were for show and phoniness. I was tightly wound, trolling for inspiration, as well as proof, indeed, that I had what it took to be more than what the Houghton Mifflin editors had once suggested might be just "a one-book boy." When I'd turned in my second novel four years later, there hadn't been enough interest at the publishing house even to read the manuscript until I called up three months later and asked them what they thought. Oh, they'd forgotten to look at it. I was insulted and took the book elsewhere—but that was a calamity too. It got few reviews or sales and no attention, and its strengths seemed even to me a repeat of what I'd done in the first, with boxing substituted as colorful subject matter for the circus.

I wanted to be a writer more than anything (certainly more than to be a husband) and my uncertainty or occasional jitters about Amy's stability seemed a drain, especially once we were back home, without the sweetmeats of traveling. I'd seen my mother's spells of hysteria, her own fear of it, and my father's concealed panic when attempting to confront it. I remembered, too, my mother's mournful accounts of how mental illness had gradually destroyed her beloved Uncle Paul's family and sent him gratefully into an early grave—perhaps the most frightening sequence of events she had ever known. It had marked her own family a bit also: her mother's sojourns in the Aberdeen General Hospital when overwhelmed by family fracases between her husband and her eldest son, Dave, who was killed by that widow-maker tree in the woods before he reached forty, or by my grandfather's infidelities with "other women" in Aberdeen. Beyond that was the legacy of shattering nervous breakdowns of two menfolk—my grandmother's father and uncle—that had caused her Hicok family's bank in Homer, New York, to collapse scandalously during the Panic of 1873 and precipitated their flight to beg a place with relatives in the Middle West.

These mysteries—why some people unravel under pressure and others don't—had bewildered my father too. Music and outdoor exercise were the only sovereign remedies he knew about that might help somebody "relax"—a very thin shield, of course, against the disintegration of a personality. He didn't believe in psychoanalysis, psychologizing, or pill-taking. They were meddling, "Jewish" hocus-pocus, or a palliative that was temporary at best. And though he wished he could believe in prayer as a solution, he didn't except insofar as faith itself can be calming. Coinciding with his climb from Kansas City to Wall Street, he'd seen his cousins' little clothing store back in Hutchinson go bankrupt during the Depression and everyone flee to southern California for new livelihoods if they could, the womenfolk in particular substantially shaken by the experience (his little brother Harold, meanwhile, long dead under the wheels of the trolley car). He believed in going forward, being trustworthy and perfectionist, sticking to the program, and—baffled by my stutter—sometimes shouted at me, "*Just stop!*" but then would be sympathetic afterwards. My own "little brother" had been born prematurely after my mother, taking a Lexington Avenue bus to save money, had been thrown onto the floor, and my father, in that era before medical insurance—unbeknownst to her at the time—had opted in the hospital not to underwrite the expensive procedures that might have saved his fragile life: a decision for which she never forgave him, because she had been damaged medically in a way that, in the 1930s, meant she couldn't have any more children.

Women's extraordinary progenitive capacities made them vulnerable, it was believed, to nervous disorders if they ran off the rails. And my male generation, looking at our mothers, bought into this idea too. The other frustrations that might be chewing at them—aborted careers, double standards in status and morality—didn't register on us as unnatural (*unfair* perhaps, but not unnatural), and so we didn't credit these as being unduly disorienting. I assumed anyway, like my father before me, that the great gamble or price you paid for all the strengths and respectability that marriage brought was the potential that the woman would go into periodic tailspins. To ride out those episodes of instability, bear with her, and survive her emotionality was part of the mark of being the head of a household, a father to your kids, a breadwinner, and a "family man," not just a self-supporting bachelor. And it was the punishment suffered by men like Mother's uncle Paul, who married for money, to find themselves saddled with a wife they didn't love whose nervous breakdowns went off like detonations among the children—and all that timber-heiress luxury now a small comfort. It was also the just deserts that were inflicted upon the kind of man who would abandon a loyal wife for a dancehall queen—that she would probably soon develop her own fancy airs and crazy spells—and why people asked (or at least the unsnobbish reason that they sometimes asked), "Is she (or he) of good family?" The hell with the money or the May-flower ancestry, in other words, if they've got crazy genes.

Apparently, then, the trade-off for the stable enjoyment of "domestic bliss," or regular meals, sleep, and sex (and I once over-heard my father, tussling on the couch, ecstatically calling my mother's breasts "The Twins"), was periodic tears, hysteria, and pills, and always had been—among a great many of my parents' friends as well, and everybody's uncles, cousins, and the rest. Women provided domestic stability but were themselves unstable: a paradoxical condition of life. And I wasn't ready for it. Didn't want kids yet, or the social or financial burden.

Amy was in a strong position financially when we separated in New York City after four years of marriage. What I've never known, however, is whether I did her wrong—whether this early divorce, so commonplace during the 1960s but in Amy's case not followed by a remarriage, harmed her in some gratuitous, awful way that became a sort of self-fulfilling prophecy. Or was it sim-ply a natural outgrowth of her own qualities? She had other affairs but not a life *with* someone else, and because I never met a better-hearted person or anyone who loved me more, I don't know whether we couldn't have made a go of it, if I'd permitted us to try. I was afraid of a slippage of focus, and being responsible for somebody who might slide off the deep end—though in fact in the next decades she seldom did. Also, having recognized that my second novel had not been an advance on the first, and that the third was not going anywhere very brilliant (they both had style and everything else hard work could give them, but not wisdom), I wanted to find a partner who would somehow feed me ideas, give me a leg up on intellectual maturity; or else, at least as an alternative, I'd benefit from the maneuverability, the lawlessness of being solo. From pain and lawlessness might spring originality.

Of course, I didn't really hit upon a voice of my own until I'd remarried and had a child. There was nothing Dostoyevskian about it, or about me either. I was Tolstoyan in my philosophical and religious allegiance, but the clichés of the time were Dostoyevskian and I'd swallowed them: that suffering was a catalyst or philosopher's stone—imprisonment, exile, mock executions. I'd suffered from and did regard my stutter as a concentrating, even somewhat purifying experience, but not cathartic, and much more of a handicap in gathering material than a lens to process it. Nor had my basic optimism been challenged, because much of the cruelty I'd encountered was unwitting. I just believed risk was what you *did*. To bridle at it—to hide in graduate school and get your Ph.D. in English, for instance, for employment insurance— was to cut your talent as a novelist right off at the knees. Many people chose that route, or worked early on as staffers at magazines like Henry Luce's *Time* or *The New Yorker* which had such settled, potent corporate personalities that their own voices were soon subsumed. Writers lose their individual voices so easily when they become technicians in the service of a collective enterprise that they often seem incongruously grateful. It solves the problems of both finance and ambition with a salary, some reflected glory, and evades the nagging challenge of whether one actually did have something new to say, because joint ventures have their own resonance, and sidemen or staffers share in that. Most sidemen should be sidemen and most well-harnessed professors should be professors—but how do you know that you shouldn't go solo until you've tried? I've seen so many writers with a certain talent avoid ever trying, yet plenty of others who only hurt themselves by burning their bridges in setting out to live as scantily as geniuses, when in their case it was just derivative. For me, I think that leaving Amy may have been good for my writing but bad for my soul, and I dreamt about her regretfully, wistfully, for years afterwards, as I never did in the wake of my second marriage, which had lasted six times longer but turned bitter with betrayal for the last ten years, so that I felt less guilt about it.

I remembered my father's jittery ambitions in middle age,

which were thwarted at a middle level as, first, he sought a law partnership, then, fifteen years later, a leadership position at Standard Oil headquarters. But there had been plenty of posh stuff in between—the immense high-up offices, the Fifth Avenue club luncheons, the dark suits he wore, so soft to the touch, the Cunard steamship staterooms, the Connaught Hotel in London, the Hotel George V in Paris, the Via Veneto in Rome. My willowy mother was sometimes an asset and sometimes a drag on him because underneath her tall, flapper vivacity, good carriage, and presentable prettiness lurked a pentimento of hysteria or delirium that was still more unsettling for being unexpected and unpredictable. I remember ninety-mile-an-hour drives on the winding roads of our suburb when she was upset. At eight or ten I didn't know why, but knew that to be a good sport you didn't complain or show fear or notice crying jags. Her high-pitched, manipulative, emotional sieges instilled in me both a soft spot for vulnerable people and a fear of being tied to them, should they become unmoored. At mealtimes she would sometimes insist that I eat with my glasses off so she could look at how "handsome" I was without them—which seemed weird to me as well as unflattering, since I was extremely near-sighted and would never be seen by anybody else in this way. She also relished fomenting quarrels between my father and me, which was carrying coals to Newcastle during my teens, except that she prevented us from making up whenever we did manage to have an ameliorative talk by coming to me when it was over and telling me how sarcastically he had spoken to her of my ideas afterwards. She and I could gab quite happily ourselves, and it was not for years that it occurred to me to wonder about the strange smile that played on her lips as she would watch my anger flare when she demolished the rapprochements my father thought we had achieved.

I learned from her that women might have an interest in what I had to say despite the trapdoor of my stutter, which no matter how fluently I might be racing along telling a story would open under me, throwing me into breathless paroxysms of verbal epilepsy three dozen times a day. Joyous things had a danger to them—travel, sex, sports, falling in love, even talking—and I learned to hide my hopes and dreams and keep my cards up my sleeve lest they be trumped and nullified. Whatever I said to her might be recounted later to anybody—strangers standing in a grocery store. Indeed, my problems were likely to be, on the theory that ridicule might cure them, or else reported to my father and acted against indirectly. So, concealing what I hoped to do (like the hoard of twenty dollars stashed in the closet), I trusted instead to the strength of my thumb to clear out—in other words, trusted strangers on the open road more than those I loved.

Was love always askew and a subsonic hysteria; never equilibrium? The shoppers in the grocery store would be told how I didn't want to go to church anymore, and dressed sloppily, and had turned down an invitation to the Greenwich Country Club Junior Cotillion. Seldom was I given a party that wasn't a surprise—walking into a room filled with the children of my mother's friends whom I wouldn't have invited if I had chosen the guest list. She once told me that she wasn't constitutionally suited to motherhood, though without volunteering how and why. Did one have to balance the sanity of solitude against the nutrition of love? This *was* love, I recognized, and not all manipulation and compulsive flirtation, just as my father's rigidity implied a permanence to family relations. The most important decision in your life, as he kept stressing, was marriage, although it was accomplished when people were the least ready to make it—panting from their hormones even as they pledged irrevocable vows. Then they woke up in a year or two and found out who they were married to, which tested their mettle. And the distinction between mother-love and father-love, he sometimes added, was that the first was unconditional, the second earned. Yet our troubles in my teens did hurt him, as he told his friends, who sometimes told me;

and later, when he lay ill the first time with cancer in the hospital, he refused to see either my sister or me, telling the nurses that our divorces and other such conduct had brought on his condition to begin with. I think that, except for dying at only sixty-three, he had a good life, but fatherhood did not contribute much to it. In his three-piece suits—wearing a tie even on most weekends—he sent money back to distressed, shirt-sleeved relatives in Kansas and Missouri, but his climb eastward out of there as a prudent, methodical scholarship boy had been so narrowly defined, so eager, obliging, and deferential in penetrating the upper social and professional echelons (as I saw when I was with him at public functions), that he lost instead of gaining flexibility.

Though my father's standards of character differed from mine (did I "live below the belt"?), he gave it primacy as a quality over other matters; and maybe that's why I do too. He never rated respectability as more important than loyalty or fiduciary rigor, and angrily saw some of his colleagues reap big windfalls from speculating improperly in stocks that he also had background knowledge of. He lacked the elixir of originality or the confidence to scarf over a paucity of new ideas with a veneer of savoir faire, as so many big-time lawyers do in order to avoid becoming staff men. And though I learned something about the importance of independence and a certain inner insouciance from noticing what he didn't have, I also observed fairness, dignity, and resilient work habits, and considerable kindness and sense of proportion in him. He did after all take early retirement after that first cancer scare, for other pursuits, and never let my mother scrub the last of his accent out of his speech—the "frawg" and "dawg" he thought lent authenticity to a man. His boyhood dog, a skinny mongrel terrier, had been named Gyp (the man next door kept a coyote pup tied to the back porch), and, like my mother in her way, he valued his origins. Those rangy Texans, glad-handing Oklahomans, and sunburnt Californians—geologists and pipeline men in

Standard Oil—were cosmopolitan in the manner of the Kansan he liked best, Dwight Eisenhower, whose famous smile was much like his.

My mother's unpredictable zest and "Western" effervescence sometimes nonplussed clubwomen at the Colony or Cosmopolitan, the two best in New York, or our own country club, and they might cold-shoulder her at receptions. That is, *women* could, but not the men—with her abundant chestnut hair and that spring to her step, and the flowers in her Saks or Bergdorf Goodman décolletage. Flirtation, not consummation, was what intrigued her, so she was not regarded as a home-wrecker, just too ebullient and gauche, or perhaps neurotic and loosely wrapped. Like my father, she felt ambivalent about their social climb, proud at times of having originated in the unsnobbish Pacific Northwest, yet so excited at others that she'd tipped over backwards in her chair from craning her neck when Queen Elizabeth walked by.

The ties that bind can bolster you and lend you a lifelong confidence, like a birthright, as well as freeing you from retracing an irksome path, whether that be too much moneymaking, social scrambling, or a marital ball-and-chain. Yet they can also make you irreparably flighty, always preparing an escape route in case your partner crumbles and collapses. Once some amount of writing success had untrussed my mouth, I was comfortable talking to women and have needed a woman as anchor ever after—would search immediately for that basic necessity when I moved to a new place, as if to stave off the emergency I invariably expected was coming as I raced to finish each slow book before the floor fell in or a deluge or a war started. Just to eat regularly and be able to sleep was a gift—not to fly off centrifugally. My parents had a rather good marriage, I think in retrospect, though they pummeled each other during their fifties, when life pinched like a shoe. My father believed that caution would stave off disaster, having graduated from law school right into the teeth of the Crash of 1929, whereas my mother, by contrast, was a juggler. Growing up with three fractious brothers, an autocratic father, and two rich uncles to placate—and the idea that she didn't really have much to say, but that dizziness in a pretty woman was puzzlingly appealing—she would try to hold her own at dinner parties with a coy, winsome manner, while advancing ideas that she had no stake in but thought might be provocative enough to set the men squabbling to instruct and impress her. Because I didn't feel scatterbrained or short-circuited (she was all pep, enthusiasm, and piquancy so nobody would notice), I didn't realize how much her vertigo might in fact resemble mine. I too could be capsized. Nor did I feel free enough to write essays—that most direct form of expression—till after my poor father's death.

I LOOK BACK, as I say, with more guilt upon my first marriage, in which no adultery occurred, than on my second, when it did. Amy was a dear, pure-spirited woman, and in four years we'd never quarreled laceratingly. Solicitous of each other, we continued to keep in touch, and wobbled on a seawall overhanging more hysteria than I had bargained for. At the United Nations, however, she found an agile, intellectual Frenchman who lent her reassurance; and somewhat later, an Hungarian diplomat—which, during the Cold War, provoked immediate FBI surveillance of her comings and goings, even within the corridors of the UN. She found out how many elevator operators and maintenance people on supposedly neutral territory were moonlighting as gumshoes. Others stood all-night vigils outside her apartment building when he slept over, and Eastern European voices would call me up to ask if I knew what she was doing: Or were we "separated?" When she finally saw her lover off at Idlewild airport, a handsome female operative contrived to stand next to her, striking up an impromptu conversation and observing the sincerity of her tears.

One looks back thirty-five years to an old love or love affair with special nostalgia because it can't be recapitulated. That was

then; misunderstandings can't be set aright, or lost verve reconstituted. The country of the blind, indeed! Headstrong, vulnerable,
and unreasonable, I seldom wanted to fathom a situation for the
purpose of reaching an accommodation with the other person,
but only to attempt to change her. I was limber physically but
obdurate temperamentally.

So was my friend, Brigit, I would guess. After my divorce, I
returned alone to Europe, living on the Janiculum Hill in Rome
at thirty-two, with a Guggenheim fellowship, waiting for my
third novel to come out. At such an age one meets a woman every
few years whom one could have married. And Brigit was *that,*
although our quarrels sometimes spiraled like water going down
a drain, counterclockwise, as if irrevocably: yet perhaps they
needn't have, if I'd been readier to adapt (or even simply to marry
again), or had appreciated my luck. She was a fastidious, lis-
some Englishwoman in her middle twenties, Folkestone-born and
therefore witness as a little child to the terror of the Nazi Blitz—
the Heinkel and Junker German bombers flying overhead toward
London, or bombing the local docks, and British Spitfires dog-
fighting with the Messerschmitts, which might crash in smoke
and flame. Then, during the early 1960s period of hysteria about
Irish Republican Army bombings in Great Britain, she had been
subjected as a young woman to humiliating incidents and public
scenes just because she had an Irish-sounding surname. Once, for
example, a stranger pulled the emergency cord and stopped a
London-bound railroad train when she noticed the name tag on
Brigit's suitcase. Brigit had left the profession of nursing, which at
the entry level she was finding hierarchally demeaning, as well as
England, to take a secretarial job in a private grammar school,
which she loved, in Rome, where I met her.

On a balmy April morning striped with sunlight, we sailed
from the Italian ferry port of Brindisi to Patras, in the Pelopon-
nese; and overnight again from Piraeus, near Athens, by way of
the clustered Cyclades and the lone island of Ikaria, to Samos—

which is one of the largest and was then among the least-thumbed-over Mediterranean islands—whose marvelous pine forests spread lushly across the slopes of two substantial mountains, Kerketeus and Ambelos. These pines had survived partly because Samos was so far away from any industrial activity and because several conquerors had depopulated the place. Not just Darius, the ancient Persian, but a fifteenth-century Turk: it was, after all, only two miles off his coast. We regularly gazed across the strait at Mount Mycale, in Asia Minor, still wild enough in 1965 to provide a home for a few leopards. One had recently swum to Samos during a forest fire and became the last free leopard ever killed in Europe. Even during our half-year stay, warships and fighter jets from Greece and Turkey often maneuvered aggressively, close to Samos's shores. Nevertheless, this had been the legendary home of the fabulist Aesop, the mathematician Pythagoras, the astronomer Aristarchus, the historian Herodotus, the poet Anacreon, and the goddess Hera, protector of all women and the Queen of Heaven.

Brigit returned to Rome after our expedition, and a decade later, when I looked her up (having dedicated a book to her), I was pleased to see her well settled in an apartment near the Tiber and the Vatican, working for the UN's Food and Agricultural Organization, with a hideaway up near Siena that she could duck off to in her car on weekends. But when we arrived on Samos that first morning we were both more innocent. After a splendid dawn approach along the mountainous deep-water bay to the micro-port of Vathy, we sat down to eggs and rolls on the quay, then hunted up a hotel room. I went to a barbershop for a lathery shave, where, in no time, gabbing around (Samos being almost devoid of tourists in those days), we were put in touch with a local attorney who wanted to rent us his tile-roofed garden house next to the water a mile out of town for about a hundred bucks a month. He was gray-faced, in low spirits, quite bereft because his youngish wife had just run off to live with her lover in Athens.

The little weekend house had been her pet project and was therefore now a source of sorrow to him. She came out once to check
on our stewardship of it, looking winsome, somber but replete.

Up early in order to read or work, Brigit and I would stop at
noon to swim below the patio and eat lunch, and again at three,
usually to make love and brew some tea to enjoy with honey and
the yogurt that we bought fresh from a dairyman who came by
leading a donkey carrying a packboard. Samos's sweet wines had
been famous since antiquity, and there were also olive orchards
and sloping pasturelands, under the forests, for sheep. We'd walk
into the hills for an hour or two, as the belled flocks drifted home,
and wind up at sunset downtown, sitting beside the dozen fishing
caiques moored for the night (each with a pair of eyes painted on
its bow), sipping ouzo, nibbling calamari or grape leaves stuffed
with rice, before moving into a taverna, after darkness fell, for
moussaka or souvlakia, followed by a moonlit stroll back to the
house.

Some days we'd catch a bus to Manolates or Tighani, Mytilíni
or Marathokambos, and hike to a high monastery, or to an acro-
batic waterfall up in the sun-shot woods, or an isolated beach
where seals could whelp, or a hidden oubliette of a cave set like a
slit underneath a cliff, or a two- or three-thousand-year-old ruin
from which a tyrant such as Polycrates had held sway. And what a
walker Brigit was! Her long-legged, swiveling stride was stronger
than mine, and I was such a jerk that although she let me be the
boss in lovemaking, I resented it when she outstripped me on our
treks. I was competitive instead of adoring. *Now* I would love it,
assuming she were willing to stop and generously come back to
dawdle.

We circled Samos in the course of our excursions, sleeping in
private houses wherever we ended up, on different trips. In the
most remote villages, such as Kallithea, reachable only by a foot-
path, people told us we might be the first foreigners to have
walked clear around the island since the Germans had occupied it

in 1941 and sent a patrol commanded by a lieutenant to look at every settlement in the hundred eighty-four square miles. The Germans had garrisoned Samos mainly with Italian troops; then abandoned most of them in 1943, evacuating their own personnel as the fortunes of war swung the other way and British bombers hit Vathy. The stranded Italians were left to be hunted down individually by Samian partisans with rabbit guns. Eventually the survivors climbed toward the waterless peaks, more than four thousand feet up, and were shot when thirst drove them out of their last hiding spots. Above Kallithea, we found the skeletons of several lying in the mouth of a cave, where the Greeks had contemptuously left them unburied. In the late 1940s, Greece's civil war had raged in miniature in these same craggy redoubts again, with the local Communist guerrillas finally losing to the better-armed Rightists—though they held out much longer, sniping from the serrated ridge tops, because their families sometimes got food to them and they knew where the springs were, high up.

Brigit and I suffered through our own meager wars, unfortunately, which we always patched up tenderly afterwards, but not before inflicting injuries. We had each learned to be inflexible and to distrust the opposite sex while struggling for independence from difficult parents, and we could be remarkably blind to one another's point of view. I was dejected, too, because my novel, *The Peacock's Tail,* when it came out, flopped. *Time* magazine had sent a photographer from Athens to take my picture, but then the review they published was bad. Brigit, walking sympathetically home from the post office every morning empty-handed, found me so uncommunicative and our prospects as a couple so dubious that she suddenly took off. The problem was that she didn't tell me she was leaving or write a note. She simply vanished, embarking for Chios, where she stayed a week or more. After searching our favorite haunts and sleeplessly imagining that she could have come to harm, I reported her as missing to the police. To my surprise, however, they reacted not by suspecting suicide, but that I might have murdered her. They put a watch on me. A female detective met Brigit's boat, after she sent me a postcard from Chios announcing her return. And she looked lovely indeed, swaying shyly, gracefully down the gangplank in a blue dress that set off her yellow hair and tanned arms—then astonished that her disappearance had drawn the interest of the police.

Another, shorter idyll ensued, of turquoise swims, good fishy meals, and work and sleep, interspersed with strenuous hikes uphill from Karlovasi, Platanos, or Vathy. But again we quarreled. Our romance had stalled. And one impeccably azure day, when Brigit wanted to choose a shortcut home from the Zoodóchos Pighi monastery, down a vertiginous bluff; and I said, *No, please,* this would be a mistake—she started anyhow. But with a heart-piercing cry, she nearly fell. She managed to catch herself and scramble up the precipice again. Yet I realized that we were in a deeper fix than I had understood; and indeed if she had fallen, I might really have been charged with murder, this second time. So we crossed to Turkey for a placid three-week tour—Ephesus, Sardis, Izmir—before parting wistfully at Istanbul's airport and affectionately calling it quits.

Again, as with my divorce from Amy, from decades later it doesn't seem to have been necessary.

PUSHING THE EDGE

When I'd turned thirty, I'd decided I was going to need a second career. My first two novels had sold, altogether, about six thousand copies, and the third was taking five years to write, for an advance amounting to a thousand dollars a year. Corresponding from Spain (where the money I had inherited from my grandmother was running out), I obtained a job at the New School for Social Research, in Greenwich Village, at three hundred dollars for the spring semester: the class to meet for fifteen weeks. Facing the students, I had to psyche myself up to outwit my stutter. Adrenaline could do it for a short while, if I felt inspired. That simple chemistry seemed to help; and being inspired itself distracted me from the sort of self-consciousness that tripped me up, rallying my own spirits as well as the students' to the honor and urgency of the vocation if you chose material that was important to you and dealt honestly with it. The natural voice and pace of story-telling could bridge the gaps between all of us with the basic reactions that we all share and that fiction ought to play on.

My breathlessness probably added a frisson to the points I tried to make about the brevity of time we had to write our books and the stamina required. But it was also a drag, and my career sputtered. At the New School, the night classes included a mix of college-age dropouts and housewives, retired businessmen, and other midlife aspirees, such a selection that I seldom afterwards encountered a student I hadn't met before. Sometimes the retired businessmen complained to the dean's office that my handicap sabotaged my capacity to teach and I should be replaced, but the women tended to favor keeping me until I got beyond the problem. After three semesters, I moved on to teach at Rutgers, Sarah Lawrence, and the City College of New York in the later 1960s, and came to love teaching. Doing it part-time lent a pivot to my monkish week and also educated me. Eventually I gained enough experience to feel useful beyond simply providing an ear as people attempted to think about their pasts and come clean about themselves—or maybe learned to read better from working at the craft. It was worth doing even if nobody in the class ever wrote professionally, I thought, because of the rhythm of analysis, composition, and reconsideration that is at the heart of writing well once your memory has been greased—the daily lope, I called it, which had that special joy of craftsmanship, regardless whether the tale being told was sad. This disciplined lope is what all work is about.

Wealthy kids from Sarah Lawrence inevitably were different from those at City College: their journals sometimes horsey, their love affairs more whimsical and peripatetic, their closets ampler, to cushion a breakup. But face to face in semi-friendship, if you could teach one bunch you could teach another by paying close attention to *what is important to this person?* The to-and-fro, if serious, conveyed the same things about literature as both a solace and a resource, and the masterpieces that they read could lie like money in the bank inside their heads to draw upon later. Rutgers, in New Brunswick, New Jersey, was my first state university, and the students were neither the alert, multicolored, overcrowded underdogs of CCNY, nor sleekly in-therapy and hyperesthetic. They were omnivorous, degree-minded, and the professor a dish on the buffet table to be devoured. I taught Thomas Mann's *Confessions of Felix Krull,* Kafka's *Letter to His Father,* Turgenev's *Sportsman's Notebook, Life on the Mississippi, My Antonia,* and other marvels. One gets unfair credit as a teacher for the books assigned, if they are sufficiently lustrous and kinetic—almost as though you'd written *Moby Dick* as well as introduced it into the students' experience. Genius is so palpable to an enthusiastic young person that great books can chaperone themselves; you need only arrange a meeting.

When I moved on, a good deal later, to stints at the University of Iowa Writers' Workshop and the University of California at Davis, I was introduced to faculty politics, tenure tension, and related anxious stuff, not on my own behalf but through friends who had academic careers to pursue. And a "godfather" was quite essential, as it was in determining at what stage poets got their Guggenheims and Pulitzers. Universities were homey places for people who had landed solid berths, or those who wished to be gypsies, like me. The offices and housing were cozy. The clamorous dining halls swarming with nineteen-year-old folk reinvigorated me, and there were football games and wrestling meets or drinking hideaways for the evening, and a big buzzing research library, as warmly glamorous as it had seemed when I was in college myself. These were pleasant sanctuaries, with a different regional climate, culture, and topography, soothing to writers trembling on the edge, like Raymond Carver—who showed up broke in Iowa City while I was there—or my friend Richard Yates, brittle and recently burned in an apartment fire—both trying to stave off a shattering fall. Nelson Algren and John Berryman, a decade or two earlier, had famously flamed out in Iowa City while trying to reclaim their self-sufficiency; but for me, not a drinker, more controlled, the need for these change-of-scenes was subtler, though perhaps as great.

I loved the brown Iowa River sliding by my hotel room; and visiting old-time, horse-plowed Amish farms out in the country but nearby; and crossroads Mexican bars where the migrant workers hung out; and the winter groves of leafless cottonwood trees along the Mississippi at Moline, where a dozen bald eagles that had migrated down from Canada could be seen on any February day. I loved the long coal trains rattling past my window at night, and the Iowa pride in maintaining a windblown optimism. Or—in California—the red oleander and white-blossomed pear trees, the sycamores and valley oaks and silver birches, the flights of ducks and egrets over the bywaters of the Sacramento River; the Mediterranean balminess, but "tule fogs" in February; the large ketchup factory in Davis, with tomato fields spread around. I lived with other transients in a motel called Ivy Towne, at 801 "J" Street (though everyone in California seemed transient to me), and formed friendships with graduate students and other teachers—much as in Iowa. Putah Creek wound through the prettiest part of Davis, where big trees had been allowed to survive. Pond turtles and carp and breeding mallards swam in the turbid water. Walking into the fields around the veterinary school, you could see yellow-billed magpies and burrowing owls; and there was a hawk rehabilitation center.

Professorships debilitate most writers who take them on long-term, I think: not so much because they have to work hard, as that they don't. They become shallow-rooted, like bonsai trees, and stunted. But irregular, gypsy teaching appointments seem to refresh a good many writers I've known, providing a break from the brutal condition of being freelance with three months of white-collar respectability, a classroom audience, "office hours," a department secretary, a salary check, and the bracing balm of living surrounded every day by hopeful young folk with every sort of possibility ahead of them: or at least who think so. The grizzled, gimpy writer, though probably not accomplishing his best work in such a setting, is nevertheless bewitched a bit during the semester into imagining that, although pushing fifty or sixty, he maybe *does* have a great book in him if he'll just keep on struggling. And it's fun and even useful to him to feel that way. He writes a better couple of chapters with that brief boost.

Davis was on the Chicago–to–San Francisco rail line, which was a kick. That's how I got there from New York, and left again for places like Berkeley or Moab, Utah. The engine of money and industry underlies the placid surface of any college town because legions of uneasy parents are toiling away to pay the bills. But almost anywhere can be like that if, for example, infrasonically you sense the subterranean tumor that, lurking in somebody's torso, is altering his face. The difference is that college kids don't have a tumor yet, so there's a blitheness as you stroll the paths. Nobody's shot their bolt; nobody's cards are eclipsed on the table. And teaching, if done well, can be the Lord's work, genuinely altruistic, though it took me quite a while to feel my way into realizing this. I needed the validation of being a "writer-in-residence" first, and the income. Though my two wives had never supported me, they'd certainly paid their own expenses, as well as providing my health insurance through real-time jobs and anchoring me in place in New York apartments where I could settle in in reasonable comfort and work with a will. Homelessness would have been an absolute abyss for me, a spiral down. Even during my interludes of far-off teaching, I needed a tether in the evening— the hugs of a Beowulf scholar in California, of a middle-aged social worker in Iowa City, of a chef at Sweet Briar, a librarian in Wisconsin. The intensity that draws some women to itinerant artists is not a put-on or voluntary, but more like a long-distance swimmer who needs a rowboat to rest in in the evening: *without you I will drown*. (At the University of Iowa's Writers' Workshop in 1978, I was told by the director, when he picked me up at Cedar

Rapids' airport, that it was "not required" that teachers sleep with some of the graduate students, but it was "expected" that they would.)

I came to Bennington College in 1987 at the kind recommendation of the *New Yorker* writer Arturo Vivante. Seventy or eighty stories of his had been published there, until they'd dumped him. Now he was locally celebrated in southwestern Vermont for teaching Tolstoy and for his gentle, white-haired eroticism, gazing into any mature woman's eyes (sitting on the sofa with her at a party) and telling her that *those* portals were much more intimate than any other. A Roman, he was trying to write a memoir about being interned on an island in the Saint Lawrence River during World War II as an enemy alien after his family had fled Mussolini (his uncle had died in a small-plane crash after scattering anti-Fascist leaflets over the city). We also had in the literature department an elegant Englishman whose father had tutored the children of real royals in math; and a rumpled Africanist, fresh from teaching English in Nigeria; and a Chaucer specialist in a sixties leather jacket whose chief claim to fame was having known Paul Goodman and who had been trying to finish his Ph.D. thesis for a quarter-century; a Dickens maven, his protégé, who was about a decade behind on *her* thesis; a poet of my own age who had published a promising first book twenty years before but almost nothing since; a somewhat older freelance scholar who had never graduated from college but over the decades had compiled a forty-thousand-page unpublished diary; and also Madame Chiang Kai-shek's (I think) grandniece.

It was a funny place, in other words, headquartered in a converted dairy barn—a fifty-year-old experimental college, specializing in radical innovation in the arts, that had gone deeply to seed. Kenneth Burke, Bernard Malamud, Theodore Roethke, Stanley Kunitz, John Gardner, W. H. Auden, R. W. B. Lewis, and Stanley Edgar Hyman had formerly taught in our literature department, but we were now a sort of academics' tag sale, the protégés of former protégés. With a declining student enrollment, Bennington was coasting downhill on its reputation, on its way to becoming history, and doubly like a cockeyed *Titanic* voyage because so many of the faculty still believed, in the 1990s, in a kind of bohemian *droit du seigneur*, whereby they could sleep with undergraduates as a sidebar to academic freedom, like being forever free not to publish or otherwise excel in their chosen field once they had obtained a professorial position. In a single semester one teacher I knew impregnated two of his students; another, earlier, had given one of his the herpes virus. Incongruously, we had the most expensive tuition in the country, yet next to no endowment fund because part of the radical premise of the place when it was founded in the 1930s had been that an educational institution shouldn't be beholden to the rich. There had been five presidents in little over a dozen years, and the high tuition had become a kind of fiction because as word of Bennington's decline got out among the better secondary schools, wealthy families ceased to send their children and the classes filled up with scholarship kids who couldn't get into front-rank conventional colleges.

They were intriguing, however, off-beat and kooky. Helping them might entail explaining to a boy why he should stop sleeping with his mother when he went home for Christmas vacation—or in an extraordinarily intensive, drawn-out process, uncovering for another boy some of the ramifications in his life of the brutal beatings he had been subjected to since infancy. A girl, too, who had circuitously wound up at Bennington after a brutalized childhood might discover in the course of writing an autobiographical senior thesis that her "aunt" was really her mother, and vice versa (a prison sentence having caused the two women to switch)—or that the wall of silence about a missing father never *was* going to crack. We had a "Bastards' Club" of kids who regarded themselves as that. One girl knew only that her father had been an actor who had once appeared as a Grape in a Fruit of the Loom commercial. Another had supported herself since the age of sixteen by slinging hash, having run off from a hit-'em-with-the-belt-buckle Seventh-Day Adventist family; and I had a Red Power Mohawk, an extremely angry young man, to acclimate; and a rattled woman who had worked in a plastics factory from the age of fifteen; and numerous waiflike foreign students. It provided real work for a teacher but because I had just one child of my own, I took to the challenge with considerable gusto. Except for the financial constraint of being a free-lance essayist, I would have preferred to have had three or four kids, so this gave me a chance to fill some of that void: not to mention the enjoyment of poring over Homer, Cellini, Dickens, or Flaubert again, new classics like *One Hundred Years of Solitude,* and trying to communicate why they were so fine.

The town of Bennington had been Grandma Moses and Norman Rockwell country, but also was steeped in the sterner stuff of Robert Frost (buried there) and Simon Fraser, one of the continent's salient explorers, born in the town to a Tory family (his father died in a Revolutionary prison, and they then went to Canada). So was that line of my own ancestry, as I was surprised to discover from family papers. Their three-story brick public house is still standing, near the Bennington Battlefield, on the present New York–Vermont border, where my great-great-great-great-grandfather, David Mathews, fought on the rebel side. He was called "Tory Mathews" later on, however, when the rumor started that he had built his tavern with Tory and Hessian gold given to him after the battle by King George III's two colonels, Pfister and Baum, who had been carried, mortally wounded, to his log cabin—one of the closest farms to the battlefield—to die. This was a time of political confusion. "Yorkers" tended to be somewhat Tory and Vermonters more sympathetic to the Green Mountain Boys, but even one of Ethan Allen's brothers, Levi Allen, had sided with the British. Though David Mathews's land straddled the boundary line, he had married into the Fay family, which owned the Catamount Tavern in the middle of Old Bennington, where the Revolutionary militias had been organized. That might have both protected him and got him enough financial backing later on, when he became a successful, glad-handing publican himself, open to all viewpoints, but the object of jealousy. He and Lucy Fay produced twelve children, and had a notable manumitted black servant named Pomp, who lent flair to the establishment. After Vermont (formerly "New Connecticut") became the fourteenth state, in 1791, Lucy and he helped start a neighborhood church alongside the purling Walloomsac River near the foot of the hill where the battle had been fought. It has since fallen in, but their marble tombstones remain in the grown-over graveyard. The same research I did for this book turned up the information that another ancestor of the same vintage, Abiel Buttrick, fought at the North Bridge in Concord, and five later Buttricks were friendly acquaintances of Thoreau in that town, mentioned in his *Journals* two dozen times: which pleased me. A couple of them shared their hunting lore with Thoreau; and "Mrs. Buttrick says that she has five cents for making a shirt, and that if she does her best she can make one in a day."

I LANDED in Bennington at fifty-four with eye problems that gradually rendered me legally blind: one reason I didn't move on. The other was that I soon fell into lasting involvement with Trudy, the college's therapist, who functioned, it seemed to me, like "the little Dutch boy" of the tale. Her fingers kept plugging the holes in the dike, keeping the seas of psychosis in our shaky student body from breaking through. Though teaching was still a secondary occupation for me, it was about time to settle down and save some money for old age; nor, if I went totally blind, would my natal city be the kindest place to live.

Except for some highway strip development, Bennington was

now a chapfallen, down-at-heels sort of town of sixteen thousand people, in a comely location. The mills and little factories nestled alongside the river had been closing and the shopfronts on Main Street emptying. The colonial houses that lined the bluff up above, like white museum pieces where the managers and professional men and other white-collar people had used to live, were instead being sold to summer folk or to couples partly retiring from the city—admen or investors who continued to keep a pied-à-terre and some office space in Manhattan for seeing old clients and going to the theater and lunching with friends. The town's blue-collar pep and the college's brainy zeal had about played out, and town and college were treading water. A battery factory and other plants had folded, and although the college's traditional disdain for conventional credentials had kept bringing it new teaching talent—like a rhizome growth somehow materializing from underground—that wasn't happening anymore. Our pro-tégés of older protégés, who themselves hadn't panned out, looked for weak candidates when hiring new teachers, who wouldn't threaten their jobs by standing out. Nor were the last-minute alumnae donations that so often had kept the place going still drifting in.

A new president, Elizabeth Coleman, had been brought aboard to attempt to remodel the place. She was an angular, intellectually pretentious, but brusque, forceful, if not slightly cruel, adminis-trator, whose style was more bluestocking than bohemian. The previous female president had carried on with an American his-tory professor, although married. But ours was a warrior, instead, who had a fuzzbuster on her car and sometimes talked turkey to errant male students "man to man," as she said. After prudently casing the joint for several years, she managed to persuade the board of trustees to fire a third of the faculty, including, as if coin-cidentally, the ones who had set themselves up as sexual emirs with student harems. She was an astute judge of character and took about six years to figure out and implement her careful moves, although nineteen of the twenty-six teachers did file a law-suit afterwards. It reminded me a bit of the French Revolution in that, besides the amorous satraps and petty tyrants being whisked offstage, good people, too, disappeared. Killing is corrupting, and once the tumbrils start rolling, they're hard to stop. You're sur-prised to see a friend of yours on one of the carts going to the guillotine and want to step in front, but the momentum of the frenzy carries it by. I'd been almost swept away myself in 1991 and was again in 1994. Academic politics are notoriously insular; and I don't believe in tenure for artists anyhow. But I felt sympathy for our sacked German-language teacher, weeping, and a Peruvian Spanish teacher, two nice-guy philosophy professors devastated, and a little later, a liberal Chinese teacher and translator of Con-fucius, who had spent two decades in hard-labor camps in his homeland. I've written about this in an earlier book, but the con-troversies involving academic freedom continued even into the millennium year, when another philosophy teacher was summar-ily dismissed in the middle of the term for criticizing the adminis-tration; and other faculty quickly left in the tense atmosphere. Free expression is at the core of the traditions of higher educa-tion in America. Without it, a campus is not a college; and my position varied according to the circumstances. We now needed a healer, and we had a warrior; and back in 1991, when I had been in jeopardy, both the American Civil Liberties Union and the Freedom-to-Write Committee of the writers' organization, PEN, which normally deals with foreign dictators, came publicly to my defense.

Yet my major anguish in this period was the onset of blindness that I've already described, when I had to "map" the students in my classrooms. Several used to drive me up to my place in Barton, in northern Vermont, on weekends, a four-hour drive, where we'd burn kerosene, eat canned hash, walk in the ferny woods, and lis-ten to the coyotes howl. Because I am primarily a rewriter and therefore being semi-blind played havoc with my work (I could just do first drafts, composing in my head, not read them over), I would also go off alone, slide under a low-slung spruce, lie on my back, and howl to my heart's content like a sobbing wolf— convincingly enough that the coyotes on the ridge slope sometimes answered me and sent a scout down close. It was a wonderful release. The kids took longer moonlit walks, or pursued a romance, or talked to me compulsively, if wounded, when they could, trying to get at a particular truth about themselves. Blindish, here in the dark or in the candlelit house, my role as a teacher was less handicapped and I could be useful. Essayists of my stripe, going back to Henry Thoreau, tend to be social conservatives but political radicals. Thoreau, for example, disliked the advent of railroads, yet worked to free slaves by the *underground* railway. And, today, political radicalism tries to oppose the megacorporate forces that everywhere are destroying what's left of nature, while social conservatives, on an oddly parallel track, are resisting lifestyle changes that also have the effect of dissolving our individual ties to nature. And although radical politics and social conservatism usually lose, that rear-guard sort of action is not out of sync with what essayists so often do.

As a genre, the essay's appeal includes an accommodation to defeat by means of the phoenix of humor, plus intelligence or postgame analysis. Generally, essayists have begun, like me, by wanting to be something else—a glamorous poet or high-flying novelist. Thus they're no longer as all-or-nothing, do-or-die, as that young novelist or poet. Having found that they weren't Tolstoy, they know there's life after disappointment. They've discovered nourishment to sip beyond what they expected: in the modesty of inquisitive temperance, for instance, and the subtleties of self-dissection, well mulched in contradictions, and amounting to a sort of sidelong narrative—or "novel." Like the mind's, an essay's circuits criss-cross in whimsical logic or ebullient cynicism. Oxymorons are its condiment. The writer might say "I think . . ." in the first paragraph yet present only emotions, memories, or paradoxes after that. Essayists are foot soldiers, solo explorers blazing the trees as they go along, but they can gain height as though jumping on a trampoline and multiply themselves if they can clarify for other people what they, too, have been feeling. Essays are not panoramic like large-scope fiction, but seek analogies, as a short story does, a deft loop-around that lets you look perhaps at your own tracks: *where've I been?* A pell-mell, devoted life is what you want, and essays compile a roster of such things.

Some degree of anxiety can be inferred when people like me become professional gypsies. Itinerancy is bliss only for the nervous, after all. But life *is* nerves, and knowing that may put you in the game. At my ten colleges (Brown and Columbia were others) I've often begun a course by suggesting to the students that they feel their own cheekbones to remind themselves that they already have a death's-head skull traveling with them, and thus to figure out that they may have a productive career of something like ten thousand days, whatever they choose to do—so make 'em count. What you try to accomplish with students is help them to recognize the real thing, whether in literature, or their own projects, or other people. Get ready to be thirty-five, I say, going through a partial list of master writers who hit their stride approximately then—Dickens, Tolstoy, Flaubert, Melville, Joyce, and on and on. Freelance teaching is adventurous, like freelance writing, because you arrive in a new town—Beloit, Wisconsin—where nobody knows you and you have to win your spurs all over again. For decades, my belt has been a money belt containing a thousand dollars in folded bills, a hidden symbol of my freedom to hit the road at any time. Coasting on your laurels is not the best way to accomplish anything, and I like not knowing where I'll be in several months. Some of my favorite phone calls have been when an editor says, "Do you want to go to south India?" Or North Yemen? We're here to see God's world while we can, and within reason, I've tried. That's not the sum of it: the images people go under with are of their children, spouses, buddies, parents, lovers, not scenery. But you report what you've seen. It's part of the reward.

To push the edge, yet loop safely around again, is what an essayist does. He is supposed to be a voice of reason (not unlike when teaching) and, although perhaps seeming to scant moderation, to be a kind of closet moderate, skating across the negligible to try to find the nub. It's hard to accomplish this because you don't really know enough about yourself to pontificate. I say I'm an Emersonian, but my dreams at night are not. Were Emerson's? Do we ever stop rehashing embarrassments? Life is a gauntlet, and the sad marks in the mirror may not only stem from divorce and blunted love, but what we forget—like fretting about atrocities of the French-Algerian war in the late 1950s, even before Vietnam; or in the late 1940s, being designated by the administration at my prep school to be a denizen of the dormitory known as The Zoo; or the alarming two weeks in 1970 when my daughter, while learning to talk, assumed that stuttering was part of what you *did*!

A writer's memoir necessarily leaves out the experiences he has already thought most accessible, in books published before. My beloved Alaska, and my beloved Africa, are elsewhere. Come to think of it, my mother used that word, "beloved," for my frequent attachments to certain ponds or people, dogs or books. And I remember, as a smaller child, being stubbornly reluctant to stop gripping my spoon crosswise in my fist—loyal to my original way of eating applesauce—instead of switching to some fancy adult adaptation. Love and loyalty remain important to me, and I will return a favor decades later. But being a Darwinian, if someone or something is sufficiently disabled, I do move on.

ENTROPY, ALAS

*I*t pains me in retrospect that I didn't give Marion more fun and a better time. We were married for a quarter of a century, and she died in the same year, 1993, that our divorce finally went through. Although from opposite backgrounds, we were both conservators by temperament, which gave us something in common and lent us an extra stability. That, with the illuminating presence of Molly, helped us last. Adultery, which by definition is embedded in marriage and is not like a bachelor screwing around, may have too, unless you assume we would have been better off wedded to other spouses, which oddly enough I'm not prepared to do. I loved Marion, and she loved me.

I'd been born into the Protestant Establishment, my father from the Midwest, my mother the Far West. But though both their families had roots going back to the seventeenth century in New Amsterdam or seaboard Massachusetts, this later scattering of ancestry from the East out to Kentucky, Ohio, Michigan, Illinois, Kansas, and Washington, on top of a failure to accrete much money along the way, had vitiated their links to any claim to an old-family aristocracy. Instead they were strivers on the Manhattan post-flapper scene. My father rode and drilled with the socially elite cavalry unit of the National Guard called Squadron A at the armory on Madison Avenue and Ninety-fifth Street, and sang Gilbert and Sullivan with a comparably select, gala, social-register organization they hoped might float them to acceptance in the subtle new parabolas that they aspired to. But he was forced to resign from Squadron A for screwing up a dressage exhibition. Nor did the Blue Hill Troupe save him from the "nepotism" which he said caused him to be passed over for the partnership at Davis, Polk, in 1940. Thus we retreated to the Connecticut suburbs, where the pressures were different: of the country club and commuter-train club car, of midtown New York business clubs and a web of acquaintances in the oil business; and for my mother, of church groups and garden clubs. At Saint Bernard's School, off Fifth Avenue, I'd had to box publicly before an audience of parents and schoolmates at the age of seven, in the manner of an English schoolboy (our masters hurled chalk at us if we acted up in class)—though I'd cried, unfortunately, while doing so—and played soccer in Central Park. Now, in the country, at a private day school, I played first-team football at thirteen, which I liked much better (I was a lineman because without my glasses I couldn't see)—but was also required to take tennis and golf lessons, which I resisted because I already recognized that these were a coded form of categorization and how important it was to my parents that I not backslide out of the station in life they had attained. The tennis racquet was a social and financial badge, like the Greenwich cotillions where Lester Lanin, the society bandleader, himself used to ask me if I had forgot how to smile. Though we made peace during the months when he was languishing with bowel cancer, I ended up mostly disinherited by my father when he died. I'd turned socialist and enlisted in the retrograde Harvard mold represented by John Dos Passos, John

Reed, and Thoreau, and my first short story had been about rodeo cowboys, some of whom I had also managed to rub shoulders with.

In 1968, I remarried. I'd dreamt of Amy for years, hearing her voice on the street or in the subway, both of us running for blocks to embrace one another—and despite my bohemian proclivities, I had acquired a distaste for the idea of divorce ever after. Better a *folie à deux*, stressed and buffeted by time, sociology, or psyche, as my second marriage may have been, than such a bland exit. Even our divorce lawyers were partners.

This woman, Marion Magid, was an editor at *Commentary*, the magazine of the American Jewish Committee, and a Barnard grad, thirty-six, dramatically witty, formidably well read. She was a master of conversational innuendo but never cruel, a high-octane interpreter of what was wrong with Tennessee Williams for *Commentary* and what was hip in London and Amsterdam for *Esquire*. Raised in the Bronx, she'd known Yiddish before English and had translated Isaac Bashevis Singer's famous short story "Yentl the Yeshiva Boy" (later a Barbra Streisand movie)—only quitting translating for him because he groped her. She'd acted a bit in the Yiddish theater, her name once in lights on a Broadway marquee, and had written two scripts that the avant-garde photographer Robert Frank made films of. She'd also written and edited for Shlomo Katz at the Zionist literary magazine *Midstream*—her girlhood summers were spent at Camp Kinderwelt and Habonim Labor Zionist Youth camps in New Jersey and the Catskills—and had worked for a TV producer at ABC, at Cleveland Amory's *Celebrity Register*, and for a New York psychoanalyst for several years. She expressed exceptional affection for some of these former bosses, like the producer and the psychoanalyst, and concern at the plight of many talented men and women (such as Lionel Abel's staunch ex-wife, Sherry Abel) whom she knew as they aged: which I recognized as part of her lifelong loyalty to friends. While at Evander Childs, she had refused a proffered transfer to the much classier Hunter College High, on Sixty-eighth Street in Manhattan, for what would have been an accelerated program; then had almost insisted upon going to the City College of New York instead of accepting the scholarship to Barnard, until her brother leaned on her about it. Her tolerance of my impediment—such a departure from her own verbal fluency—was doubtless linked to this largeheartedness.

Marion was compelling, with handsome legs, a wonderful whiskey voice with which to launch her bon mots, a wide generous mouth and cheek structure, shoulder-length reddish brown hair of the coarse, pleasing texture of a fox's pelt, and when she dressed for success in those salad days (which was not ordinarily her habit), she wore short leather skirts, net stockings, and what she called "Krafft-Ebing" fantasy boots. A woman of parts: and I was now marrying into the Jewish Establishment. New York's chief judge of the court of appeals performed the ceremony, and for twenty-eight years my medical insurance continued to be an American Jewish Committee policy. Though I was not her first WASP, nor Marion my first Russian Jew, we were amused by the contrast when she rattled off the names of previous admirers, like Klaus, Gert, Werner, Baruch, Maier. She hadn't been married before, but the love of her life had recently married an Israeli girl, so, like me, she was at loose ends. Her mother, short and intense, met me with alarm and confided to Marion that my Ivy League teeth looked too good to be true, must be bridgework. My mother, tall and limber, sailed to Europe the day before our wedding.

Yet the difficulty I had in speaking, which pushed me into essay writing and nature writing, may have been as big a difference as all this ethnicity. I could scarcely say anything of complexity to a stranger—indeed, such a person was likely to wince just watching me try—whereas Marion was celebrated at parties for lines like how "it should be as easy for an Arab to move from the West Bank to the East Bank of the Jordan as for a Jew to move from Grand

Concourse to Mosholu Parkway"; or the term *semicolon*, coined at the end of her life when, like my father, she lay dying of bowel cancer. Amy's kindness in the face of my handicap had been of the simon-pure, innocent variety, but Marion's patience was also leavened with her sophisticated interest in psychiatry. And her city-woman's curiosity was piqued by my being a nature writer (though of the Joseph Wood Krutch variety, a New Yorker traveling to Alaska for refreshment, not as a naïf), as well as my having been born into the casually anti-black, anti-Jewish, anti-Irish, anti-Italian *joie de vivre* affluence of the majority Anglo culture that had so frightened millions of new immigrants like her own parents, even if I'd subsequently rejected it. Indeed, some of her Habonim Labor Zionist friends visited us one weekend when we had borrowed my parents' house, bearing a ceremonial sugar-glazed ham. During Israel's Six-Day War, Marion had grabbed some kind of journalistic accreditation and flown to the Sinai and slept on the desert floor with a tank commander, and she kept a model tank on our coffee table to remind herself of that victory (also hung paintings by her ex-lovers).

I'd been partly formed by influential Americanist teachers like Commager, MacLeish, and Kazin, though my personality was more like that of the fragile, fractious Berryman, who killed himself (as did my prep school mentor, an English teacher at Deerfield I was fond of, named Dick Hatch), and I'd driven, hitch-hiked, or ridden a train to forty-three of the states before I left college, in my Thomas Wolfe/Steinbeck/Dos Passos fervor to explore America. So when my dreams of publishing my first books were fulfilled, I found that the established writers who championed me in the 1960s were not my fellow Ivy Anglos, but rather Jews like Saul Bellow, Philip Roth, and Kazin. That was no accident, because I'd admired their work and sought them out, whereas I had ambivalent feelings about the suburban stories that John Cheever and John Updike, for example, were writing about settings where I had grown up and which I believed I knew from the ground up. They were not really putting the warts in, I thought (as Cheever's diaries, in his case, later proved), much as E. B. White's Manhattan essays, written for affluent *New Yorker* subscribers who had a stake in what he said, were less complete, convincing, or let-the-chips-fall-where-they-may than when he felt able to speak his unvarnished mind about Maine. Both Cheever and Updike, as well as Malcolm Cowley, did later assist me, especially Updike, my college classmate, who on the strength of his humanity and his ancestral Pennsylvanian roots turned into an outright genius. But in the sixties the anguish that Philip Roth evinced about Jewish bigotry and complacency in *Goodbye, Columbus* was almost a mirror image of what mine had been as a boy in anti-Semitic Connecticut—just as Bellow's boisterous themes in *Henderson, the Rain King, The Adventures of Augie March,* and *Herzog* captured my hobo heart, as Cheever at the time did not. The *New Yorker* that my parents' anti-Jewish friends had comfortably subscribed to did employ Jewish writers, but their role seemed to be to play either the zany, glassy "smart Jew," like S. J. Perelman, whose verbal pyrotechnics were like a crossword puzzle, or roughneck, lowlife specialists like A. J. Liebling, who rubbed shoulders with gangsters, boxers, and corrupt politicos, so that the WASPs wouldn't have to—and who, despite his general mastery, I thought, sometimes sweetened the prizefights and other rough stuff he witnessed for his genteel audience, too. As Norman Rockwell and the *Saturday Evening Post* writers touched up the hard truths about America for a different audience, *The New Yorker* was not entirely truthful about the worlds I knew, either in the city or beyond; and writers I admired more— Faulkner, Hemingway, Nabokov, Robert Frost—were not staffers for anyone, dwelt in no one's pocket, and palliated nothing.

Eventually I was to discover in part of the Jewish Establishment an equivalent grandiosity, a self-preening, callous exclusivity, a cynicism and arrogance, and the leggings of bias and racism just as ready to balkanize America, a Neoconservatism just as sneering and polarizing as the WASP country club set I had grown up with. This was disillusioning, and in our marriage excruciating. But it was a decade hence. In the meantime, Marion and I had met at an Upper West Side party given by Linda and Aaron Asher, good-guy facilitators, whom I had met through Bellow and who had introduced me to Roth. The former, whom I had met through Berryman, was there on this particular evening also.

Marion, like her *Commentary* boss, Norman Podhoretz, was more of a Mailer than a Bellow fan, and more attentive to Irving Howe or Irving Kristol than to my old teacher Kazin, because in that time—cheery as it was—as always, there were intellectual camps. But we were drawn to each other immediately and didn't talk much about credentials, drolly plucking instead at the juxtaposition of our names, Magid and Hoagland. I nodded toward the woman I had come with, a Vassar blonde from Boston named Cindy, who was chatting with Jules Feiffer and who would soon go on to win a Pulitzer Prize for newspaper reporting and marry Robert Morgenthau, the city's district attorney. But I was nettled with Cindy because I'd just introduced her to Feiffer and she had told him flirtatiously how pleased she was "to meet the Shakespeare of our time." Though I liked Feiffer, I'd thought this gauche (more likely was jealous) and so had walked away to meet my future wife.

I called *Commentary* the next day and we fingered the appeal of our exoticism again. My fragility had not put her off and I sensed in her a kindred odd duck. Her poly-sci, Nietzsche specialist and life's love had recently married the Israeli woman, and she was suffering bad bouts of panicky depression, getting by on deli takeouts, and already plagued by the writer's block that would become her principal grief for the rest of her life. Postcards from Edmund Wilson, hobnobbing with John Hollander, Richard Howard, Jason and Barbara Epstein, and chums like Ted Solotaroff, Diane Arbus, Andrew Sarris, Mary Frank, Justin Kaplan, and Dan Wakefield can only carry you so far, like the kudos that I on my side had won. I was more manic, a trifler with tigers and elephants at Ringling Bros. and later in India, as well as with death in its Arctic and later Antarctic guise. I was not much use at anything except writing and hoped to complete my allotted span without diving over the rail of a ship somewhere along the line.

We needed as well as amused one another. I was a professor and professional interviewer who could scarcely speak; she a bachelor intellectual frightened by writer's block and the prospect of an interminable single life. But more important, we quickly recognized that rare and basic affinity: each being a conservator. My work consisted of going out on long forays to try to reconstruct the reality of the frontier by talking to old men in shacks alongside great virginal rivers, or beached in nursing homes with bad legs and cataracts, about old-growth forests and bears and ice. (I nearly called the book *The Old Men of Telegraph Creek.*) She at her magazine and in the cafés of upper Broadway, because of her elegant, deep-water knowledge of Yiddish, was besieged by lonely, audienceless poets, memoirists, and fiction writers, whose only market was the *Jewish Daily Forward*. This was before Irving Howe had published his marvelous anthologies of translations of Yiddish writing, before Cynthia Ozick wrote her short story "Envy," before Isaac Bashevis Singer won his Nobel Prize—and people were thrusting thick manuscripts upon her in which they had invested their lives but *had no translator.*

Our heartstrings were thus tied in a parallel fashion to doomed but historic enterprises that remarkably few people cared to pay any attention to in that winter of 1967–68. Though ignorant of Yiddish, I'd spent hundreds of hours in the same cafeterias on lower Second Avenue or upper Broadway, knew countermen with numbers tattooed on their forearms, and had lived for two and a half years in Europe without ever setting foot on German soil in reaction to this. Marion, by contrast, had gone directly to Berlin in the mid-1950s on a Fulbright fellowship to study Bertolt Brecht, thereby outraging her father—that she would go to Germany so soon after the Holocaust, and indeed would even aspire to be an actress—much as my own contrarian acts and wanting to be a novelist had vexed my father from the opposite side. She was now more into R. D. Laing than Brecht; and in marrying rather than just experimenting in an intense affair with one another, we were both, I think, consummating a wish to be further Americanized— she to enter, me to re-enter, the proverbial melting pot or main-stream. It was not silly. We were both thirty-five, established in our skins, personalities, and careers, and knew what we were doing. But the country's cultural currents soon reversed to our painful disadvantage. The notion of a "melting pot" was ridi-culed. Israel, not America, again became the focus for Marion and her friends. In the 1970s identity politics became the rage, and we were not annealed enough to weather the change, though we tried for a good twenty years.

Both complex, feisty souls who lived by our nerves, we had tried to set our own course in life, and after two or three dates she asked, "Do you ever sleep over?" She had funny tales of other writers who would carefully study the books on her shelves instead of making a pass and then try to put her down for authors she didn't have, while mainly grousing and whining because their own books weren't there. She hadn't expected to experience motherhood, but to burn with a hard bright thinker's light in-stead. Yet, by and by, her pregnancy energized us to marry, as we might have been too dithery to do otherwise. I'd needed to be prompted to marry the first time also (by a stepbrother-in-law)— this passivity in my relations with women presumably being a legacy from my mother, who I liked to say gave me "the fright of my life," as Marion, who knew her, agreed. But no woman who wears fishnet stockings, short brown-leather skirts, and black soft-leather boots should object if her suitor likes to play the gawky, dominated boy in lovemaking; and she did not. The skit just gradually came to seem inappropriate to us after we'd got married and had a baby on the way, and she confessed anyhow that her own kinkiness consisted in not being able to make love as freely with somebody she loved as with people who didn't matter. If she loved them, her libido shut off. Our marriage, with a honeymoon at the Plaza, a happy, proud pregnancy, the birth of our daughter, and our semi-Freudian, demi-Joycean, hemi-Brechtian wordplay—which erupted spontaneously like arm-wrestling (Marion much more adept at puns, less at word choices)—and the quite amazing collage of far-flung lore and expertise that we commanded between us, was a lark, anyway: it being a bit as if my friend Edward Abbey had married her friend Cynthia Ozick. And she phoned our neighbor James Beard to learn how to cook, winning him with her intonation of the single word *Help!* Or she'd begin mocking Elie Wiesel's pretensions at his incessant Park Avenue parties, where he invariably paused for a minute at the tables of canapés and delectables to murmur augustly, *"I never forget the camps."*

She would try to relieve my ignorance of the German philosophers; and then we'd swing over a hundred degrees and begin plotting the points of a board game we hoped might earn us some money, based on frontier predicaments: *"You have lost half your horse herd in a five-day snowstorm while crossing Big Pass." "You have found a nugget worth $75 on Spindle Creek but a claim jumper has just burned your cabin." "You have traded cloth with the Blackfoot Village for a hundred beaver skins but you gave them the flu and they are laying for you." "You have broken your leg but are bartering your potato crop for firewood and meat." "The caribou have changed their migration route. You will have to haul grub a hundred miles farther."* Pioneer Pinochle, as we called it.

At the parties she took me to, I saw and envied an extravagant camaraderie, such as Protestants seldom if ever mustered. Her middle-aged friends, Stanley Engelstein and Sidney Morgenbesser, changed shoes with each other halfway through an affectionate evening and went home like that to demonstrate their love. Her mother, too, and brother Henry were more wholeheartedly cinched together as family than I was used to. It made me glad that I had crossed the ethnic line.

At the Podhoretzes' parties the mood turned tenser, however, as politics, not literary gossip, became the primary focus. I watched Albert Shanker courted and poor Bayard Rustin cozened, around the time of the 1968 teachers' strike in Brooklyn, when black community boards squared off against Jewish administrators. Neoconservatism was an embryo at these *Commentary* soirees, as former liberals reconfigured themselves, feeling that the Civil Rights movement had gone too far toward what would become pro-black affirmative action, and enlisted allies. Or an Israeli visitor would stand up before our seated group and describe with visible relish how abjectly a Palestinian ("South Syrian" was an alternative, jeering term) prisoner might break under the scientific beatings administered off-street in a police van in Jerusalem. Norman and Midge Podhoretz did not betray a visible glee at this, but writers like Malamud, Kazin, Howe, Bellow, Roth, and Mailer no longer came to their apartment, and I remember scene-hoppers like David Halberstam and Gay Talese, who had no emotional investment as yet in this liberal-apostate-versus-liberal sort of battle, dropping in and leaving with a laugh: "Tough stuff." It was like the Stalinist-against-Trotskyite bitter quarrels of an earlier generation of intellectuals all over again— *Partisan Review* veterans who at first had been pals but then made the fur fly in a lengthy, internecine, unforgiving scrimmage— though we didn't know it was ever going to get as bad as that. American blacks and their demands; the Palestinians and *their* demands; hawkishness versus dovishness in the Middle East: and Vietnam gradually crystallized as an additional issue. Marion and I had our first fights that I can remember over the invasion of

Cambodia by American troops and bombers. "Steadfast" behavior by America in Southeast Asia seemed to her to translate into future support for Israel in the Middle East. To back out of one commitment, no matter how wrongheaded it might turn out to be, could precipitate a worldwide withdrawal of U.S. force. Softness at the sight of Asian dead meant softheartedness toward Arabs also.

IN THE GAIETY of being married, then seeing Molly born, and being up with her twice a night, scribbling ideas between times, the knack that I had fashioned in my Canadian travel book for speaking directly to a reader turned into my first essays. I was scarcely aware of how this happened, wasn't imitating any previous model, but at thirty-five inventing my own. Essays are a form which fits a middle stage of life because essays require a certain tone or persona and some perspective or actual thoughts and ideas, not just the passionate narrative of a rushing first novel. I'd found a way to speak to people without stuttering and therefore poured it on, a bookful in just two years, about a fourth of which Marion published in *Commentary*. And Molly was triumphantly inventing herself, too, as we went along.

At her magazine they had realized that Marion was serious about me when, as managing editor, she'd yanked an article by somebody else out of an issue that was going to press and inserted an early piece of mine. After we had wed, she also muscled her friend Willie Morris, the editor at *Harper's*—he looked "like a Mississippi state trooper" and enjoyed being muscled like that, she said—into taking two. But most of them wound up at the *Village Voice* or in later manifestations of *Harper's*, which became my natural outlet. My publication party for *Notes from the Century Before* was given by Random House and the *Paris Review* at George Plimpton's plump duplex on Seventy-second Street with the usual suspects or glitterati, like Elaine of Elaine's. But though I went to Elaine's bar a few times with friends like Wilfrid Sheed or Pete Hamill, who could get tables, Elaine would refuse me entrance with a barely perceptible shake of the head to her maître d' if I showed up alone, not recognizing me as germane. Though I'd been born in a hospital on Eighty-eighth Street near Elaine's, I was categorized as a downtown person, and indeed chose The Lion's Head, in Greenwich Village, as a place to meet friends or go for a break at the end of the day. Oppenheimer, the poet, photographers like Billy Powers, novelists like David Markson and Joe Flaherty, plus sportswriters for the *Post* and *News* like Vic Ziegel and Larry Merchant, were my confreres. An Irish brand of jokey, do-or-die expressiveness prevailed—people calling bookies, wangling tickets to the fights at the Felt Forum or at Sunnyside Garden in Queens. No one was dropped from the rolls of friendship because his career was not going well; the sweet sadness overspreading all of life was assumed—that's why you hugged, drank, bet on the races, and watched football on TV. It was aggressively masculine, but the masculinity was supposed to be earned and eventual defeat presumed. Flaherty's father had been murdered for asking for a clean election at the union. The bartender, Paul Schiffman, was a bitter beached sea captain; Reardon had been an actor; Wes Joyce had tried commercial fishing. Joel had gone to Black Mountain College (not yet a sprightly credential), but mostly set hot type for a living. And Al Koblin had seen too much of the Miniver Cheevy aspects of Bleecker-MacDougal Street hangouts like the Figaro, the San Remo, the Rienzi, the Feenjon, and the Bitter End: the Lethe/Circe ideology of young women in black leotards who offered you acid and beakers of carrot juice if they invited you home, of hip-hop sexual splurging, while time stood still. (Between my marriages, I once fell for such a soul and took her to the Five Spot, the jazz club on Third Avenue at St. Mark's Place, to hear Thelonius Monk play the piano. But when she got inside, she dropped me for the bearded hipster Seymour Krim, author of books like *Shake It for the World, Smartass,* and went home with him instead.)

There were poleaxed people, klutzy people, Kafkaesque people, and one of my former classmates shot himself in the empty chess club he had tried to start a few blocks away. I suppose, to put it in a nutshell, the difference between the "uptown" writers and me was what my friend Frank Conroy did at his publication party for *Stop-Time,* held at Elaine's around this time. His publisher had hired a stripper, and Frank knelt at her feet in front of a hundred rubberneckers and pulled her panties off with his teeth. Not that I disapproved. On the contrary, I would have wanted to do it for real in the privacy of some basement room, but couldn't have performed it under lights as a campy stunt for the occasion. And indeed, whereas Frank told me his best solace between his marriages had been the kindness of Kurt Vonnegut, mine had been the breasty empathy of my Twenty-first Street chum Leonore.

Our family lived almost next door to Oppenheimer's in a huge so-called Artists' Housing Project, one block square and government-funded, called Westbeth, on the Hudson River near Twelfth Street. It had a lot of actors, painters, jazz and other musicians—Gil Evans, Ornette Coleman, Billy Harper, David Del Tredici—and on the top floor, Merce Cunningham's dance studio, with troupers and students coming and going. His own limber stride and riveting face lent justification to the whole funky place, and it seems to have been a good spot to grow up, because a quarter of a century later my daughter and her actor husband still chose to live there. I thrived, too, and Marion was wryly fond of Westbeth, claiming that she felt comfortably middle-class, ensconced in a thirteen-hundred-square-foot duplex in the midst of so many bohemians, whereas uptown, in a smaller, more expensive apartment in a well-heeled building, she would have felt comparatively poor. The West Village maintained its stamp and character better, was cozier and more livable as the years went on than many fancier neighborhoods. Everyone and practically everything coexisted, the drug deals and leather clubs and prostitution in the blocks beside the river, the bachelor career people getting started, the middle-level couples, hetero- and homosexual, raising children or living quietly, and the Gay Revolution engineered in their spare time mainly by other middle-income people, assisted by frenetic "bridge and tunnel" visitors from the Boroughs—plus the throngs of customers enjoying our savory little food joints, our Indian, Burmese, Ethiopian, Italian, Vietnamese, Thai, or Tunisian restaurants, or oddball, raggedybag, cosmopolite shops.

Marion was not a walker: in fact by preference was an extraordinarily *slow* walker. Her mind was her speedy vehicle and worked on indoor matters. But she liked the European low-roofed charm and continuity of Greenwich Village, the stable quality of neighborliness, of greengrocers and wine-sellers whom you knew, eateries with only eight tables, and little triangular parks like Abingdon Square's playground near us, with zigzag vistas of eccentrically colored buildings and a sky that remained close and accessible. The Village had an edge-of-city flavor, and not just because you could walk from these mild climes to Midtown's gridlocked, electric scramble in hardly more than half an hour. It was also because we lived alongside the Hudson, which is so big that it retains its magnificent out-of-city majesty, yet feeds raffish New York Harbor, where banana boats were still tying up in downtown Manhattan during our early years, next to miscellaneous barges, lighters, fireboats, Coast Guard patrol craft, and glamorous Holland-American passenger liners. And because I wrote about this stuff, for me the gritty streets were always juxtaposed to the jumbo flow of Adirondack water and Mount Marcy where it came from; or else the tugboats that I went out on for other stories. For Marion, the nearby area had been an incubator for experimental theater, zany sculptors, Spinozan loners cogitating in walk-up cubbyholes, or refugee intellectuals struggling in

the fashion of Pnin to adapt to the strange New World. From
Bertolt Brecht's son, who lived across the street, to Thomas Pynchon, hiding incognito on Charles Lane, the neighborhood had
remained hospitable to strugglers. But the reality for her was a
slog and then a subway trip uptown to a nine-to-five commitment
of generous but wearying time, editing the work of others, which
drained her of the energy that she had hoped to devote to writing
books of her own. This effort often continued in the evenings and
through the weekends because as *Commentary*'s politics shifted
from the sort of conventional liberalism that most intellectuals
and writers continued to adhere to and it became a spearhead for
Neoconservatism, it lost its dependably graceful roster of well-
known authors and began to publish a new crowd that, however
innovative their ideas were, wrote with their thumbs and required
exhaustive penciling.

REACHING FORTY without ever having broken a marital vow,
and quite a rara avis in uptown or downtown circles for that, I was
restive. Marion used to joke that men ought to have two wives,
one for company and one for sex, and knew virtually no man of
mature years who had been sexually faithful. We'd loaned our
apartment to one of her closest buddies for his assignations.
Another went around town showing off photos of his estranged
wife nude to strangers to "get her married and cut off the
alimony." But she said that what distinguished a decent from a
tacky man was whether he exempted his wife from the messy
experience of hearing at second-hand that he'd seduced her best
friend. Or in another context, powerful editors in the magazine
world divided the ingenues they had access to between those they
slept with and those they brought home to their parties. It seemed
a time of "general copulation," in the phrase from Peter Weiss's
exemplary play *Marat-Sade*.
    Marion said tactfully that she had never had an orgasm and

believed herself not good at sex, though I tended to blame myself because I'd never given my first wife an orgasm either, at least not till after we split up and she came back to visit me and taught me how. It had required the patient yet peremptory tutoring of a couple of women whom I knew between my marriages to rid me of the boyish selfishness that marked my sexuality until I was past thirty. But, absorbed nowadays in a different phase of life— helping to find an adept pediatrician, a lively nursery school, and carrying Molly back and forth, morning and afternoon, on my shoulders—I'd turned into a less selfish person, though more tired or perfunctory as a sexual partner. I was writing at a pitch: my best spate of essays.

Muriel Rukeyser, Ed Sanders, Joe Chaikin, Edward Field, Gilbert Sorrentino, Galway Kinnell, and other writers lived in Westbeth for a while. Kinnell was a friend of mine in Vermont as well, yet Oppenheimer, the shambling, prolific, slightly smelly Beat poet (I don't know *why* smelly; it was more than citric; it was acidic), was my special chum. A good father, baseball fan, mentor to numerous young women who aspired to write free verse (I remember his relief when one of these pretty novices proved still willing to sleep with him just after all his teeth had been pulled), Oppenheimer seemed too often a sad, neglected, impoverished man, and quite bitter at Sorrentino, his old friend, who had published him in the magazine *Neon* in the late fifties but then satirized him in the novel *Mulligan Stew,* in 1979. Sorrentino was very straight and spruce, even natty, when I knew him; did not accept the ethic of voluntary poverty that he had formerly embraced as a Beat writer anymore; and soon left us to become a full professor at Stanford and habitué of faculty clubs. Sanders, on the other hand—a stockier, more athletic guy—was performing with The Fugs, a scatalogical nightclub act whose panache helped inspire Philip Roth to write *Portnoy's Complaint,* Roth later told me. Sanders left us to live simply in the Catskills and become an environmentalist and literary journeyman.

One block square, eleven stories high, Westbeth had been the Bell Telephone Company Laboratory, where several long-distance technologies, as well as the vacuum tube for television, color transmission, transistors for radios, a 1937 computer, and a 1926 movie sound system had been invented. So I used to claim that geniuses *had* worked here. Nearby, Pynchon tiptoed in and out of his midget, cryptic, hidden house, and just off Sixth Avenue, three rather distinguished, very likable writers were living: Stanley Kunitz, Grace Paley, and Donald Barthelme. I used to lunch every month or so at Alfredo's on Hudson Street with the latter, each of us wrestling with our demons—his alcoholism, my stutter: not too different, as I had thought when in the company of Berryman also. Paley and I, besides teaching two semesters together at Sarah Lawrence—riding back and forth to Bronxville in a car pool— had in common our itch to save the world: in her case as a pacifist, a feminist; in mine by describing endangered wildlife.

At strobe-light parties on the less sedate streets around St. Mark's Place in the East Village, I used to see William Burroughs looking on as resolutely impassive as Andy Warhol at the antics of the crowd, and Krim and Allen Ginsberg—two other Beats who believed in stylized stances—plus Philip Glass (my fellow-father at parents' meetings), and perhaps John A. Williams, Richard Yates, Ivan Gold, David Markson, or other nice guys and fellow strugglers. Yates was a John O'Hara figure, Ivyish but pained because having had no father and no money during adolescence, he had missed going to Yale, and did his best work *(Revolutionary Road)* relatively young because of the astringence of that. Markson wrote his best novel *(Wittgenstein's Mistress)* at sixty instead, and Williams *(The Man Who Cried I Am)* and Gold *(Sick Friends)* seemed to stall out earlier along the way, while Glass, the composer, went on to become an international figure. Yates divorced the mother of his daughters when they were young, while I knew him, and therefore was memorable to me particularly as a father because of his conscientiousness, which I wanted to emulate when my turn came. At least he tried to be conscientious, as far as his pills and liquor (or the mental condition requiring him to use them) permitted. Watching Kazin, Bellow, Berryman, Kinnell, and so many other writers I knew undergo the trauma of divorce, or else split their lives with the most flagrant infidelities, while the inevitable bubble of distress merely fed their fertility, made me suspect that I might too.

Uptown writers who were taken seriously included Jerzy Kosinski (who used to call you up and, when you went to see him, hide in his closet until you found where he was), Renata Adler, and Gay Talese. In this transition from the sixties to the eighties, the question of what constituted "making it"—knowing Jackie Kennedy, or making piles of money—was up for grabs. Norman Podhoretz's memoir, *Making It,* brought him ridicule and grief for being cheeky and solipsistic, especially from brother intellectuals amused by the famous closing scene in which two subservient black waiters "vie for the privilege" of tending to his needs. My impression was that he veered his magazine rightward from mainstream liberalism not just for the sake of what he saw as Israel's interests, but the simpler motive of having been wounded by these reviews. Yet my wife, and *his* wife, Midge Decter (some said their marriage resembled the Chekhov story "The Darling"; others, that she was the *Direktor*), who had been a long-time mentor to Marion, veered with him step by step, as well. Marion's aesthetic sense of fiction and sense of ethics were different from Norman's on some matters, and she didn't attempt to change her style of living as the bandwagon began rolling and the sumptuous grandiosity of Neoconservatism increased—didn't wish to move from the West Side to the East Side or ratchet up her party-going—but I could never detect an iota of distance or time lag between her boss's political views and hers, as these swung around by ninety or a hundred degrees. This surprised me and gradually caused me to feel a bit sandbagged—that her political convictions should shift so drastically and identically in harness with Norman's, after the bad press *Making It* received. Of course, there was a larger shift. Richard Nixon and Henry Kissinger were in power, and other Democratic hawks switched parties to support the idea of a brute projection of American force worldwide and a slow-down domestically on issues such as civil rights, or concern for the homeless and the poor.

Podhoretz was abrasive and ingratiating, like many people who are shaped like a fireplug. We had in common a taste for political novelists like Dreiser and Dos Passos and a practical side, disliking excuses. I remember, at one of his cocktail parties, him talking of people who employ the bogeyman of anti-Semitism—pointing at me, stuttering badly in another conversation—"as if he was a Jew applying for a job as a radio announcer and after-wards he said they didn't hire him because of prejudice." Norman was nervous near dogs, however, afraid they might bite him under the table at dinners, and later came to claim that nature and envi-ronmentalism were a left-lib fad. Several men I knew through Marion who had worked for him had quit because "he took up all the oxygen in the room." But I wasn't in that position. What both-ered me was his proprietorship. Once at a small publication party early in our marriage, he grabbed Marion's haunch with his right hand, staring at me, and kept his hand on her buttocks for several seconds without resistance on her part. That I hated him for. I ceased attending these functions, and since the U.S. invasion of Cambodia, had published my stuff elsewhere. The adventures of Elliot Abrams, Podhoretz's bizarre son-in-law, who as assistant secretary of state lied to Congress about the Iran-Contra Affair, and the pronouncements of Jeane Kirkpatrick, his Cassandra protégé, or other stalking horses echoed for me only in the num-bers of her magazine that Marion brought home and the Sunday talk shows featuring her boss that we watched.

The fight for old things whose survival engrossed me—wetlands, wildernesses to be preserved—had no cost to America, even if you didn't care about them as a cause, whereas it began to seem to me as the years went on that this championing of the South Vietnamese regime, the shah of Iran, the Argentinean junta, the Salvadoran and Guatemalan dictatorships, in what appeared to be a screened strategy for assuring hard-fist support for Israel against the Arabs, come what may, did have a price. It warped our foreign policy away from a Jeffersonian involvement with emerging countries struggling for democracy all over the world that would have dovetailed with our best interests and traditions, and perhaps those of Zionism also. (The fanaticism that ultimately led to Yitzhak Rabin's assassination in 1995 had never been confronted, for example.) And I came to believe that Marion's focus had shifted from Isaac Bashevis Singer to Menachem Begin and Yitzhak Shamir. From this point on, we felt an undertow in our marriage, and I suggested, not joking, that we move to New Mexico.

These were patriots who cared about America's welfare, also—and I'm speaking from an acquaintance stretching across two decades with dozens of Neoconservatives. But they simply didn't believe that America needed their attention much. Like the WASPs in the rich, sealed-off suburbs, whose money was withheld from decaying metropolises like New York just when our cities most needed money and attention, the wing of the Jewish Establishment in which I found myself stranded thought that America could drift along quite nicely if their focus was upon Tel Aviv instead. The results for New York, Detroit, Cleveland, Los Angeles of this neglect by both the people I had grown up with and the people among whom I was now living soon became plain. And so many friendships were breaking up over politics in the seventies and eighties in this Neocon vs. liberal, or *Commentary* vs. *New York Review of Books,* little world that our situation differed only in being marital. I was determined that the gravity of divorce not evolve out of it, but especially missed friends of my wife like the stellar writer Ernst Pawel, biographer of Kafka, who were banished. Such a list would be extensive, and the quarrels were so bitter that eventually the American Jewish Committee had to launch a new magazine, *Present Tense,* to represent its other members. Better yet, *Tikkun* was started.

The scathing contempt that friends of mine like Malamud, Kazin, Roth, and many less well known liberals expressed for what the Neoconservatives were doing to Jewish humanism let me know that I was in good company in being alarmed. Lakes of ink were spilled. But what happened to us in particular was that Marion's first love, the Nietzschean poly-sci professor whom she had fallen for way back in Berlin in the 1950s, lost his young Israeli wife to cancer; and this—as he began telephoning daily for solace, a man with heart problems but a roly-poly, untidy vigor, a wispy spade beard, and playful irony—together with other callers, bachelors who were dependent on her in Toronto, San Francisco, and elsewhere for company at night on the phone, doubled the strain. It seemed to me a platonic form of promiscuity, though since I was in The Lion's Head two or three evenings a week—after picking up Molly at school and taking care of her during the afternoon—I can't really say whose loneliness had precedence. We still sometimes had happy weekends, when Marion might bring home the desperate, half-English, half-Yiddish manuscript of a frantic refugee wetly escaped from the Soviet Union, who had showed up in her office clutching the hollowed-out hairbrush in which he'd concealed the microfilm of his Gulag memoirs. Losing sleep, lavishing her free time, she would somehow transmute his anguish to publishable prose, and after it had appeared in the magazine, the guy would win some kind of book contract or teaching post and, safely launched, maybe send her a dozen roses.

My own twenty essays for the *Village Voice* had got me *Sports Illustrated* assignments in the South, and trips abroad—to Cairo for *Harper's,* and on to Cyprus, Jerusalem, later Khartoum, later Sana'a. (I first flew into Nairobi on an El Al plane from Tel Aviv after guerrillas had fired a bazooka at the preceding El Al plane, which provoked much furor on the airstrip as we landed.) We hadn't moved to New Mexico, though we did buy a house in northern Vermont. But it wasn't distant enough, and the five-year itch toward sexual infidelity, which I suspect is built into most men, was chafing me anyway. I bridled before the wall of the taboo against adultery, procrastinated, took refuge in my lack of confidence, dodging possible seductions and making the barriers inconvenient as well as explicit and thus tougher to scramble across. Trips had seemed too temporary for sex, and one-night stands too grubby. But at last I took the easy way—the elevator—on what I billed to myself as a visit to a painter's studio.

There was so much "work" to see in our building—painters' entire oeuvres, actors trying out scripts, and poets poems—that a lot of liaisons occurred. This person, a bar-stool friend from The Lion's Head, was a talented, blue-smocked, demonstrative, zaftig woman of my own age, who drew, as it happened, mostly genitalia. You sat on a board couch, drinking herbal tea and looking out at the magnificently shimmering Hudson, or else at heroic-sized, multicolored vulvas and penises. She was a friend for years, considerate of me (indulgent too to an eminent art critic who was dying of face cancer at about this time; when many people had abandoned him in his disfigurement, she would have supper with him, though he was far too important to have helped her career even if he'd wished to), and stocked with exuberant stories of sailing around South America as cook on a little freighter, and of the young Jimmy Dean and Marlon Brando. But her feminist paintings of women impaled on the spire of the Empire State Building, though they helped break the ice, did not render lovemaking easy. Most of her boyfriends, she said, were jazz musicians; and with me she'd end up in a hammock she had, where we fondled our fantasies, rocking, resting from the world, which I guess is what an affair is for. Like so many of us in that building, she was injured, divided, self-entangled, obsessive, and yet inconclusive, and as musky as her perfume, which afterwards I had to try to scrub off.

Nevertheless, this venture breached the taboo for me, and down in Texas, I fell in love. I was on a jaunt to write about red wolves, and Barthelme had given me the number of a friend in his hometown of Houston who had kicked out her husband of umpteen years a year or so before. She was an art teacher with two teenage sons, and invited me to sleep on her couch, but slipped to me in the small hours. Later, we would meet in the towns of Winnie or Liberty, Texas, or in Cameron, Holly Beach, or Johnson's Bayou, across the state border in Louisiana, and drive the clamshell roads at night, admiring the nearly wild Brahmin cattle silhouetted against the sunset or the dawn, grayish bluish humped animals that could survive the winds, mosquitoes, drought, heat, rains, and frost. We'd listen for wolf howls—these last beleaguered wolves of Texas—howling, ourselves, to stimulate an answer, and one time homed in on an un-oiled windmill that in the moonlight sounded like a lonely wolf.

I hustled another assignment to go out with a bunch of Cajun trappers in their pirogues—some had outboards on them, some were still poled—while they collected their night's worth of raccoons, mink, nutria, muskrats, and a few otters. It gave me a horror of furs. Twice, I stayed for two weeks in a camp on an island in the vast salt marsh near Hackberry, in southwestern Louisiana, ten miles by boat from the closest road, where my four companions, men in their forties who spoke patois French, caught piles, hundreds of creatures, skinning all afternoon and into the evening, with a Cajun radio station in Lake Charles playing softly, or country vocals from Beaumont, Texas—the animals stirring in their heaps because they were easier to skin if kept still alive and flexible, in a coma from a blow on the head, not yet stiff and dead. It was January, cold at sunrise, but not in the afternoons; and all night the coal-like red eyes of big alligators glowed around the banks of our little island, as they hunted for scraps of meat off the carcasses, until the wading birds' braying hyena-chorus marked the brightening dawn. We ate ducks and rabbits that had got their feet caught in the traps, plus gumbos of crabs, fish, or crawdads. When I encountered anybody who spoke English I'd embark on an orgy of note-taking, but whether I knew the language or not, the splendid diversity in how people live and react was always thrust to the fore.

One lantern-jawed gator hunter walked out to my car after his grandkids hollered for him to "come talk to the magazine man." "Yeah I got lots of stories I could tell you," he said. "But I'm dying, I got lung cancer. I don't have time to talk." However, another man, blind, in a different house, who also said that he was dying and about to be carted off to a nursing home, had the opposite response. He grabbed my hand to hold me there while he poured out the intricate tale of his life, his bag of tricks when hunting gators, going right into the water after them with a knife, feeling with his feet, and his prowess at outwitting the rest of the hunters, who often tracked him, and also the wardens who were after him, and the natural history of whole passels of denizens of the swamp, till twilight finally darkened the room and I couldn't see to write.

I went to the annual muskrat-skinning contests and cross-dressing balls and jambalaya fests of the region; to pepper-sauce factories; egret and stork sanctuaries; and sometimes showed up at midnight at our agreed-on motel with mud to my knees— eating shrimps, oysters, and chicken-fried steaks with my friend. She drove to these Gulf Coast beaches from her Texas-style patioed house on Bissonnet Street in Houston. She was slim, lithe, small-faced, and frizzy-haired like my first wife, but less innocent, more socially and professionally ambitious. Her accent was of her birthplace, New Orleans, with hints of the French Caribbean behind that, the ultimate in sultriness for pillow talk. If I wasn't going to New Mexico, maybe I'd move here! My infatuation was so intense that at Houston's airport, going in or out, I groaned.

I wangled other assignments—went to Pilottown, at the Mississippi's mouth, to watch commercial garfishing, and into the freshwater swamps upriver to eat squirrels with bobcat trappers, or visited plantation houses for *Travel & Leisure,* and went to Big Bend on the Rio Grande with a puma hunter. The very name Bissonnet Street would catch at my heart when I murmured it to myself back in New York, but what held me up was the daily delight of waking up in the same house as my daughter, not as an absentee father two thousand miles away, and the fact that I did love my wife to her dying day. And abruptly the momentum broke when my Houston friend's elder son told his father I was at the house and told his mother that his father was coming with a gun. It was no idle threat. We fled hastily to a motel, and I returned to New York alarmed that she should have stayed married for so long to somebody who, months after their separation, would resort to a gun. It was southern enough but too southern for me, and indeed, ten years later, when we met casually, she told me another man she was breaking up with had just threatened her with a gun. That passionate tongue and that thrilling voice came with a price.

What she did when her divorce went through and her kids finished high school was sell her house and move to a bleak windy loft near City Hall in Manhattan, not in order to follow me but to pursue her dream of being a painter in the great hub of world art, instead of as a housewife-professor in Texas. She slept on a mattress on the floor, garret-style, much as I'd done in my twenties; and although I sympathized with her aspirations, the exotic quality that had charmed me was broken. Here on my home ground I didn't want to go through the romance of bohemianism all over again. Her paintings became constructs of slits angled into the canvas, partially laced up, which made me jumpy, and our relationship ended suddenly when Marion's doctor discovered cancer in a lymph node in her throat. Priorities seized me. Fortunately Marion was soon well again.

At some point around then, Marion went up with our daughter to visit her Nietzschean widower at Cornell, who was phoning every night with his Germanic Santa Claus voice, inserting himself as a kind of uncle in my daughter's affairs, to see whether she wanted to leave me for him. At least so I interpreted the trip. But she came back. I doubt whether she could face leaving the city, which apart from Israel was the only place in the world where she had ever felt at home, and she also said that she didn't consider the jumbled household of her friend, with two motherless girls, would be an improvement for Molly upon life in our more focused home, with a decent school. She said she felt guilty too, though, on behalf of her friend and those motherless girls.

There were fewer exhilarating episodes at work with dazed refugees whom her editing skills could dramatically help, and fewer first-rate literary scholars and fiction writers sent stuff in. The old stable of authors was gone in favor of polemicists banging the drum for the Cold War and fisting the Arabs and backing what were called "authoritarian" dictatorships in the Third World. These required laborious blue-penciling, compared to the former stars, twice the time to inject a literacy into their work, as Marion used to complain. Nonetheless, she was wholly enlisted in the war being waged to attack "the culture of appeasement," undermine Jimmy Carter's administration, and with Midge Decter's lobbying group, The Committee for the Present Danger, weld Neoconservative support for Ronald Reagan. I later thought I'd seen a precursor of the ethnic balkanization that— different from class conflict—plagued America afterward.

In a sense the Podhoretzes, often on the lecture circuit, were juxtaposed for Marion with the memory of her father, a furrier who used to come home smelling of skunk pelts and occasionally would push his hands under her nose as she sat doing her homework, to remind her of how he was paying the bills. He had hated militarism. *"General Who?"* he'd say, if somebody farted; and, *"Never desert the Democratic party."* Generals were not just the heroes who won the good wars; they were the fascists who had started them. And like me, and without sacrificing religious autonomy, he had believed in the dream of a New World melting pot, which was now being ridiculed by many Neoconservatives. That idealism of the Depression thirties, like the ideals of the sixties—from voting rights in the South early in the decade, to the Stonewall Inn riot in our own neighborhood in 1969 which had launched the Gay Revolution—had dwindled, however, to mere self-expression. And the black-Jewish alliance of the sixties had similarly frayed to a pernicious jealousy on both sides. The idea that the long epoch of suffering embodied in slavery could be compared to the tribulations of the Jews throughout history seemed galling, infuriating, to many people whose conversations I sat in on. And the Arabs were not simply rivals for a patch of homeland, but surrogates for the Nazis in Germany who could not and never would be properly punished—as well as descendants of all those "Egyptians" who had been battled with biblically, and not just in the Yom Kippur War. At our Seder service, read at a large family celebration each spring, the Haggadah text singled out Arabs inimically, somewhat as Roman Catholic liturgy had demonized the Jews until Pope Paul VI's *Nostra Aetate* changed it in 1965. I felt as if maybe I'd left Anglo racism for another toxic brand, or more anyway than I had bargained for. What now seems like a time capsule was then a buzz saw.

LIKE NUMEROUS MARRIAGES of the era, one could argue with equal cogency that adultery splintered ours—or temporarily preserved it—enabled it to last or shattered it in pieces. Adultery, like "adult" books, has little relation to *adultus*, Latin for "grown," because it can be that still-nineteen-year-old mind sidling down the street looking into lighted windows for a woman alone. Yet it only occurs within the context of a marriage and may really be a negotiating position, not primarily about sex— although I think that nature did in a schematic sense design men for polygyny, once each successive child's period of toddlerhood is gone. Men have a sack of seeds to sow; and such a theory does not contradict the adolescent aspects of cheating on your wife because men were not built to live very long. My wife's telephonic polyandry, as I called it—half a dozen men counting on the intimacy of her wit to buoy their lives daily, nightly, or at least three or four times a week—may have been built into her too. A survival tactic: men waiting in the wings. We stuck together by attending school plays, and for wee-hours warmth, and book collecting, and to confront the bureaucracies that everywhere try to make existence as difficult for you as they can. Her relationship to her mother was exceptionally close—through her fifties, she would converse or cry out to her in her sleep—and that oddity also, while at first an obstacle, may have wound up as a balancing factor that helped our marriage to last. So much of life is spent spinning one's wheels or in the company of lost souls that passions, when not hateful, are a savior. And though I wished for her sake that she'd stop, I liked the rituals of her smoking, the messiness of our apartment, which, like smoking, was not my mode of doing things, but—earrings on the floor, stained coffee cups on novels— enriched our partnership just by its difference.

The phone lines hummed; the streets were priapic; the restaurants seemed filled with forlorn people whose spouses had recently left them. There was a feeling to the seventies as of a creaking, corniced avalanche in the making. In a deteriorating society conduct tends to be improvised, and the sexual license of the counterculture, as well as the Vietnam War and Watergate, had soaked the underpinnings of the country. Union members who might have sheared a hirsute hippie a decade before looked pretty hairy themselves. Traditional loyalties of many sorts were eroding toward the great greed-grab that was to follow, and plenty of people were getting divorced or having an extramarital affair who didn't need to. A friend of mine, in separate years, found two men she loved dead of heart attacks in her apartment—waking up to discover their corpses in her bed, or on her couch—and asked me whether orgasms were all that important: that we, and especially men, should search so hard for variety. I had settled into heterosexuality when I was soldiering as a medic and thus escaped the AIDS epidemic that hit our Greenwich Village neighborhood so cruelly twenty years later. It was unfair that promiscuity of one variety was punished with a death sentence and others not at all. Yet my fragility or brusqueness prevented me from sleeping with anybody I didn't like, so I wasn't tempted to forget that it's the friendship that matters—whether true-blue or a more lemony and slippery-fish connection—and, probably in order to cut the sin of my own infidelity in half, I didn't sleep with married women, or with undergraduate students, or with the loves of friends. I regretted the failure of my marriage, yet not many of the specifics of my conduct, just as I wouldn't have regretted writing a novel that ultimately failed.

While teaching a semester at the University of Iowa, I fell into an involvement with another conservator, a woman who headed a social agency that helped the local elderly to find housing and shop for food. She had written her master's thesis on a nearby community of Amish farmers whose Sunday services she used to take me to, and an earlier thesis on the Indians of the Kuskokwim River in interior Alaska, whom by chance I also visited later on. She was interested in old customs, old heroes, and was a Texan—willowy and yet statuesque, dramatic in gesture yet sympathetic to people who weren't. She lent a comfort and glamour to the Mississippi-midwestern milieu that had attracted me to Iowa City in the first place, and our lovemaking, which was amateurish, blundery, and delightful, was like the high-school sweetheart, star of the graduation musical, that I'd never had. She, again, was my age, and an appropriate partner, but I was too New Yorky to uproot myself and she too bound to Iowa by temper and by her career to move.

I may have been a bit like Marion in the quirk that Marion had warned me of: that psychological damper which throttled love-making with a loved one. It may have reinforced our original attraction to each other, which was honest and in earnest and continued for a decade both in the city and at the country place we had acquired. My best writing in Vermont was done during the years when I was sexually faithful there, the directness of a clear conscience matching the springwater. I'd meet Marion's sleeper at the Montpelier train station on weekends, when she liked to pretend that we were in a Russian novel—*"You will find us very dull in the country, Sergei"*—mimicking the accent. Her sense of humor redeemed the tedium of being housebound, because she didn't like going far from the house outdoors. We were a rare couple, not just as a sort of Ozick married to an Abbey but because so few writers or readers cared a straw about either *shtetls* or wildernesses in that period. My companions in Vermont were generally the back-to-the-land hippies from several communes around. But they would shoot a moose or bear out of season like any poacher, and applauded the parceling out and auctioning off of priceless stretches of wild land. Bookishness, respect for the classics, a real work ethic, and elite causes such as conservation were part of what they were rebelling against. Along with their LSD and cocaine and the pot they peddled as a cash crop to the city, this was what divided me from them.

Marion continued her round of generously painstaking editing of young writers to get their first short stories into print, and of older, all-thumbs ideologues who grew increasingly chesty as their views reached fluency, though her own essay projects remained mired in a writer's block. At the magazine, there was

the disappointment of Senator Daniel Patrick Moynihan, a former contributor, converting from Neoconservatism to Neoliber-
alism, but the concurrent conversion of many Truman liberals to
being Reaganauts. At a Park Avenue party, Leonard Bernstein
achieved the ineffable with Podhoretz on behalf of many angry
radicals by unexpectedly leaning close to him in the midst of the
AIDS panic and kissing him on the lips. Marion began a memoir
of the Bronx which should have been a dazzler, from her stories I
had heard, although that, too, didn't get the time it deserved. At
night her polyandrous retinue of callers kept unbosoming themselves in her ear—sometimes speaking unpleasantly to me if I
picked up the phone. One guy might spin his rotary dial to pro-
duce a long-distance Bronx cheer of clicks. Another mocked the
latest essays of mine that had appeared; my subjects were "derelicts or animals," he said. I did keep riding tugboats through Kill
Van Kull to Newark Bay, or going into the woods with bear scien-
tists, or revisiting the circus for what I might have missed, while
prowling newsmen's haunts where tabloiders hung out, in one of
which I found a bar buddy who became a friend.

To make love with a woman you must pay some attention to
her; and, in the fin de millennium, that had become heterosexuality's saving grace. Otherwise, the proverbial war between the
sexes nearly ensures you will start scrapping with one another.
She will remember her callous ex-husband or oafish dad or the
last chump who tried to manipulate her, or just plain feminist
exhortations. In part, I think, we resent the opposite sex because
of the utter helplessness with which we lay for years in some
big person's arms without having had the later satisfaction of
gradually growing up to replicate them. And thus the wholesale
anonymity of bathhouse same-sex promiscuity that pervaded
Greenwich Village in those remarkable years would not have
worked between men and women, even then. Love is love and sex
is sex; but heterosexual hedonism—including the bold, incessant

infidelities of the married poets I knew, which far surpassed my own—is forced to be different.

My friend was a photographer's model who was finding modeling hard going as she aged. I was hobbling around with a hernia and parathyroid problems and what not, and was touched. Women who make their living with their bodies have always reminded me of athletes, such as the boxers I wrote the novel about in the 1950s and the baseball players I'd admired in the 1940s, with the mortality factor telescoped and accelerated. Her red flare of hair was turning crisper, her figure thicker, and she discovered with alarm that she was descending from glossy pages to newsprint, from top-of-the-line airport magazines to bottom-shelf "skin rags." The brisk professional photographers who paid a decent wage and made a game of it were calling younger models (she showed me her portfolio to test my sexuality through my breathing, the first night she invited me home), and she was left with the Brooklyn shutterbug clubs, where ten or twenty cheapskates got their kicks from ogling her for a few bucks in "dues." Or a solo operator would put aside his camera and try to corner and paw her, having hired her presence for an hour; then in "revenge" trade her phone number to a scary deviant who phoned at midnight to ask her measurements, discuss poses, and threaten and revile her. She did do kinky posing for a comic-strip artist in dominatrix costumes that he supplied, but his wife watched, joking about it, and afterwards they would order in lunch.

Frightened—because where would it end?—she liked men more than women, nevertheless, and understood that her livelihood was grounded in their vulnerabilities. Outrage seesawed with empathy when she spoke of them. And what she wanted from me, apart from literary talk and chat about trips to Africa that she didn't get from her dinner dates, who were mostly business or professional men, was the simple reversal. "Kiss the Queen. Kneel to the Queen," she whispered as I licked her and she came six or seven times, purging those humiliations of the camera for the time being. Nobody should ever enter her again, she promised herself, without first doing the same—while I, for my part, sought spellbound to climb head-first into the primal womb, in our deep-swimming, almost pelagic sessions. Then she'd do air force exercises while I unwound by watching Johnny Carson.

Trotting back through the sweet Village streets—Christopher, West Fourth, Bank, Bleecker, Bethune—with the lights of New Jersey glistering on the wide Hudson at the end of our block, hinting of trips out west to other rivers that were the inspiration of so many writers whom I adored—Cather, Twain, Anderson, Faulkner—I felt I was sideslipping trouble like a quick coyote and assembling a doable life. But when I actually entered our homey apartment, dodging into the bathroom to scrub myself in the shower, I felt guiltier than a rat—trying to figure out if the perfume was finally off, if the soap's scent would mask it—before sneaking into our bed and trying to lie on the far side so Marion wouldn't smell my body if she awoke. Unless, on the other hand, I heard her purring into the phone in the next room, blowing into the ear of one of her polyandrous crew. Then I didn't feel like a bad husband. She was "the darling of our hearts" (as the phrase came to be used) to so many men, each half in love with her, that I was merely sad.

Infidelity can be a cliché, like trying to flee death, or sexual insecurity, or the more casual hoist-a-beer cheer that you "only go around once." It may seem to alchemize lies into white lies by siphoning off the poisons that otherwise might lay low a marriage. I prefer to think ours didn't fit any such truism, but was unique. Would we have found monogamy if we had moved to New Mexico? Instead we stayed put and provided a stable framework for our daughter to go to school and for us to work hard for twenty years, turning out two or three hundred issues of her magazine and my own set of books of the period. We played our word games, read classy novelists, ate good meals, and shared a mostly comfortable bed.

If you teach college students, as I do, you see the results of pell-mell divorce and concupiscence—homes that have fractured into shards, kids whose parents are no more than a ready credit card, who have nearly lost track of where their titular pater familias actually is; kids who are sleeping together not for sex but only for company. I've met the father of a student of mine at a New York party who didn't know what his son was majoring in. An honest-to-goodness sea change has occurred, an Antarctic convergence of katabatic winds and sea currents, and Generation X is a name the young accepted for themselves for a while because so many basics remained undercertainties. The torque applied to marriages now is unprecedented: the speed of travel, of electronic simulation, the cultural crosshatch and dissolution, diverse titillation and rudderless liberation, the no-fault method of reckoning everything, changing jobs like a suit of clothes. Adultery is not biblical, but "acting out." "My Sweet Erasable You." Nothing is binding or even binary, not sexuality or ethics.

What can happen—to choose a down-to-earth, painful example—is that, through the miracle of TV, you can see people dying as you sit in your living room. You can see children shot on the West Bank of the Jordan River by Israeli soldiers for the crime of stone-throwing, and remember meeting, on a visit to Israel with your wife and daughter, the man now responsible for an aggressive new policy of shooting more children—sharing a Shabbat dinner with his family, in fact. And because you disagree with your wife on this matter of shooting stone-throwing children, you wonder how long the marriage can last. You write for a liberal magazine, *The Nation,* which she refers to contemptuously as edited by "self-hating Jews," whereas you tell her some of her associates have been created by peristalsis. But this is not how life is supposed to be lived, with fidelity to party and not person.

And I doubt Marion knew any woman of her generation who
didn't have reason to fret about being cheated on, or any man,
hetero- or homosexual, who wasn't promiscuous.

THE INTIFADA, when it burst out in Israel's Occupied Territories in 1987, was like the Tet Offensive in Vietnam. Although the
Palestinians lost, it proved that the conquering power's assumptions were wrong. In my weeks in Israel and a hundred New York
discussions, one of those assumptions, at least at the leadership
level, had been that Palestinians weren't quite human beings.
Their grief, pride, courage, and feeling for home weren't real,
and reprisals could forever grind them down. For some of my
acquaintances, Arabs were a kind of unsleeping preoccupation,
fully equivalent to the worst bigotry I had ever seen in the WASP
neighborhoods in the Northeast where I had grown up, or the
Deep South in my travels from the 1950s on—though with the distinction that the deeds of the Nazis, or Christian anti-Semites,
were rung in to justify any oppressive measures visited upon the
Arabs. I came to believe that the reason I would hear Gandhi and
Martin Luther King spoken of so slightingly was because of an
unease with the reality of how a King or a Gandhi would have
fared in the Occupied Territories, tortured, with broken bones.

Marion, meeting friends of mine like Edward Abbey or Jona-
than Raban, expressed a corresponding disparagement of their
intellectual integrity, and the character of their books and mine
on nature or the Middle East. I was enduringly touched by the
angry slump to her shoulders, her disappointment and irony
when I would come home sneezing because my allergy to cat fur
had been triggered (most single women keep a cat): "*Have you
caught cold?*" But our allegiance gradually tore, despite the sympathy for each other we still felt. I remember a specific moment
when it registered on me that I was traveling with the wrong
crowd. We were driving to the Upper East Side with a man who, as

evinced by his deep tan and good car, had done pretty well, like so many of her friends, riding the Neoconservative wave. We were passing the Martinique Hotel, a welfare dumping ground at Thirty-second Street and Broadway, whose haggard beggars this lunchtime had spilled over the curb. They weren't blacks on this particular day, so the crux was their poverty, not their race. They were Appalachian-looking whites—bony, vitamin-starved, despairing kids of ten or twelve with faces out of Walker Evans or Dorothea Lange, the product of some social cataclysm in coal country. This man's father, if I recall, had had a horse and wagon hauling junk in Winnipeg fifty years before, and he had taken rabbinical training for a while, but when these hungry-looking, country-looking children asked for change for groceries at the stoplight, he rolled his window up, exasperated that he hadn't had clear sailing all the way uptown. It was of a piece with the idea that the problem of homelessness was being exaggerated by liberals, and the Reagan policy suggestion that ketchup should be considered a "vegetable" in school lunch programs; and I made up my mind with a kind of abrupt finality that I had better cut and run. Yet the twist to the situation was that Marion herself gave almost daily to homeless people, lived comfortably with Molly and me in integrated housing, and like her brother, of whom I remained fond, was never grandiose or swank or cruel. In twenty years I saw her nurture, cater to, and act as a disciple or mentor to many sleek and tony Neoconservatives who were tailored like WASPs and employed the code words of bigotry as skillfully as the most repellent of them, yet neither absorb nor object to the toxins herself.

I WAS IN LOVE with Alaska—and in Alaska—at this point, with a person who had shown up at 7 A.M. at my door in Fairbanks, where I was teaching for a week. We'd talked, and after a side trip I flew down to Juneau, where she lived, and, wildly, we did more than talk. In June it's the loveliest state capital in the United States. She was a public-health nurse who had been flying out alone to half a dozen Tlingit villages on the islands of the Alexander Archipelago on a schedule of troubleshooter visits for total health care, from prenatal to easing old people into a gentle grave. And, like me, she loved hearing old lore and pristine stories, loved seeing wildlife and sizing up individuals who had rarely encountered a bureaucracy or even piped-in electricity before. On a ferryboat we went visiting some of her clientele, now that she was preparing to take up a new job in Anchorage directing the nursing care of all the tuberculosis patients in the state. Our curiosity, our enthusiasm, our sexual personalities jibed in what was the strongest infatuation I've ever had, though she was a good deal younger and more radical politically than me. Linda was a woman of salient mercy, her heart tied to the fortunes of a great many people, fighting for the best she could get for her patients— doctor visits to the remotest places, medevac flights, surgery, preventive measures. She was the kindest person I've ever known and as intrepid as any. Our sorties to Eskimo hamlets and trappers' cabins, traveling all over Alaska together checking on Athapascan, Yupik, or Inupiat people who had caught TB, would imbalance this chapter if I put them in. We stood on the ice of the Yukon River in January and the Arctic Ocean in February, bathed in the hot springs of Chichagof Island, and flew in tiny ski planes, seated on the floor, clasping each other in tandem, to see how a child in a winter camp on the Koyukuk River or the Holitna River was doing. Crooked Creek, Sleetmute, Red Devil, Point Hope, Kotzebue, Bethel, Nome, Tanana, Ruby, Galena, Dillingham, Angoon: we saw them all. She left nursing and eventually became an anthropologist, working with Central American Indians, preferring the single life to do that—then married a Guatemalan revolutionary: her father having been a CIA agent, alas.

Not surprisingly my marriage broke up by and by, though years after some of my friends had expected it to. ("We thought you liked being unhappy," one said; and I have not really elaborated here on how unhappy I was.) Our daughter was at Harvard and headed for graduate school, but because it had been a full decade since more than a couple of my friends had been welcome visitors in our home, Molly knew almost none of them while growing up, only Marion's circle, an exclusion I'd come to resent. I felt quarantined—with Marion beginning to jeer generically at WASPs—distressed to the brink of wanting to jump out a window when I left.

I had formed the long-term attachment with Trudy in Vermont meanwhile, and one day announced that I was taking the bus there, expecting that Marion's first love would at last move in. But he didn't, and so it was I who shared with Molly watchman's duty at Marion's deathbed in the hospital several years later, when cancer caught up with her again. I was not an inappropriate presence, because I still loved her and respected her as a brave partisan for what she believed in. I admired her passionate motherhood and her faithful affection for her many friends, and was present to the last, when the morphine the doctor had prescribed very peacefully suppressed, first her fierce, ebullient wit, and then her breathing, high over 168th Street of the city she loved. Not yet sixty-one, she hadn't written her wonderful book, and that, too, is sad.

My father would not have approved of our marriage because Marion was Jewish, but would have disapproved of our getting divorced more. He broke off his friendships with people who got divorced, and once told me the only excuse for indulging even in infidelity was if you were married to someone who was mentally ill, without specifying whether my mother's spates of hysteria had made him do so. I've said that my mother gave me the fright of my life, but have never been able to define it through a series of incidents which connect like dots. Usually I felt quite at ease with her, confident of her love, though she was so manipulative it could become rather like rassling a python to avoid her snares. In the warp and woof of my marriage, my mother and Marion's passionate father were heavy bettors, although both of them were spirits from a world eclipsed. Yet I think our failures and betrayals were mutual and common to our era, driven by our era, and that our stopgap solutions were improvised in a fervor of stubborn conservatism. I don't think anybody should enter a marriage they later regret. And I never have.

GREENING UP

*L*oving the city didn't prevent me from needing some country. So in 1969, when my daughter was seven months old (and at the same time as I'd begun to write essays), I took another plunge and bought an eight-room house on forty acres near Barton, in northeastern Vermont, plus an old Volkswagon Beetle to get to it.

Marion and I dug out the gravity spring up the hill, where our water flowed from, put in a heater to make it hot, a bathtub, and a little gas furnace to supplement the 1921 cast-iron wood stove. We hired a carpenter to jack up the sills and resettle them (the price of the house had been $5,000), a mason to rebuild the chimney, and a roofer. We filled the woodshed from the discard heap at a dowel-mill down the road, bought more lily bulbs and cultivated the roses, the rhubarb and horseradish, limed the worn old lawn, and spread ashes on the lilac beds, rented a P.O. box, and acquired a library card.

The place, of course, snowballed in importance for me during the next three decades. I wrote about it frequently as I gained familiarity, and in the 1980s dictated a good number of *New York Times* nature editorials from the nearest pay phone, six miles downhill, because our road had no electric or phone lines. We kept chickens, goats, dogs, and Molly grew up with memories of kerosene light in the evening for at least a part of every year, and the sight of deer and the occasional bear, of foxes hunting woodchucks and killdeer soaring, woodcock diving, and snipe wheeling in lariat loops. It was an eight-hour drive from New York to Wheeler Mountain, which curved around in front of us and the house of our only neighbors, Karl and Dorothy Wheeler, but seemed farther because the cliffs looked more like Idaho than Vermont. Bobcats had colonized them, ravens nested on them, and people came from Montreal and Burlington to climb them.

While house-hunting, I'd found that the real estate agent I was looking for in town was married to the owner of the gas station where I stopped to ask directions (which, passed from father to son, was still in the same family at the millennium, as were Barton's other principal businesses; and the village still had about a thousand people). Avis Harper took me along a few back roads where a guy might step out on the porch with a shotgun to see what we wanted; then passed me on to Em Hebard, who had kept a general store, served as a Republican state legislator, and later wound up as Vermont's treasurer. Em had enjoyed, however, a secret, early "socialist" period in Washington, D.C., and Greenwich Village—a job in the Agriculture Department at the tail end of the New Deal, and then a sublet over a jazz club in New York City, where he could sit out on the roof and listen to jam sessions all night. So, whether just through luck, or else insightful fellow-feeling, he brought me straight to the raw corner of Caledonia County where I fell in love.

The Wheelers, though almost eighty, weren't selling their land. Karl had been stationed in Brownsville, Texas, during World War I—and his only child, Hilda, was there. Then after the army, he was employed as a railroad fireman near home, until the Depression derailed that job, and he took over his father's farm, under the twenty-four-hundred-foot mountain that bore their name. Unlike Dorothy, he had plenty of kith and kin around, who, like Dorothy herself, gradually became my friends. Dorothy had grown up in the Shaker colony in Canterbury, New Hampshire, where her father was the handyman after her mother's death from TB (and she took an unsentimental view of those crabby Shakers). Making do with Karl, she had sold cottage cheese and buttermilk, cream and pies, eggs and cakes to the summer folk on Willoughby Lake, going the five or ten miles by horse and wagon, and had boarded a few of the jitterier single ones in her spare room, when that sort of arrangement flourished as a custom in New England. Best, she'd liked writing a weekly column for a newspaper during their salad days while Karl was on the railroad. Now, the big cow barn had fallen down, as well as the sugarhouse. Even their "Wind Charger" windmill for sporadic battery power had broken. But they were comfortable on the old place and called Karl's nephew at suppertime at 5:15 each afternoon on a CB radio to tell him they were okay.

Next door to the Wheelers, in the only other house on this four-mile stretch of dirt road—and no road paralleled it in either direction for at least another four—lived the Basfords, who *did*, however, want to sell. Donald was a housepainter seasonally and otherwise made a poor living brewing corn whiskey that he sold for $1.50 a pint, and bathtub beer for 35 cents, if you supplied the bottle. Kay, the humorous English war bride whom he had brought home a quarter-century before, cleaned house for the pharmacist's family downtown, and warned me in all fairness that in the wintertime it got so cold here that their rabbit-dog would jump into the oven in the morning when she first lit the stove. Also that the man who had built the house, around 1900, had shot his mother-in-law and, a few hours later, himself. She pointed to the bullet holes and said, not her, but other people suspected the presence of a ghost.

Kay was eager to achieve the benefits of electricity. They had given up their couple of cows, and an attempt at Christmas tree and ginseng farming, and did subsistence vegetable growing and ate deer meat. In the family Bible Kay kept a clipping from the *Caledonia-Record* of the time when Donald had caught a $65 bobcat skin. I got to know them pretty well after they had ceded their house so gladly to me; and their story is a sad one. Donald beat her; she fled one midnight, hitchhiked to safety, and returned to Britain for three years; then came back to nurse him through his strokes and decline. Donald was a saturnine, unrelenting iconoclast, a north country agin'er from the get-go— about politics, religion, social norms, and what-have-you. Unlike Karl's relatives—sometime hunters and trappers who also ate raccoon or bear or bobcat meat—Donald didn't maintain a wider net in the community than that which bootlegging provided him. *They* paid their taxes much quicker, worked at the high school, served on the Rescue Squad, joined the American Legion. Nevertheless, an acidulousness like Donald's raffish outlawry is a kind of shirttail cousin to the cynicism that goes with lawyering or writing. And Donald benefited for a while from (besides mine) the powerful friendship of our most distinguished citizen in Barton, Lee Emerson, Vermont's "last balanced-budget governor." If the snowplow hadn't pushed up Wheeler Mountain Road for a week or more, despite Kay and Donald's standard bribe of a glass of apple cider and a deer meat sandwich for the driver, Lee would leave his office over the bank and walk across the hall to the Town Clerk's office, or place a potent phone call to the Town Garage, and the truck would be there in an hour: and no sandwich necessary. Donald used to paint Lee's big house on Park Street, with the mansard roof and distinctive turret.

An unfortunate feud with the Wheelers had begun when Donald accused Karl of molesting Donald's stepdaughter, Mickie, while dandling her on his knee during her visits just up the road (accurately, Karl's wife Dorothy said). Karl thereupon cut off Kay and Donald's access to the original spring that the two houses had shared for fifty years, and for a while they had no running water. Mickie herself became a friend of mine briefly, years later, after her parents' deaths, and before her own from alcoholism. And her bitterness was directed at Donald, no one else. She'd seen him hold a meat fork to her mother's throat and rape her on the living room floor, next to where we were sitting as we talked. Or force the two of them, with a pistol at their backs, to face the wall for hours on a Saturday night, his "English whore and her little bastard." Mickie had escaped through marriage after high school, but she had picked a crook, who earned her a year in jail as an accessory to one of his burglaries. (Hiring a lawyer, he got out sooner.) She said her favorite husband had been the one who beat the shit out of Donald once on a visit home, and left him hog-tied on the floor, after Donald had bloodied Kay, and told Kay to burn the house down when they were gone—which was a tried-and-true method of dealing with unwanted relatives in Old Vermont.

Mickie was a blowsy, commonsensical, attractive sort of woman with a drinking problem, visiting her mother's grave before she stopped to chat with me, with a young son in tow, or her new fiancé (a guy twenty years older than her and missing some teeth, whose chief charm seemed to be his social security check, but certainly quite ga-ga over his good luck), and worried about her children. She had returned to Barton, her hometown, after another shipwreck. But the children's switch in schools was being blighted by the memory people had of Mickie's return another time—one August maybe twenty years before—when, as if to spite her parents, she had danced naked on the stage of a girlie tent-show at the County Fair. Her kids needed to fight with other kids every day in order to defend her name. She told me her drinking had started when she was nine or ten, a "little waitress" carrying glasses of bathtub beer downstairs to the customers and secretly sipping from each one.

Kay Basford used to tell me that she had had "two daughters," the bad and the good, but I didn't realize at first that both were poor Mickie. Mickie had been so loved by boys as a girl that two separate fiftyish men stopped in, the year of her death, to revisit the house where they had felt her spell. Her worst early experience, she said, was when Donald had sold a darling, cast-off horse that he'd picked up for her a few months before. Sold it to the local mink rancher for drinking money: and hadn't warned her. She happened to be standing in the schoolyard at recess when she saw it rolling by—her precious Blacky—tied in the back of the knacker's truck. She screamed and screamed, but there was no way she could rescue it, even by jumping on her bike.

I mention all of this as a prelude to the ambiguity of driving around Vermont. I found Donald himself companionably amusing and irreverent in an axe-swinging sort of way, and Kay flirtatious, tasteful, rather wise, until Donald stopped me one noontime outside the drugstore and told me he was going to kill me because his wife had just run off to England and I must have helped her because how else could she have gotten the money? Actually, from the pharmacist's wife—yet he couldn't prove it, and didn't kill her either, but moved into a trailer down the highway with a woman who was rumored to have killed her husband (ruled a suicide, though supposedly the pistol was left out of reach), until Kay came home and Donald had his several strokes and lay abed, cursing at his helplessness.

We had a district attorney, elected by the county at around that time, who was not an attorney; he had to hire a green law school graduate to do the lawyering for him. And our postmistress referred to almost anybody with a foreign accent as an Eye-talian. Not more than a few years back, nightriders from the next town had shot into the house of a black minister, a newcomer, and driven him out—a spasm of violence that was condoned by the state police who investigated it, as well as by our county newspaper. More recently, the local sheriff lost his bid for re-election after being accused of sleeping with the game warden's wife . . . It was that kind of place; and when Neil Armstrong and Buzz Aldrin walked on the moon, Marion and I went to the Hotel Barton to watch the spectacle in the lobby (plus take baths for a dollar a pop—we hadn't hot water yet). Though the sight was breathtaking, at dusk the clerk turned off the TV set and went upstairs to bed at his regular hour—sent us home laughing. But this lovely, rambling, three-story, eighty-year-old white building with a wraparound porch burned on the night before Thanksgiving a couple of years later, when the interstate highway construction crew was bunking there, and probably lonely: the price of progress.

Other "flatlanders," "from away," besides us were showing up, but they were mostly of the generation ten or fifteen years younger than Marion and me, the so-called hippies of the Baby Boom, born during the hyper-sexual years of World War II, not in the depths of the Depression, and thus less cautious and skeptical, more communal and programmatic, settling year-round on other hundred-dollar-an-acre abandoned farms, with the secondary aim of trying to change the world. I wanted the world changed, too (and Lyndon Johnson, on our honeymoon-weekend at the Plaza in New York, had renounced his candidacy for re-election because of the debacle in Vietnam), and so have remained fascinated ever since by the flower-child experiments of some of these Boomers, and the complicated fallout.

A leading edge at the moment was the commune movement here along the Canadian border, near the sources of the Connecticut River and in the watershed of the St. Lawrence. It had been Rogers' Rangers raiding territory during the French and Indian War, and of disaffection during the American Revolution and the Civil War. Disaffection, insurrection, slave- and alien-smuggling, draft-dodging (one of my current friends was regularly guiding draft resisters into Canada about now)—so why not a bit of potgrowing and free love in the name of brotherhood? Although

North country folk were often offended by this new counter-culture, they tended not to go and snitch to the narcs. Their grandpas had outraced Customs men in low-slung roadsters during Prohibition, or hidden the dudes that did. And thus one of Barton's leading businessmen, after hearing confidentially from the local state trooper that a certain single mom who had shown up wearing a peasant blouse, earthy skirt, a glassy look, and windblown hair, was really a federal plant, tipped off her neighbors, so that she fished in vain for information from them for a whole year.

As a New Yorker, I disliked what drugs were doing to the city, and the hippies' notion that shuttling the stuff down there was a romantic livelihood and a lark. But I was in the mountains for the wildness; and one of the commune leaders joined me for a forty-mile walk through the forests (twice as far as I went with an official Fish & Wildlife biologist) and became a dear pal. Another dropped in unexpectedly on me at Wheeler Mountain with three cohorts to check my bona fides, but thereafter allowed me a free run at his Farm, where some of the women gardened bare-breasted because they thought it helped the veggies grow. And another let me watch him snort cocaine, if I chanced to be around—though a dealer from the city who was making a pickup told me that if word got out, I would be tied up, put in a bathtub, and the hot water turned on. The only law I knew of that was being broken which seriously angered me was when some hippie hunters would shoot a moose—of the first, protected few that were wandering in from the faunal reservoir of the Maine woods, where they had survived the nineteenth-century slaughter—and hold a barbecue.

LIFE SPORTS A JANUS FACE, spendthrift and yet miserly, with both a grin and grimace underneath. We often weep in seizures of intense happiness, for instance, and smile in grief: just as, in my stint in the army, working at the hospital morgue, I'd noticed how commonly the dead had managed at the last moment a benign or temperate sort of smile. This circularity is neither alarming nor incongruous, but rather seems to make things whole and complete. In the summer, dancing butterflies of pretty colors will congregate where I've gone outside to piss in the grass. The glint of tiger yellow or cobalt blue in their beautiful wings may be enhanced by the minerals that they so crave and that my body has declared surplus. And if a nesting phoebe soon grabs one, she is going to profit also—which is a foretaste of the myriad uses that more extensive portions of me will be put to eventually.

As during my three trips to northern British Columbia in the 1960s, I was in the country to take risks and seek linkage, in a place where the very reason that change is slow is because of those many links and risks. My neighboring writers, Wallace Stegner and Howard Mosher, doubtless felt the same. Stegner, whose literary and teaching careers were in the West, willed that his ashes be scattered in a bed of ferns at his half-century summer house in Greensboro, Vermont, because he said it had been altered less destructively during his lifetime. And Mosher has constructed, over several decades, a "Kingdom County" in his fiction from Vermont's Northeast Kingdom's ligaments and legends. We would go around, Mosher and me, sometimes together, scribbling at a hot-rod race or a cattle sale; and I ceded the old-timers mostly to him (after my British Columbia book, which had been entirely about old-timers), just as he left the counterculture, and the mud-wrestlers at the county fair, and most wildlife to me. When the British Columbia book came out and got few reviews and skimpy sales, however, I found myself vomiting blood, because I thought it might be the best I'd ever write. But the doctor in town headed off an ulcer for his standard charge of three dollars for an office visit, and I walked over Moose Mountain, behind my house, into

Big Valley, camping in a flyweight tent, with my brown hiking goat named Higgins, and Bimbo, a savvy white collie who had lived with the Basfords.

To recapitulate the stages of my education in Barton is difficult because the biota itself has been evolving; the people and land values changed. Vermonters began playing golf, traveling like summer people, and voting like Oregonians. And the moose and coyotes—which are such players on the scene now—came in after I did. The Wheelers' pastures grew up to woods, changing the populace of birds. Winter wrens, hermit thrushes, and ovenbirds supplanted the meadowlarks and field sparrows and bobolinks. Fishers (having been all trapped out, for the fur market in "sable") were reintroduced to the state about the same time that I was, primarily so they could control the oversupply of porcupines, which had no other natural enemies. I'd had to shoot nine porcupines—which were gnawing at my house for the salts porcupines seek in their diet—in the first year alone. But in another dozen, the "hedgehogs" and the "fisher cats," as people call the two species, were back in balance. Meanwhile, warming winters brought wild turkeys, as well as turkey vultures, north from gentler climates—right up to the Canadian border, to shake hands with boreal birds, like blackpoll warblers, three-toed woodpeckers, and spruce grouse. My Connecticut woods and circus days and British Columbia trips of course connected as a preparation. I'd live-trapped weasels, seeded baby turtles in different ponds, kept gopher snakes and homing pigeons at the age of ten or twelve, then had cared for menagerie tigers, and wandered in grizzly territory. So, meeting a black bear in a beech wood or a gawky moose in a cattail glade was not an unprecedented experience. And the pairs of barn swallows, chimney swifts, the green-and-yellow garter snakes, the flickers, pewees, and chipping sparrows that Kay Basford had protected (the one cruelty of Donald's that I witnessed was when, while painting my house, he caught a snake and painted it red), were already friends of mine from boyhood.

I've now accumulated more than thirty years of close observation of the matriarchal colonies of garter snakes that live under my house, not to mention underneath the Wheelers' (which was next inherited by Dorothy's niece). Though not big, they are relics, to me, of the dinosaurs, and superb survivors, more anatomically advanced than pythons, for example. Through having caught and released them by the many dozen, I've known individuals for long periods—old blackened males that finally needed some help with the special exertion of shedding their skins, or perhaps a week of in-the-house heat in order to digest a last meal in September, after a lean dry summer, before going underground to hibernate all winter. These snakes breed in May, immediately after emerging, but a pregnant female will fast for a month or two, as her womb swells by August, displacing her stomach. And so, when she ages, she will live and breed for a few extra years if you capture her and feed her earthworms during the crucial couple of weeks in early autumn, between when her babies are born and when hibernation must start in such a rugged climate. Otherwise, in her exhausted condition, she may not be able to muster the energy to locate, grab, subdue, swallow, and digest enough prey to put on fat for those eight months of suspended animation (and wriggle out of her old skin). Though by now she is a confident hunter, she may get caught, still engorged, by a shift in the weather—a freeze, a snowfall. If the sun that is the engine of her metabolism loses heat before her innards process that last meal, it will rot inside her during hibernation and burst and poison her.

I've watched many births and seen the twenty or so babies distribute themselves afterwards in little (I think, same-sex) yearling bands. Also the later confrontational hostility between garter snakes from different maternal colonies, and especially between the mothers themselves, if they are suddenly caged together—although the crisis of captivity dissolves their belligerence after a day or two, and they'll coil amicably, just as they hibernate every winter balled in a common mass together under the wood bin in the Wheelers' basement, or under the Basfords' old milk cooler, buried in the ground outside my garage. Each house had had two colonies for a long while, until Dorothy's niece decided that she wanted to rent the Wheeler house to summer people and asked me to transplant her snakes to mine. *Four* breeding females and their individual colonies now established around my house and chicken coop and barn have made for inevitable complications.

THE BEARS I'VE KNOWN—because of the eight thousand acres of state-owned forestland close around—seem to have been able to maintain a continuity of vastly larger, but possibly somewhat comparable arrangements. Five to fifteen square miles is said, by those who study bears, to fill each breeding female's needs; and I would guess that in the broad vicinity of this notch I've kept aware of the resident sow's biennial birthing of her cubs, and then eviction of them the following year, when a series of males revisit her in June and the baffled yearlings begin blundering about in search of footing for themselves, except for a daughter from that or a previous pair who will remain within her mother's territory, as a sort of understudy. I've watched the amorous, rangy, burly males, and the disowned, panicky cubs, at that summer juncture when the world turns upside down for them. The physiology of bears' hibernation, their method of breeding and parturition, and later nursing and nurturing, are obviously different from a snake's methodology. Yet she defends her boundaries and food sources as punctiliously. I've lain on the ground in many cherry seasons and listened to a feeding trio—the mother and her cubs—munch fruit close to my house after dark has settled down. Though they were well aware of me, the old female knew I was harmless, and was only intent on warning off other bears—who wished to descend from the ridgeline of Wheeler Mountain to my chokecherry bushes and apple trees to fatten for their winter's sleep—with deeply directed growls. The clocking of her seasons and her years, her shifts from cave to cave for different winters or different pregnancies, her quarrels with my dogs, and nattering vocalisms while educating successive pairs of cubs (and bathing in the Wheelers' tablewater spring, until the niece's husband fenced it in), have engrossed me as much as the coyotes' more recent advent—who howl so personally in July, once their pups are mobile, from the vicinity of their den on the slope above my house.

Constancy is what we want—the snipe and woodcock whickering in lariat loops every spring during their mating flights; and killdeer even earlier. Barred owls and white-throated sparrows also making themselves heard, about then; and "a ton of" robins landing from the south, flocks desiring to beat the crowd—fifty, ahead of the next fifty, and foraging in a skirmish line. Wood thrushes, mourning warblers, waxwings. And the later sharing of the land, by which my local doe deer delivered a fawn in mid-June in the waving grass and full-leaved willow trees alongside the same stretch of stream, a hundred yards in front of my door, where the coyote pair had flirted and bred repeatedly for a couple of hours, till sunrise, four months earlier—coyotes that would have nourished their two-month-old pups with the newborn fawn if they had known. So would the bear have eaten it, if she had been alert to the matter and not perhaps distracted by a June-moon suiter. More meaty was the moose calf born the last week of May in a glade three or four hundred yards from my house, and closer to the coyotes' den. But the succulent plant life right there permitted the cow moose (as big as a horse) to stay close for a while, and neither the coyotes nor the bear would have been fool enough to mess with her.

LIFE IS FLUX, but habitat in Vermont has lately been turning somersaults, when it's not state-owned, as everyone tries to make his mark with a chainsaw, skidder, bulldozer, or fancy landscaping—or simply double his money by buying and splitting up a bunch of acreage. Given an opportunity, the red-tailed hawks are likely to return to the same nesting tree, if it's not cut; and blue goshawks will drop by every fall to try for the adolescent snowshoe rabbits that no bobcat has ambushed. The years that you live on your place acquire a bounce because you know that the wood frogs will sing again in the snowmelt, and spring peepers right after them, when the red squirrels are nibbling maple twigs for the sweet sap, and song sparrows get back—once the zero nights are well past, when you had puffed your own feathers like a nuthatch and sat mute. Red-winged blackbirds, yellow-bellied sapsuckers, rose-breasted grosbeaks, scarlet tanagers, yellow warblers, indigo buntings, yellowthroats: this is wild plumage, not civilian, and the names speak to the effect that spring has, as birds materialize variously in migratory pulses, and the sow bear rummages in the swamp by Wheeler Pond for jack-in-the-pulpit and fern roots and sedges, and the waterthrushes strut, the treefrogs climb the poplars, and ovenbirds make the woods ring with *teacher-teacher-teacher,* just as teachers like me feel that the term may end.

My life was bifurcated between New York and Wheeler Mountain—*that* carbonation, and these still mineral waters. I loved the kerosene lamps, and then the city's electricity, in six-month bouts. And my marriage provided me with a solid flooring to write essays, because employing the pronoun "I" appeared to take more assurance than working anonymously as a novelist. (In 1970 not a lot of writers were using it.) The problematic part, however, was that Marion could never learn to drive; and although she gladly gave our daughter over to the life of the country every summer and did enjoy being in a small town, I doubt in twenty years she ever walked more than two hundred feet beyond our house except on the road. She was a city person, as was I; but she was so wholeheartedly a metropolitan New Yorker that half of my life, half of what I loved, we couldn't share. The country, with its mysteries, frightened her—its tracklessness and shifting skies, night cries and octopus-armed vegetation. We were good company indoors in Barton, as well as in New York: affectionately amused that her endearing mother, Peshka, when she came north to visit, was reminded of the *shtetl* in Russia, Semiatych, that she had left at twenty. For *these* cramped rooms and oil-burning lamps Peshka had crossed to the New World!

We'd married for the backup we provided one another—the layers of enthusiasms, authors, historical perspectives that we filled in for or lent to each other—besides the sexual chemistry and limber parrying of marriage. Marion had never dropped a fallen friend, and hadn't a pennyweight of New York brutality. Had been so loyal to that high school, Evander Childs, in the Bronx, that she'd refused the transfer to the much flossier Hunter College High, near midtown in Manhattan. But Marion's alternative to New York (and most New Yorkers do need one, whether it's Nova Scotia or a charter boat in Jamaica Bay), was Tel Aviv, rather than anywhere to the north, west, or south. Her heart was there; and over time, like two Roman riders—with legs spread, each of us straddling two galloping horses as though around a circus ring—we drifted apart, because only one of our plunging horses was shared.

I never went to the country to leave the cruelties of the modern world behind. Like Marion, I loved New York and didn't stop considering myself a New Yorker (nor did Marion regard herself as an Israeli) or think the rural matrix kinder. In Barton we had a wild, cruel county fair with cunnilingual girlie shows—three dollars for a lick—famous among carnie types as far south as Alabama, and that the Quebecois poured across the border by the thousands to pay to see. The director employed prisoners as cheap labor at his cedar sawmill and limped, it was said, because he had been shot in the foot as a kid by a farmer he'd stolen a turkey from. His son was one of the men who had driven the black minister out of Vermont. And our dog-catcher once shot a stray dog in his own living room in front of his small, crying children, according to a friend of mine who was drinking with him at the time. I could go on with tales of the spiritual penury and hardscrabble misery in these ice-rasped hills. But I wasn't in Vermont for a respite. I'd experienced mostly kindness in my own life anyway, whether on the highway with strangers, or a long-distance pay phone, when trying to place a collect call home in the pre-touch-tone 1950s, with four or five or six operators, plus their supervisor, hanging on the line attempting to decipher the numerals I was struggling to say. In prep school I'd sometimes been made fun of as a "commie" because my politics were liberal, or a "fairy" for wanting to write novels, but never for my handicap.

Under Wheeler Mountain, I peered out my windows as if in a bathysphere, watching birds of passage or random mammals—a stalky bobcat, a sinuous fisher—and the wide, ancient, homely cliffs that towered up with cracks across them like the pentimento of a thin-lipped grin, and two slightly mounded, snoutlike nostrils near the top. The rock itself was not a monochromatic granite, but striped with dark. And stunted spruces clung to precarious indentations, like green brushstrokes along the face, except where recent avalanches had marred the visage, stripping it of hard-won soil, like a vertical palsy after a stroke. As I'd done as a boy, I transplanted nesting turtles to different ponds when I found them egg-laying on a sandy road in June, or the hatchlings in September. My pace on a moose trail was city-quick, like the accommodation to congested agendas and scrambled viewpoints you make in a metropolis—but not so unlike a countryman's improvisations either, except in tempo. Then, during a rain shower, I'd duck under a tree, where city-time stood still. The canopy of leaves deflected most of the falling water; and I'd woolgather, or watch a mink twist underneath a boulder after a salamander, and notice beyond it—where a stretch of soggy ground had drowned an aisle of trees—a vista opening toward a concave facet of the cliff that I'd never seen in all my previous walks.

I might become aware, also, of a scent from quite another sort of prehistory: a personage whose black hairs had rubbed off against the bark over my head, and who had left macho claw marks reaching idiosyncratically here and there above where I was sitting as a message not to me but other beings. Strolling on between rain squalls, I'd find perhaps another kind of bear tree, a nursery birch with two cubs hunkering in the upper branches while their mother fed in a swale a mile away—or an ample, large, old, nutting beech, smooth-skinned, that generations of bears had climbed, impatient to consume its fruits even before they fell. It was claw-scarred wherever bears had shinnied up, ten, twenty years ago, as though with archeo-handprints that had fossilized. These spoke to me, like the moose tooth-furrows that had stripped the bark in a poplar copse, or a buck-banged willow trunk by a stream's ravine.

The "ledge hawks," as Dorothy Wheeler used to call the peregrine falcons that nested on the mountain before pesticides wiped them out, are reappearing in a tentative fashion—already well established on Mount Pisgah nearby. But raven pairs have been thriving way up there throughout, hollering like howler monkeys as they school each annual quartet of chicks—flying them down off their fledgling ledge into the maple trees and firs, the butternuts and basswoods, the orchards and meadows—all of the complexities of humor and food. Hazelnuts and carrion, squirming or pouncing things, berries and bugs. The parents instruct their young in eating a shrew: and then the mouse that the shrew had been eating; then a spider on the apple that the mouse had been gnawing; and the apple itself. Hearing a coyote bark, they all flap over and spot her gobbling grasshoppers in a hayfield, and gobble lots of those, while staying out of her reach. Seeing a bittern from the air that has been fishing in a marsh and is poised with a perch crosswise in his beak, they stoop and startle him, bully him, and lift it when he drops it, take the fish to a tree, and make a little meal of *that*. In the pasture above the bittern's pool, a cow has been giving birth. So, wait with patience on a branch until she finishes. Then seize the afterbirth before a fox that's circling, sniffing the prize, feels brave enough to dart close and grab part of it—beating out a turkey vulture, too—vultures being more instinct-ridden and slow, like a roadkill bird.

The ravens' acrobatics enable them to finesse some of the mincing of habitat that is under way below, as people shop about for patches of property like new habiliments that they can try to construct another persona from. Having done mergers and acquisitions, or worked in malls or cyberspace, they hope raw land may be a new costume to get comfortable in, plus a hole in which to park some money, and a keepsake to leave to the children, if nature ever becomes their bag. When I chat at the soda fountain in the drugstore with a new guy for a while, it can become like watching amateur theatrics. Landed gentry, or Natty Bumppo—*How'm I doing?* he asks. Or I may learn that he had won a dismissal on embezzlement charges in a previous domicile. One aging neighbor of mine roamed through the woods in a killing fever, shooting any bird or animal on sight, as if their deaths could postpone his own. Quite the opposite, is a friend I have, beached here by divorce, who is a former Green Beret and has quit killing. He confronts poachers on my land with his AK-47 and asks if they want a duel. Or else, in a more suicidal mood, he'll spread his arms and tell them to blow him away—"I want to die." He sometimes fantasizes that the CIA has posted snipers on the cliffs of Wheeler Mountain to wipe him out because of the villages in Vietnam that he saw flayed. Another friend, with memories of combat as a marine in South Korea to exorcise, will blacken his face before dawn and creep into the woods, sneak behind a poacher, and put a chokehold on his neck. Up the road, however, is a fourth-generation farm family whose daughter is studying to be an opera singer, and who, when they notice that the mother bear whose territory we share is hanging out with her cubs, just witness her activities without wanting to make her into a rug.

A quiltwork, if not a crazy quilt, of landowners has spread across the old farmsteads that other families jettisoned. A gentleman not far beyond them, who was both a Seventh-Day Adventist and a psychiatrist, was raising llamas, but died taking off in his homebuilt airplane. We still do have an elk farmer, growing antlers for the Chinese medicinal trade. And a man I know produces South American parrots and Central American king snakes for pet wholesalers in what used to be a dairy barn. Rainforest birds and reptiles, even when replicated in ski-climate Vermont, coincidentally may come in designer colors because in the course of eons the jungle endowed them with striking tints of camouflage that are flamboyant when removed from the surroundings that germinated them. The hues and tints, although perhaps originally intended to conceal the creature, now become a drawing card (like the comedy of a "talking" bird) and appeal to our jaded and disoriented optic nerves because the russet, emerald, brick, or blue has been mediated through eternity by a logic that inseminated us, as well. The snake's lovely colors—in a sort of contradance with its slither—fetch us back to the emotional content of Creation, when alarm and delight were marbled together.

Across the road from this former hippie, breeding tropical parrots and serpents, lives another flower child, who bid good-bye to his commune's disintegration by setting off alone on his stallion, Ace, and rode from Vermont to Oregon. But after that heroic effort, he didn't stay; just visited his mother and trucked Ace east again to use for logging and plowing right where they'd started. Similarly, a woman who crewed a couple of years on a yacht in the South Seas returned to work on a weekly newspaper. And a man and woman who had established modern dance careers as a touring duo came back to build their studio and base themselves in the Northeast Kingdom.

To feel at home is the essence of adulthood. And when I poked around with Bimbo, my white collie, looming like Sancho Panza in the backseat window, I'd drive for an hour or so and park where some back road ended, scramble across a beaver dam, a moosey bog, and then up to the top of West Mountain (which is actually east of East Mountain), or one of several others, tuck my sleeping bag under a white ash tree (for its quiet rustle), boil a pot of rice-and-something in spring water over a wisp of fire, and gaze at the roll of the forest and sky. The wind's seethe was soothing to dream in, once I'd caught my breath and eaten. Notch Pond, South America Pond, Seneca Mountain, Bull Mountain, Ferdinand Bog, Unknown Pond, and the spread between, without houses, barns, cabins, or pavement in any direction as far as you could see. Only a gaudy lightning storm in a menagerie of clouds—or the cerulean blue that we know the physics of, but not the more significant explanation for why it evokes such a sense of equanimity in us, and peace and glee. I'd lie and look and almost seem to join the sky, as water vapor is sucked up. What I like to call serene turmoil—or the Brownian motion undergirding life—is not dispiriting, because it never stops. If the seas did quit sloshing, the moon tilting its crescent, clouds scrimmaging, leaves falling and sprouting, we would promptly wish to bury ourselves.

And human nature being nature, I've often found the effect not different to walk ten miles in the city. The moil there also produces a serenity in me because underlying the swarm of sights is the same sensation of enlargement, though it may tire me more and not last as long, for lack of (let's say) bandwidth. But the equanimity and, cumulatively, the jubilation are quite the same. Although each of us wants to be unique and important, a deeper satisfaction arises from yearnings that seem the opposite, and make a city different from a suburb or a grid of summer cottages. To be a mote, to blend into a vast and celebrative mass, as part of a collective voice, with bells ringing—whether in Saint Peter's Square at Eastertime or Times Square on Victory Day—linked and swaying, not only with blood kin but other people, including and especially strangers, is exhilarating. It's why hymns sung by a congregation have a collective, ethereal sweetness surpassing the voice of any individual parishioner's, or those particularly glorious days when you are glad that everybody is in Central Park, not just you, and that life isn't crimped and measly: not for them, and therefore in the largest, deepest sense, not for you. Mobs, of course, don't engender our best instincts, but crowds occasionally parallel, I believe, our intricately wild and teeming beginnings. And—taking advantage of the calendar in some of these climactic fests at the turning of the year or midsummer Independence Day—we gather confidence, amidst the anonymity of numbers, to reclaim our birthright of hopefulness, and rub shoulders not against but *with* other people, as the seat of the brain that we call the heart wants to anyway.

I HAD A FRIEND who lived in a busted trailer by the lake in Barton on his old-age check and from the trotline that he kept rigged for fish and the nightcrawlers that he raised and sold to daytrippers who put their boats into the water at the public-access point near him. He owned no car, but, come October, would hail a Greyhound bus on the highway and go to Florida on his fishworm money, living in a roominghouse a few blocks from the ocean, and (as slim and funny as he was) dodge proposals from the widows there. Though born in Vermont, he had the open gaze that vastness lends—the bigger sky, huge spaces he had encountered when he went west as a kid in the 1920s and homesteaded on the Alberta prairie, in the grand mix of Indians, Métis, Mounties, outlaws, and railroadmen. He was a blithe man when death took him.

Another neighbor is a former dairyman, a practicing Christian, share-and-share-alike. If somebody robs his house, he'll say they needed the stuff they took more than he did. He used to try to convert me to accepting the Lord, but lately seems to recognize that our ideas of what is sacred aren't so incompatible, and equally under siege. He sees things as Creation, as I do, but, perhaps fearful of being disillusioned, is less interested in the biological details, and—again, like me—foresees the end of the world we love, or else unnerving alternatives. I sometimes attend the evening services of his Solid Rock Assembly of God Church for the hymns and tears and general hugging, which can be a mild catharsis for me too, at least at lonely moments and mostly watching others do it. We both know that true religion is not teary for long, but ebullient, even in the face of unnerving alternatives: that Brownian motion (to use my metaphor) will override the changes.

My friend, having retired from milk testing, tracks the headwaters of every nearby stream, the movements of our moose herd, besides going fishing, and fulfilling his paternal duties to five grown children caught in the current venal whirl. Being a Bible believer, he envisions a God more immutable than mine. Immutable, however, in what way?—mercifully, implacably? Like the endgame of the new technology, that remains a mystery. We're less bewildered than suspended in a state of dread. Our faith itself makes us more vulnerable than a cynic or an atheist. We are ebulliently in dread and under siege.

The other friend—that combat veteran who gets a chokehold on some of the poachers who hunt my land—once held a buddy's severed head in his arms all night, lying hiding on the ground while a Korean "gook" patrol searched for him also. When staying in my house, he's been known to shoot a hole through the woodshed because a woodpecker had tapped on it and he thought the knock might be an intruder. Like the ex-Green Beret who imagined CIA snipers on the cliffs who wished to terminate him for what he did for America in Vietnam, he's in the woods partly for his wounds. But he says that he was injured more during his childhood, before he ever joined the marines, when his father threw his mother down the cellar stairs and nailed him underneath the back-porch stoop to improvise a cage. The Green Beret came home, bought a piece of pretty land and put a trailer on it, but then the man he'd bought it from shot another man and the sale dissolved in legal riddles. For relief, I've seen him shoot his crossbow at a straw target. A Navy Seal I know was forced by his mother to lick her spittle off the floor, when he was small: and now is a commando.

In other words, it doesn't end. Yet that is how the West was won, the frontier settled—by wounded folk like us. And the regularity of the arboreal and faunal cycles, the rolling weather so dependably unpredictable that it jounces you as air pockets do a plane and you can't go on autopilot—and the bronco-ing landscapes, pummeled not just by recent glaciers but, in the case of Wheeler, a three-hundred-million-year time frame—medicates us. I prefer a house that looks upward at a natural panorama, instead of down, as if you'd conquered everything you see (which will soon be webbed with roadworks, anyway). Gazing up at fastnesses that the clouds, in a mime show of animalia, alter almost hourly, I watch the mountain go from being a sperm whale's broad profile, to an immense, snouty sphinx, and then a pubic travesty of a vulva-and-bush, four hundred feet in height. Or just a surf wall of rock, a breaking, gray comber taller than that.

The solidity of the town I'd chosen, Barton, lay in its longtime grocery-and-meats family, the Comstocks, and the Harper family, whose garage likewise went from father to son, as did E. M. Brown's feed and hardware store, which mixed its own grain formulas from freight-carloads at the Canadian Pacific Railway siding, and constituted an anchor for the dairy farms for twenty miles around. Almost everyone in the village ate at the counter of the Ruggles' drugstore once in a while (also a business that passed from father to son); and when Lee Emerson retired, his law practice, in the brick bank building, was taken over by Bill May, from one of the town's oldest families. Since the 1860s, there had been water-powered mills and little factories alongside the tumbling falls at the outlet of Crystal Lake, manufacturing tables, rockers, toilet seats and water tanks, piano sounding-boards, Peerless ladies' underwear, and wagons, buggies, butter tubs. Also a woolen mill, a gristmill, an iron foundry. The water-closet seats were fashioned out of oak or cherry to look like mahogany; and the carriage-maker was equally classy. This considerable commercial history underpinned Barton's middle-class pretensions, although by now the only factory of any size was Ethan Allen's furniture operation in the next village, Orleans. Dairy farming and pulp-logging for the New Hampshire paper industry were Barton's other economic mainstay; or cutting yellow birch and rock maple for Ethan Allen, or cedars for making fencing, tamaracks for railroad ties and barn floorboards, or sawmill spruce and pine. Real estate wasn't much of a factor in 1969; you simply went to the agent's home and drove with him to look at hundred-dollar acres. Or insurance: I insured my home through a retired shop teacher who told me on his front porch how—as an infantryman in an advanced platoon in northern Italy in 1945— he had watched Benito Mussolini being hustled away from his last mountain hideout at Salo by German soldiers, before the partisans seized him at Lake Como and strung him upside down. And how twice, as a good buddy died, he "gave him his (morphine) shot."

The suburb of my boyhood, New Canaan, had been a regular Connecticut town in transition toward becoming a high-end bedroom community, when we moved there in 1941. It still had a two-story Checkerboard feed store to supply the relic farms around; a rinky-dink railroad station on a trolleylike spur line; volunteer firemen who responded from their homes to a code of whistles blown at the firehouse that told them where to go; and a local tackle-football team that grown men played on in games against the neighboring towns. The golf course was a modest nine holes (though I remember watching Babe Didrikson Zaharias swatting an exhibition round, and Don Budge and Bill Tilden once on the tennis courts). The genteel scramble began in earnest after the war, with titans such as Thomas J. Watson, the founder of IBM, occupying dachas, Philip Johnson building his glass house (much ridiculed at the time), and narrow roads named after real Siwanoy Indians—Ponus, Oenoke, Wahackme—becoming grandiose. My father, in fact, wrote an article for the historical society about "Indian Rocks," a traditional campground a mile or two from us, where corn had been pounded in hollows in the stone. It soon became a forcing-bed for advertising, technophile, and banking wealth of the postwar decades, however; and as a small boy I used to walk the putting greens of The Club with my father and a few proto-captains of the new industries. He occupied a middle level in the pecking order of all this ferment, so before puberty I learned to recognize some of the ethology on display.

Barton, by contrast, didn't get a golf course until twenty years after I arrived. Instead, town softball teams played on a diamond on the river bottom behind the drugstore, as a main event all summer long—and not just the Little League, and then the Babe Ruth League for teenagers, but the Frontier League, or Northern Vermont League, for adults. There are still some local games between teams sponsored by nostalgic merchants who buy the uniforms, but fewer; and the men's basketball league is gone. The funeral director, on Church Street, was a charitable man who had wanted to be a priest when he was young. He used to put on movies for the kids in the Town Hall, at cost, on Friday and Saturday nights, and make popcorn. But that is over. A friend of mine bought coon skins and other furs to sell to New York dealers, but he is dead. Next to nobody traps. The mink are doing so well that they prowl right into the sporting-goods shop in the basement of the drugstore and eat the bait fish, kept alive in a tank there, waiting to be sold to day-trippers.

The fluctuations in how land and the houses on it are employed puzzle many people (being occupied intensively for two months; then not for ten), and require considerable elasticity from the wildlife, too. New cottages spring up, but the owners live like suburbanites, in their cars, if not indoors; and the mammals and birds will form concentric circles of minihabitat around each dwelling—robins and flycatchers exploiting the lawn, wood warblers and woodpeckers out beyond the fringe. Foxes hunt and den closer to a house than the coyotes (who will eat a fox) normally choose; and deer feed and bed down closer than a moose. Although accordioned into ever smaller parcels, the land can yet retain a certain stubborn ecological value if it's manhandled less: if, that is, the people are away somewhere, or mostly on the Internet, or else in front of the TV, instead of being out sugaring, or driving cows around, cutting hay and corn and firewood, trapping bears, and shooting owls and "chickenhawks." Wild critters can swing right into a summer person's dooryard in the early fall and grab whatever rabbits, squirrels, and the like that have been sheltering there. Or when the snow flies, you'll see a bobcat's tracks go into the cellar and out again, and mouse nests demolished. The people bought the cabin to kick back in, watch the wrens, keep a boat, a diary, and entertain eccentric thoughts, dodge extraneous conversations—plus possess the inestimable privilege of merely thinking about it when gridlocked in the city.

The woods become a proscenium for many folk to strut their stuff in particular roles they may have picked: whether as a sandaled Gandhian; or a "beaver-trapper" clumping about with a full beard, green wool pants, and mud boots; a Mafia don with a pistol in an ankle holster and a cultivated manner of menace; or an old-time fiddler, hirsute and picky, with a yoke of oxen, to boot. In the 1970s, cropped-headed women and Prince Valiant men hilled potatoes, home-schooled their kids, argued at public meetings, and bid for a grain-sack full of laying hens at Souliere's Tuesday-night animal auctions. I was chameleon enough myself that I hung out more with these heterodox hippies than with either the middle-class pillars of Barton society or the guys who turned dowels into table legs and stained furniture for Ethan Allen.

Now, newcomers tend to try to dilute the character of any place they move so that it won't seem unsettlingly different from where they left. But the hippies only sought to alter Vermont's morals, not its wider mores, and for years put quite a brake on change. They burned stovewood, plowed with horses, maintained numerous farmstands, helped or bartered with their neighbors, and disdained pecuniary ostentation. But, having few fixed rules and private spaces, there also was a trickster, totem-pole quality, a sliding variability to some of these communes. The faces and personalities were often tiered, as if piggyback, until, next week, the arrangement switched. Scouting up a humpy road to reach one of them, you never knew what you'd stumble on, a buttermilk picnic or a bad acid trip. Would they build their New Jerusalem or piss it away? Eventually they did piss it away, for the most part, in six-pack binges and false starts; left dozens of jerry-built dwellings abandoned in the woods. But all this took at least a decade of merriness and angst. And some tough nuts did hang on, such as the friend I'd bushwhacked the forty miles of forest with. A Bronx boy and Coast Guard veteran, Al had run Dorothy Day's Catholic Worker soup kitchen near the Bowery in New York and was a committed idealist, though more of a loner than a leader. The leaders crashed.

I had my dog and sleeping bag, so I could stay over if it suited. But usually I wouldn't, because I liked to be at home at work when the sun rose. There were anomalies in several of these Brigadoons, such as the medieval enthusiast who had floated in on the tide of Heads yet was said to be sleeping with his own daughters to tutor them in sex, because that's what the thanes supposedly had advocated. And some lesbians were reported to have fertilized themselves with a turkey baster from a wooden bowl that a few men had volunteered to jerk off into, so none could later claim paternity and the women might bear their kids in simultaneous solidarity. But in general, a commune visit was cheery—the ballooning conversation and the good salads. And the hippies blended with the locals better than contemporary uplink people, with their bicoastal assets and cyberspace income. The hippies and the farmhands, or an assembler from Ethan Allen, might meet in a beer joint and begin to trade car parts, or else ice-fish and do a little redneck pot together. They could all use a chainsaw, pound nails, drive a bread truck, or kick cow shit. In both cultures, all work was regarded as of equal dignity and futility, and a night's mischief (if not the underlying alienation) was fairly similar—the junker cars and woodpile winters, the beer runs and disheveled children.

Now that everybody wants a "place" somewhere, people bump into each other with far less rhyme or reason. The guy training a pair of coonhounds on the weekend to clear his lungs of the reek of furniture stain, and a matron walking in the woods with a cell phone and a mushroom guide—who has a chalet down on the lake but winters in Arizona—are gingerly when they meet at a foot-log across my stream. Ours is a town where three bank robbers used simply their deer rifles for the stick-up (directing traffic outside the bank as if the barrels were batons), and then perhaps put the money in a boxcar that rattled into Canada, while the cops were tipped off to search through several manure piles. And who knows if the showoffs who scattered play-money in front of the grandstand at the next demolition derby—from a jalopy painted THANK YOU, HOWARD BANK—were really them? Around the same time, the grandstand roared to life when the then-governor of Vermont was officially introduced to the crowd by the master of ceremonies, before giving a speech, as "a Porky Flatlander." Our *later* bank robbers, on the other hand, were just three vacationers from New Jersey, doing it (as they told a friend of mine, who saved their newspaper clippings for them, after they had got away) "for the rush."

If farmers live by the weather's vagaries, the hippies were directed by their daily shifts in mood, and saw the cycle as rather analogous, drawing on food stamps and other poverty programs— if not a trust fund—in the meantime. Thus, the self-proclaimed "Woodchuck" type of Vermonters, who hibernated as much as they could through a frigid winter, weren't so unlike this dogged class of hippie, who slept in their long johns in a yurt or a tepee, a geodesic dome, or a remodeled cowshed, in January (not just during the summer), and pulled on bib overalls in the morning and went and kicked the ice out of the pigs' and chickens' water dishes, and bundled their children off to school. It wasn't much like bohemianism in the East Village in New York, where the city's jitters percolated and, for example, the genius of the Abstract Expressionists lay along the edge—where people slept less and knew that life was short. Here, they might just bliss out for the rest of the day, once the kids were fed and in snowsuits and the basic carpentry of winterizing the sleeping-loft was done. Yet the hippies' suspicion of the mercenary economy they had fled from dovetailed nicely with many farm families' poignant reluctance to shatter their traditional long view of the value of land and simply cash out to a summer person, run to Florida, and watch TV programs. A hustler in our county was going around to impoverished elderly couples, speaking French to the ethnic Canadiens, and carrying a bottle of whiskey, a suitcase full of stacked money, and the paperwork all filled out. But by and large, the entire state's resistance to cheapshot change was reinforced by the counterculture's choice of Vermont as a real focal point: while the sexual promiscuity they also brought with them was a national tide that was rolling in upon New England anyway.

The hippies were anti-bookish, in the main. Even the college graduates soft-pedaled the idea of education in favor of what they could prove or accomplish with their hands. This, like their lack of interest in money, made them unintimidating. Herbert Marcuse had had some philosophical influence: but the sandaled marginalia was what had fostered Gandhi, Buddha, Christ, not the buttoned-down, bought-off universities, with their rich endowments and literary/scientific canon. Nor was *Midtown* where anything was at. Midtown was where the Vietnam War was hatched, and Nelson Rockefeller's savage state-trooper riot at Attica Prison in 1971, in which forty-three people died, and where investment bankers swaggered down the sidewalk. If you were a Green Mountain hillbilly who had never set foot in a city except maybe delivering a load of Christmas trees, you had nothing to fear from chumming around with the hippies. They wouldn't embarrass you by suggesting you'd missed anything—just tuck ten pounds of pot in the back of your truck next time, underneath the wreaths.

That's changed. Divorce, job-hunting, the interstate, and electronic thruways have inoculated nearly everybody against an Appalachian sort of localism. Even bear hunting is done by radio-collaring the dogs and driving around in a pickup according to where the signals turn; then punishing the dogs with electronic shocks to the neck if they mess up. My own reaction is to pull in, be more private than I used to be: as, indeed, most people are, with their on-line aliases and faceless e-mail. It was fun the old way, dropping in on people who had no phone and what-you-see-is-what-you-get. I was fortyish and therefore spared the sort of juddering blunders I might have stumbled into during this fevered period, even as an onlooker, otherwise. The herpes, smuggled from Brooklyn, that some of my friends caught; the bar fights with cue sticks in the Osborne Hotel in Island Pond (a guy laying his pistol down next to his drink); the rollovers in vehicles that other friends of mine kept suffering, or near-death episodes from pneumonia in fireless cabins. The "Smash Monogamy" hippies, the "Free Vermont" people, the "New Morning" individuals, and the "Weather People" stayed downstate, like the Red Clover and Red Mountain and Pie-In-the-Sky communes, and others who preferred a more political, less offstage stance—though some Yippies from Berkeley did establish an anarchic, populous commune called "Earth People's Park" right on the Quebec border, with a "Ho Chi Minh Trail," where drugs could be backpacked across.

It's a wonder that I can only think of a couple of young people who were murdered in the Northeast Kingdom probably over drug deals that went awry; and one aging man who overdosed on boron in a weird kind of potency health craze. And I remember only the suicide of a boy who lived in a treehouse at Mad Brook Farm: after a spell of riding the rooftree of the main farmhouse on nice days, and hollering a lot. People from the age of twenty to thirty were trying to hack free of extraneous edicts and restraints, surmount their own makeup, and retune the rest of the world; and the remarkable thing was how few of them met with a trainwreck. Mostly, they lost half a dozen years or so, and some laps in the race, lamed their children a bit, and were sidelined. But the booming American economy carried them along without desperate consequences. They got boozy, sheepish, lunky—as the fallen often do—but were soon not noticeable as a bloc anymore. Summer people swamped them. Golfers outnumbered them. Gun nuts enlisted a few of them; or the fad for organic gardening, which meant that they could sell their vegetables at a farmers' market to the leisure class and maybe venture inside some rich Stowe housewife's pants. From disillusion, a person can slip into the notion that all life is a con; and as the hippies lost much of their enthusiasm for the showy, frenetic promiscuity that had aroused widespread disapproval in the towns around, they saw Vermonters themselves begin going overboard with divorces, live-ins, love swaps, bed-hopping (or "jumping the fence," Vermonters call it), gender-bending, toke-puffing, and other longhair stuff.

What didn't catch on during the 1980s and 1990s was the hippies' fastidious disdain for money: which is the only thing they were fastidious about. For example, although they were nominally pacifists, in my thirty years of writing about Vermont, the only person who has ever threatened to burn down my house because of what I'd said was a hippie, not a regular old-fashioned, hawkish, crew-cut Vermonter. Unmercenary communitarianism has never been adopted much in America (it's not a hallmark of the Mormons' signal success); and so the hippies who didn't morph into go-getters were stranded, delivering newspapers, laying flagstones for patios, and pounding studs and plasterboard, as if their gambit had fizzled. Nor did they believe they'd actually proved anything, because they lost faith in the 1960s' mantra that all work is of equal dignity, honor, and fascination. They'd gotten sick of life underneath-the-house or underneath-the-car, fixing the plumbing or the transmission and differential in freezing weather, when you're existing on a minimum wage and fighting off the flu and the multiple lovers somehow haven't added up to one true partner. Now they worked just to eat. Work was another con.

My curiosity faltered when the experiment collapsed, although I remained sympathetic to my hippie friends who seemed as baffled as dolphins suffering after running up on a beach. The 1960s had been like the 1930s for an earlier generation: a failed revolution in many ways, but which did leave a sea change in the culture, despite its know-nothing dimensions. The Vietnam War—like the stockmarket Crash of 1929—had magnified and helped delineate a national emergency. In throttling the war and passing civil rights legislation—as with the New Deal's social security, welfare, and Fair Labor laws—the country as a whole had been upended in unforeseen, ancillary respects, its hierarchies mutated. Transience and egalitarianism were boosted; dress codes and lifestyles changed. So, when I go to hippie reunions nowadays, I remember the wistful men I saw hanging out in Union Square in New York City in the middle 1950s. Twenty years had passed, by then, since those grunts from the trenches of the proletarian revolt had had their heyday during the Depression, and they, too, had wilted. Mainstream culture had digested what it wanted of their innovations in union-organizing and the rest, and spit them out.

The hippies' aims struck me as more nebulous because, in

keeping with their dropout stance, they seldom participated in politics. On the communes, they practiced women's liberation, consensus government, legalized marijuana, and nonmercenary self-help, but thought that corruption imbued "the system" so pervasively, you should live separately. Just by being there, however, they liberalized the interior of New England, when formerly there had been a disjunction between the working-class, manufacturing towns and rock-ribbed, rural viewpoints. They could plow snow, chop a log, sew clothes, hold up one end of a reasonable discussion, and cook "American chop suey," just like a "Woodchuck." The differences, of course, lay in their imported sense of an emergency, whereas the local families had lasted in these tough hills through the Civil War, two world wars, and various economic recessions, when land might be worth a dollar an acre or a hundred an acre, yet provided a steady living and would anchor you to the nth generation.

The hippies admired *that* idea, but the farmers, too, were eclipsed not long after them, and partly by the money scramble. Money had been a scrimmage before—in 1900, 1925, 1950, or whenever—without dissolving so many family farms. Not everyone had joined the Gold Rush or gone to the big city, and land values way out in the sticks were not in play as asset management. Nor did people hop about in lifestyle phases or via electronics, as they do now. The hippies, though building on the grungier kinetics of the fifties city Beatniks—that low-rent nihilism, combined with social rebellion and impromptu, circular travel—had added a cleansing, country dimension: a place for women and for Gaea, the Earth Mother, for multicultural music, a green thumb, and an egalitarian self-sufficiency that dropped out of ordinary society not as an end but as a means. ("God is dead" disappeared as a mantra.) Hippie women weren't supine. They cooked and hugged and marched in protests the way Neal Cassady drove, and didn't value unhappiness as a spiritual talisman the way the fifties groupies had. They believed in the virtue of other people, in other words. And yet it was a thin Buddhism, and they bathed in the elixir of nature without much thought for its survival. Not a total solipsism, like the Beats' had been, or the Yuppies' that followed: but living by the day was their motto, with a little help from Mary Jane to bend the mind.

CONTINUITY. How fast the poplars grow; and how slow the oaks. The staunch white pine that I still can't see the top of when I am standing underneath, although a forester told me it would be all but dead of blister-rust disease a quarter-century ago. The barn and house have new metal roofs that ought to last them much longer than that. My marriage didn't last, yet the place somehow did. The continuity of reddish-sided jumping mice and white-throated sparrows, two-lined salamanders and blue goshawks, shorttail weasels and starnose moles. The smell of the cedars, and the joe-pye weed (like vanilla ice cream), while a nighthawk dashes softly overhead, and a mink frog brusquely calls. A toad starts singing; and a big green frog—and one of the cliff's pair of ravens seems to mimic the green frog. A male bear descended steeply from his den overlooking my house in late April for a stillborn calf that had been left for him, while the resident female roamed sideways separately on a gentler gradient that her cubs could handle from *hers* (catty-corner in the V of this mountain notch from his wintering spot) to find the one left in order to get her off to a well-nourished start.

Thirty-some years of yellowthroat song from the apple tree and raspberry patch in back of my house, and a Nashville warbler in front. Spotted sandpipers out by the pond, and a pair of young beavers trying to colonize that stretch of stream, but beaten back by shallow water every fall, though they may have pooled enough for a kingfisher to hunt. Two moose, heading there, slanted across my back field last evening as I finished this. But they would have been deer, looking toward my window, when I came to Vermont.

REACHING TIDEWATER

*D*ivorce means divide, turn aside; and "two-time loser" was the term for somebody twice-divorced, in the argot of my youth. A colleague of my father's who married his secretary was exiled from Rockefeller Center to a sort of stringer post in Saudi Arabia, because if *that* contract, "till death do us part," was violated, what did it say about the person's probity in lesser partnerships and agreements? Of course, so clear a sense of right and wrong has long since blurred. "Quitter," "loser" aren't epithets we hear thrown around, any more than such an idea as "probity." Many people marry temporarily or try alternative lifestyles, and "losing" has to do with income, not integrity. But even money has begun to play second fiddle to mobility now in plenty of alert and comely people's minds. And mine was the generation, now sixty-ish, that coolly oversaw this change—neither protesting nor quite yet reveling in it. The kind of integrity embodied in trusting a man's handshake for a business deal had also countenanced egregious racism against "jigs," "kikes," "wops," and "Chinamen," and thus we converts to the newfangled moral fluidity that accepted easy divorce and what in my father's day might have been called "checkered" personal histories were achieving an advance in democratic values at the same time.

I've written of my marriages: How sending Amy, at twenty-eight, to Mexico to procure our Spanish-language divorce may have been the worst thing I have ever done—good for my writing, but bad for my soul—and how I dreamt of her in poignant scenarios for years afterwards: us hearing each other's voices and running from opposite directions for two city blocks to embrace. Then of my ten fine first years with Marion, thickened with the nectar of "raising" a child (nice word, and finally I had one of my own). Marion was a deft, intuitive mother and because we were late first-time parents we were smart enough to go slow, pay attention, and savor pushing a swing, the first bus ride, ferryboat, birthday party, overnights with both grandmothers. First movie (*Fantasia*—too scary), first puppy (Va-Va, a mongrel beagle), first visit to the zoo. *Sesame Street* and *Mister Rogers* are knitted into my memories of writing in the afternoons, and for brunch on Sunday we would push the stroller to a clam bar on Bleecker Street at Sixth Avenue, stand on the sidewalk and eat oysters on the half-shell for a quarter apiece, squeezing lemons on them; then munch a wholewheat Italian roll from Zito's as we went along. The zigzag narrow streets and rhomboid little parks and playgrounds; the dusty sunlight angling across the aging stone of quirky, shabby buildings; the private-looking, sauntering people who drew Hallmark cards or children's books, wrote Camel ads or radio shows for a living, frame my memories, and harbor no episodes that make me want to flee the place on visits now. On the contrary, if our happiness curdled a decade or two afterwards, that was not the city's fault. The city was our comfort.

The changing city. I overheard one babysitter we had hired, in talking to our pink-skinned infant, threaten to toss her out the window in furtherance of the Black Power revolution: "How would you like it if I threw you out the window?" But another woman, also African-American, attempted to kneel and kiss my hand in all sincerity when I gave her a present, as if it was still slave-time. The blonde neighbor we tried out was usually high on drugs, and at the kooky progressive school that we chose, math, spelling, and reading were accomplished by trial and error, while the teachers (believing they had more to learn from the children than the kids might ever learn from them) fondly looked on. Later, after we had gotten Molly out of there, I was amused to discover in a collection of E. B. White's miscellany that he had been infuriated as a young father by the same nutty methods at the same school.

After twenty-five years, a divorce is like dropping a whole houseful of glass. Can't tiptoe, although you try. You stumble toward wide-open, vertiginous behavior with no rim to it, and the cheerful lawyers in the offing are employees and noncommittal. Friends commiserate about the "split," not as an abrogation of responsibility to be abhorred, but a natural phase and pitfall. And yet the restive pain, the chalk-squeak jitters are not much mitigated by the fact that British royals and every other TV celebrity are doing it, and the moviehouses and museums are sprinkled with crestfallen souls who are also undergoing a downsizing to bachelorhood again. From the cocktail shaker to professional wrestling and our blurry, shifty cast of celebs, a whole range of American enthusiasms is based on agitation. My mother, born the same year as Charles Lindbergh, spent much of her considerable passion fascinated by unconsummated flirtations with Episcopal ministers, or else elegant dancing partners whose true tropism lay elsewhere.

I can't imagine hating one's former spouse. But people sometimes did, when they couldn't get divorced. Singly, we're so much freer now that we can scarcely burn our bridges because we've got so few; can't become black sheep because so many alternative life styles are in vogue. The script for splitting up—burning up the wires with phone calls, visceral pain, sedative pills, terrible bills, children weeping, messy lawyering, gnawing guilt, sleep lost, friends sought—is a tale oft told. Yet splitting isn't severance; your memories are not painted over. You may stand blinking before your next wife, stalling while you try to recollect her right name, thinking she's the old one; and in bed at night, lacking the assistance of your eyes, left with scent and grope, plus the weird surrealism of your dreams: *Who is she?*

Generic pals—*Which one?*—is that where we are headed? With e-mail, jobs, and neighbors, it's surely happening. We shuffle along, buy, sell, sign on, sign off, shed, or are shed by different people, call up texts and erase them. The entry-level job, the early marriage, the starter house: and then of course you go from there. We think our moves are self-directed, but have we partners? Then various deaths start chiming in, as we grow older. A thinning crew, both quick and dead, inhabits your head. I have few regrets outdoors, having seen the juicy Himalayas, Lake Como, Mount McKinley. That's half of what life is about. But indoors I often tripped over myself, so intent upon being independent as a man and a writer that I denied myself some pleasures just because au courant acquaintances were immersed in them. I didn't realize that what was chic was probably interesting. So I didn't go to the Cedar Tavern on University Place to try to drink in the same crowded room as Jackson Pollock, Willem de Kooning, Franz Kline, and Motherwell; or hear the jazz I now listen to on CDs, live at the time it was being created at the Half-Note, Jack Delaney's, Eddie Condon's, the Village Gate, the Village Vanguard; or hang out at Bradley's or The White Horse, in the Village, where I might have run into Dylan Thomas, Edward Albee, Truman Capote. Fortunately, this abstemiousness didn't extend to universal stuff like football, baseball, fireworks, parades, Coney Island, or the wind-down of old-fashioned vaudeville and striptease in houses like the Old Howard in Boston. I liked being in a stadium, a colosseum, a street market, a Billy Graham crusade, a bell-pealing public wedding, a sixties protest march, or simply in the midst of rush-home hour in the city, as long as I was wading in it, not compelled to rush, myself.

I did get to love Stan Getz and Benny Goodman in the sixties—between my marriages—while briefly keeping company with a gangster's daughter from the Florida Gold Coast, on West End Avenue. Her dad was terrible, one of the last of the Jewish mobsters, like Bugsy Siegel, Dutch Schultz, Meyer Lansky, and had died cursing at her from his oxygen tent when cancer caught up with him, because she was going to outlive him. Pale, slow, zaftig, and still wounded—remembering lying on the bathroom floor with her mammy-nurse on top of her, when a hit man came searching for her father, and they were all alone except for a bodyguard who shot it out with him and saved their lives—she'd sometimes lie emotionally like an invalid on her futon, only crawling over to open the door for me or fetch cigarettes or dose herself with pot or change the woodwinds on her LP turntable. I was injured too, and the constant music of a clarinet or sax was like an antibiotic lotion. Not a narcotic, but like the lungs of the wind, that blew and blew and blew (as sex itself is merely nature transported indoors).

We age at different rates, just as our pacing in adolescence and later is different. Hampered in talking, I was instead precocious as a writer and published my first novel before I'd lost my virginity. Thus my twenties became like other people's teens, as far as sexual experimentation was concerned. My thirties probably corresponded to their twenties, and my forties rather to their thirties: and perhaps in that aspect of life was my prime. It seems to make it easier to be in my late sixties now because I don't have to look back as far in my memory to locate uncommon adventures.

Sex is hardly the only form love takes, however, and most of us become better friends and parents as we mature. The ripening thirties and forties bring some patience and perspective. You learn to make the most of an hour with your daughter at the zoo, or lunch with an old classmate who's resettling and needs to find a job. Dawn in June, when you're my age, with the songbirds singing; and a mother merganser flies over an otter swimming ahead of your canoe, and suddenly dodges as a duck hawk sweeps out of the trees—she had been decoying you away from her knot of half a dozen bobbing babies. But down she splashes into the river, immediately diving to escape the falcon, and succeeds. Great swamp maples and willows; a wood turtle; a mallard family that appears to have eluded the peregrine's notice—he's gone after a blue jay. You're with a friend who is saddled with heart trouble, and this is just the kind of spectacle that concentrates your mind. Not only the glee that you two felt when you were young and predatory like the otter and the falcon, or the mercurial delight of being alive with the sunrise and a breeze on the crinkled water, but the wistful awe of knowing you won't always be outdoors in a canoe during the spring in what looks awfully like God's heaven.

Summer won't be endless now; nor episodes of drama and romance. The well takes longer to refill. Even walking, I pant when going uphill—a nice healthy sort of pant in my case, I hope, because I think that in our day our life spans, unless we drive like maniacs, are determined by our genes. My father died at only sixty-three, my mother at ninety-five, and I've always felt closer to her. People tend to gain in tolerance and grow more generous-spirited as they get older, but on the other hand, we often lose connectedness and some degree of interest in what's going on, so our generosity or tolerance is not all that expensive to us. Bring a cruel conundrum to our attention and we will certainly sympathize, but we are quite inured to the impossibility of combating injustice and to the corruption of the sort of powerful people who otherwise might try. And, much as our backs slip out of whack at some small sidewise tug, so do our minds skid off the point when fatigued a little or short-circuited by a spark. I've been publishing books for forty-five years and I don't have a fastball anymore, just a knuckleball, spitball, and other Satchel Paigey stuff.

You're only as old as you feel is a refrain one hears enough that it must have some truth to it, though your oncologist might disagree. The remissions he sees uplifting the spirits of so many dying people a week short of death—when they think that they are going to live on for years—could be interpreted as the exuberance of fetal angels confused by a passage toward ecstasy, or as an aspect of the anesthetic that commonly tranquilizes creatures that are being engulfed by death, whether a wildebeest in the jaws of a lion or a frog in the mouth of a snake. In that army morgue, most dead people smiled.

Yet in some respects we are indeed as young as we feel. Life is moments, day by day, not a chronometer or a contractual commitment by God. The digits of one's age do not correspond to the arrhythmia of one's heart or to the secret chemistry in our lymph nodes that, mysteriously going rancid, can betray us despite all the surgery, dentistry, and other codger-friendly amenities that money buys. Nor do good works keep you off the undertaker's slab. But cheeriness, maybe yes. Cheery, lean, little guys do seem to squeeze an extra decade out of the miser up above, as if feeling young were not as important as having a peppy metabolism and appreciating being alive.

Blurry eyesight, fragile knees, broken sleep, the need to pee a dozen times a day (when somebody honks at my car, parked at the side of the interstate, I assume it's a man my own age), are not inherently fun, though the smoothing-out of temperament does help you cope. Your ingenuity, your curiosity must find a new focus, not simply exploring the world as a kid does. When I watch from my canoe a tall blue heron stalking field mice through the grass, then washing them down with minnows and tadpoles, I don't experience the surge of ambition to be a zoologist I would have felt when I was fifteen. I just want to go on seeing these intricate things next year.

Among my friends who have been notified that they were terminally ill, those who died least miserably, most gracefully, were people who could be intrigued and absorbed by the peculiar changes their bodies underwent. They didn't stop observing the incongruous handicaps, the bemusing treatments that they were subjected to. The music they loved, snatches from books that had meant a lot, the news of friends who stopped in to visit, the civil war afflicting their bodies, the total novelty of dying—comprehending such a crush of sensations took all their waking time (a last hearing of *The Children's Corner Suite*!) and emotional resilience. It was a voyage they stayed on deck for.

During my spell of semi-blindness, I found myself, too, registering the dismally curious stages of what was happening to me, as I gave up driving, lost the capacity to see birds in the sky, then gradually the crowns of the loveliest trees, and my friends' faces close at hand, a fascinating catastrophe. Before surgery rejuvenated me, I learned how life itemizes exactly what you are losing. With the binoculars around my neck, and then my telescope at the window, I put off curtain time. (The moon you can watch endlessly, or a lilac branch bounce in the wind—though people object to being gazed at.) As my daughter dropped in, and the leaves outside turned yellow, I was scrambling to improvise solutions: how to get a particular errand done, how to read three paragraphs by closing one eye and focusing the other ever closer. But would I see her face again? I was reviewing a day at the beach I had had ten years before in San Francisco with the love of my life, stripping the rubber band out of her hair and kissing a pimple she tried to hide with her free hand, as the purple underbelly of a rainstorm rolled in, but reminded myself that since things hadn't worked out, she wasn't really the love of my life. Or was she?

Life is minutiae, and aging progresses by two steps forward

and then one back, as jerky as one's legs become. And though I was rejuvenated by millennium-type eye surgery (when nature had had it fixed for eons that people my age should quietly go blind or have heart attacks without bypasses, thus decently sliding offstage and leaving enough space for younger people and other mammalians), my memory kept slipping out of gear, as if a cog was chipped, at the same time that I had more to remember in a lengthening life span, and my temper grew crankier, though in fact my true balance was becoming more benign. While less in a hurry to get places, I drove worse because my mind was absent. My eyesight had been sharpened with plastic implants, but my mind coughed like an old car's motor and I would pull out into traffic without using my eyes. My chest ached a little after this happened, as it does when my waking-dreams go wandering into uncatalogued drawers of my memory where they have no pleasant business being. Yet I don't glance back and notice missed opportunities. Wanting so passionately to be a writer, I grabbed what I saw as the main chance at every turn, avoiding offers to become a tenured professor or a media editorialist in favor of staying freelance. Living frugally came naturally to me as a stutterer who had wondered how it would be possible to earn a living anyway. The only regret that accompanied this choice was not feeling free to have and educate more than one child, instead of the three or four I would have liked to raise if I had had more income. I've never treated anybody scurvily (at least by my lights) and don't experience chagrin of that sort, looking back. But of course I debate my two marriages and the crossed wires that sometimes threw sparks, or other friendships that lived or lapsed. At parties, you recognize why old-fashioned women tended to be matchmakers. Couples seem so much happier than single people above a certain age. You rarely meet a widow or a widower who is sighing with relief. And I'm with Trudy.

Marriage as the long-term pairing of men and women is such a hunter-gatherer sort of idea that its durability testifies to how primeval we still are, despite the voltage and velocity of our compression-chamber days. Our guns and murders do too, and the over-the-mountain infidelities that entertain us, our greed for swapping stacks of greenbacks ("frogskins," they used to be called) for goodies, and the special appetite for travel that seizes us, young and old. We hit the road as kids; and then again as old scouts, furloughed from the city, we retire to cruise ships or Winnebagos forty years later, feeling we've been bottled up, and forage in foreign markets, roaming for the sake of roving, watching the sun's progress as immemorial theater across the sky.

My work enabled me to travel even during my bread-winning years—in Europe or close to the Arctic or below the Sahara. I found that the more you do, the more you're up to doing. Camping in the Rockies prepares you for Alaska, and Alaska for Africa. As you grow relaxed about the procedures of distant travel, you get resourceful about the details, locating a tuning fork within yourself that hears the same note in other people wherever you go. Even in war or famine or dictatorship—because we are not speaking of Pollyanna travel—your intuitions are valid because all of us have a rendezvous with death, however humble and anticlimactic that may finally be, and exotic disasters should not be incomprehensible. Like Mobutu or Mussolini, we've been cruel and grandiose, have strutted, lied, and postured, known sneaky lust and theft and opportunistic betrayal. The spectrum of behavior we witness in going abroad is seldom all that foreign to us.

The eye surgeon had warned me in 1992 that my blindness was going to recur and I should see whatever of the world I wanted to take in rather soon. So, at around sixty, I visited India and Antarctica, each for the first time, and India again, and returned to Africa twice. It was different because in the case of India and Antarctica I was treated to blue-ribbon, well-financed wilderness tours of sights I could never have reached when my legs were young and strong. And in Africa I was already known for a book I had written there years before. The day after arriving in Nairobi, I got a call at the New Stanley Hotel from a stranger named Rob Rose, who was with the Catholic Relief Services agency and asked if I would like to accompany him the next day on a two-week trip into guerrilla territory in the civil war raging in the southern Sudan, where two million people have died. During the 1970s, in peacetime (and when I was twice as fit for hard travel), it had required months for me to win permission from the Sudanese government to visit the same high, wild, tribal redoubts on the Upper White Nile.

We set off by Land Cruiser for Kampala, in Uganda, spent a night, then ventured quickly off through disputed territory in that country's own separate simmering civil wars with factions of the Acholi and other tribes, up to the town of Gulu, with only one car breakdown. Next morning, we continued north through the hamlet of Atiak, and choppy, evacuated grasslands and acacia forests and two military outposts, then a no-man's-land, and finally a spindly bridge to the Sudanese village of Nimule. Famine country was just beyond. The Dinka and the Nuer peoples had been allied against the Arab government in Khartoum, but now had started fighting against each other as well. Their positions had consequently been shattered, their cattle and grain supplies destroyed. The Dinka had fled to Ethiopia, and been defeated there again, and retreated in a starving condition back to the Nile. But the aid agencies that had been feeding them, frightened by the lethal infighting (in which three relief workers and a journalist had recently been shot), had pulled out.

I felt sheepish for not having foreseen more than a hint of these developments during my previous trip. Yet I was white-haired now, which changed the character of my reception, even allowing for the impact of the emergency. One elder thought I must be a "King." When I said America didn't have kings, he amended that to "Millionaire," looking at my hiking boots. He was barefoot. A white-haired white man, to have come so far, must be at least a high official with the United Nations who had heard that a hundred thousand people were starving here. Pathetic, short, hand-contoured little mounds paralleled the networks of footpaths where we walked the next day. Each was marked by ragged tokens of the famished body newly buried—a broken doll, a tiny skirt, or holey sweater had been laid on top. Dysentery or pneumonia might have abbreviated the child's suffering, but surely a potent senior figure like me, beholding such a tragedy, would intervene.

My friend Rob, half my age, by dint of sleepless, dynamic initiatives, had indeed brought fifty-eight truckloads of corn from the Catholic Relief Services warehouse in the Kenyan port of Mombasa, the first food delivery in a couple of months to the refugee encampments we were visiting. In my eyes, he was a genuine hero, braving the dangers here and the UN's tacit boycott. But at Aswa, Amei, and Ateppi, smiling desperate children by the many hundreds ran to me, a mere itinerant journalist, to touch my hands and cheer me in the Dinka language as the godfather or patriarch who seemed to have arrived to save their lives. If only more food came! It may have been the most poignant moment of my life. Some of them, boys and girls of six or twelve, had already shrunk to skeletal wraiths, monkey-faced from malnutrition, and I saw newborns who would die without ever tasting milk. Their mothers, stretched beside them on the ground, were themselves dying and, prompted by our guides, partly raised their bodies to show me their flat breasts.

Seven women were said to have been grabbed by crocodiles on the bank of the Nile, where they had gone to try to harvest lily roots or fetch water or spear a fish. Wild dates and nuts and the ricey tufts of wild plants had long since been exhausted; the rats smoked from their holes; the grasshoppers roasted. The local streams had been finger-sieved for shiners and crustaceans, and every songbird slingshotted. The very air smelled burnt. And inevitably, we Americans ate only sparingly, twice a day, whisked out of sight of the Dinkas to a church compound at Loa, on a hill-top ten miles away. Africa doesn't get any prettier or more pristine than this mountainous region of the southern Sudan because its splendid forests have not been logged—or even the gold lode sought whose nuggets from the Kit River you could buy in the village of Opari, near us—due to the guerrilla wars that have been subsurface here ever since the British left in the middle 1950s. Driving, you may pass a man dead of a bullet hole on the road; and just during our stay, as Amnesty International later reported, the Dinka leadership had executed twenty-two of their own soldiers at Nimule, and were torturing other out-of-favor commanders near Loa, nailing one man's foot to the floor. Rob became quite disillusioned the next year, when he moved from Nairobi to Nimule with his wife to be helpful, and guerrilla soldiers clubbed to death an African whom he was paying to guard his house. In 1995, I went back to Laboni, on the Ateppi River, and then Chukudum, and lost some illusions too.

But lives were being saved by our trip. Even divided among a hundred thousand souls, fifty-eight truckloads of corn staved off the agony of hunger pangs awhile, and my white pate was winning me more credit than I deserved. The hospital was the worst place, ringed by hungry irregular troops, the famished patients lying bedless on concrete, rationed to one cup of cornmeal per day. No antibiotics. The nurses were so weakened that they could scarcely function and were distracted by their own children's frantic straits. It seemed shameful for a well-fed man from Vermont to be touring this furnace unscathed, with boys and women rushing to him to intercede in Washington and bring it to an end. I did write about what I had seen, and at the time did shout at the guerrilla general who was thought to have helped precipitate this immediate calamity by setting up the killing of the UN workers (not realizing that white people are as tribal as anybody else), as I would not have had the confidence to do when I was young. At roadblocks I was more at ease when ordered out of the car by teenagers with Kalashnikovs to be checked; less edgy when we broke down in Uganda in lion and bandit country. As on my more ambitious journey two years later in 1995, I knew that mines are more of a danger than lions, and malaria more than mortar shells or kids at a roadblock who are looking for other African teenagers to kill, not a cautious, courteous white man.

AGING IS NOT a serene occupation. You stumble physically and tire quickly, maybe even indoors, and your mind can be tricked by threadbare circuitry into surreal or simple confusions, like the proverbial second childhood, when for a moment you don't know where you are. Not in Africa, though: you're on your toes. And I don't think of travel as a vacation. I'd love to see Venice again, but doubt I have anything to say about it that hasn't been said better. So I turn for trips to the new phenomena of the Third World. I want to work out toward the brink of what I think is going to happen—the widespread death of nature, the approaching holocaust of famines, while Westerners retreat in veiled panic into what they will prefer to regard as the realer world of cyberspace. (Old age will not be an enemy, in that event.)

The distractions, ruses, nostrums you used to employ to foil depression, such as sexual flings or mountain climbing, are not in the repertoire of most old guys; and their suicide rate can nearly approximate the febrile teens'. But they're also freer of sexual unease and self-esteem or money compulsions. They may lack money, yet not care as much; can better do without. And "seniors," after all, are living on borrowed time—borrowed from the unborn whose world they're using up. I'm twice as old as an average American expected to live in colonial times. Just a hundred years ago, I'd be blind, crippled with hernias, if not already dead from asthma, appendicitis, or parathyroid disease and other stuff I've had before.

And money can be an equalizer. On a ferryboat from Martha's

Vineyard to Cape Cod last summer, I noticed with some sympathy an oldish man standing on the deck, who the whole way
across the water, and as if for dear life, hugged a sturdy, gaunt,
blond, young-fortyish woman. Balancing uncomfortably against
the boat's rock, she patiently allowed him to do as he wished,
nursely in manner if not in fact. The two young boys traveling
with them looked on, amused or embarrassed, though it was not
clear whose kids they originally were, his or hers. From his cling-
ing hunger, needy passion—stock-still on the deck hugging her
for forty-five minutes, except when she excused herself once to go
to the bathroom—she was a new, important acquisition for him.
He felt thankful and lucky. Though of normal build, he looked
frail and unsteady, as if he might have just had a major health
scare and was not making her a spectacle for the sake of the other
passengers, but his own. Though she didn't care for the compulsive, public part, on the other hand, like a good sport and with a
kind of good-hearted, working-class honesty, she appeared to recognize that it was part of the deal. If you become the third wife
of an ailing businessman twenty-five years older and very much
richer than you, and he's recuperating from surgery at his summer
home, you let him hug you round-the-clock, with or without an
audience.

In my fifties, I had that sizable love affair with a woman seventeen years younger than me, the nurse who took me all over
Alaska on her supervisory rounds. In chartered Cessnas, we flew
to remote Eskimo or Indian villages, sleeping on the floor of the
health clinic or school gym while she consulted with patients and
the local nurse. Frigid, wild places where in January my eyelids
sometimes froze shut and I would not have gone by myself, but
with her felt both bold and safe, knowing that whatever happened
to me, I would not be alone. And somehow, like the Eskimos', her
eyelids did not get sealed shut by the frosts. Nor was she winded
or chilled on our strenuous walks. Whatever risks we met, surely
she could wiggle me out. I remember hugging her intensely for her

sex and youth and like a lifeline to safety and my own youth. Sometimes she would pull my head next to hers and look in the mirror to see how others visualized us—was I conspicuously wrinkly and gray?—but decided no. We made love extensively every night for weeks, and the age disparity seemed to add spice. A tutor indoors, a dependent outside, I clung and pumped as if doubling my luck, my vanishing span on earth; and if I died I would be in her arms, which would make it all right. Now, I couldn't possibly do the things we did, in bed or out, flying all over Alaska, landing on rivers at hamlets where a white man was not welcome unless he couldn't be ejected because he was with the head nurse. It was delicious to bask in my friend's protection, a further frisson to fanciful sex. And chums who are eighty tell me how much more I'll lose by seventy, not to mention at their age, of the physical capacity I had at fifty-three.

But did we—we tend to wonder—catch the spirit of our times? Did we grasp a piece and participate? We know how a composer like George Gershwin captured the expatriate zest of the 1920s with *An American in Paris* and then in the democratic 1930s wrote *Porgy and Bess.* Aaron Copland, too, not a weathervane, spoke for the thumb-your-nose 1930s with *Billy the Kid* and then did *Appalachian Spring* in the patriotic, heal-the-wounds mid-1940s. Our telescoping century, from the Edwardians through two world wars to cyberspace (my mother saw the first electric lights and automobiles come to her town), has made it hard to keep current. One wouldn't even *want* to have been a flapper in 1929, a Red-hunter a quarter-century later, and then a bond salesman and cyber-master in the fabulous 1980s and 1990s.

I left the city for the country in the 1980s, preferring at that point, I guess, to watch the carnival at one remove, and haven't shifted from typewriting essays to word-processing screenplays, as so many good folks have done. Indeed my politics and style of dress (both shabby-Ivy) have scarcely changed since I left college. I pounded cross-country during the 1950s; heard Martin Luther

King, Jr., deliver his radiant speech at the Lincoln Memorial in 1963; protested against Vietnam; and saw tickertape parades for FDR, Truman, Eisenhower, Kennedy, Johnson, and Nixon, plus Churchill, King George VI, and Charles DeGaulle, in Paris. Didn't do drugs, but saw action enough, and didn't drop out of the domestic brouhaha until ten years ago.

I wished to know shadbush from elderberry, dogwood from chokecherry, bluebirds from indigo buntings, yellowthroats from yellow warblers, the French horn from an English horn, a trombone from a sousaphone, Red Grange from Red Barber, and Newt Gingrich from Joe McCarthy. We opt for what we want as daily conversation in the privacy of our minds, and whether on most days we get to watch the sunrise and listen to a snatch of the genius of Bach. It's not expensive to pay attention to the phases of the moon, to transplant lemon lilies, and watch a garter snake birthing thirty babies and a catbird grabbing some, or listen to the itchy-britches of the Canada geese as autumn waxes. We will be motes in the ocean again soon, leached out of the soil of some graveyard, and everlastingly rocking.

That is my sense of an afterlife and my comfort. The hurly-burly of streambed turmoil will be our last rush-hour traffic— thocketing through boulders, past perch pools and drift logs. Enough, we will say, reaching tidewater. We saw enough.